ALSO BY MARK SHAW

The Reporter Who Knew Too Much:
The Mysterious Death of What's My Line TV Star
and Media Icon Dorothy Kilgallen

Denial of Justice:
Dorothy Kilgallen, Abuse of Power,
and the Most Compelling JFK Assassination
Investigation in History

Collateral Damage:
The Mysterious Deaths of Marilyn Monroe
and Dorothy Kilgallen, and the Ties that Bind Them
to Robert Kennedy and the JFK Assassination

FIGHTING
for JUSTICE

FIGHTING
for JUSTICE

The **IMPROBABLE JOURNEY**
to **EXPOSING COVER-UPS** *about the*
JFK ASSASSINATION *and the* **DEATHS** *of*
MARILYN MONROE and **DOROTHY KILGALLEN**

MARK SHAW

Post Hill
PRESS

A POST HILL PRESS BOOK

Fighting for Justice:
The Improbable Journey to Exposing Cover-Ups about the JFK Assassination
and the Deaths of Marilyn Monroe and Dorothy Kilgallen
© 2022 by Mark Shaw
All Rights Reserved

ISBN: 978-1-63758-644-0
ISBN (eBook): 978-1-63758-645-7

Cover design by Cody Corcoran
Interior design and composition by Greg Johnson, Textbook Perfect

Post Hill Press
New York • Nashville
posthillpress.com

Published in the United States of America
1 2 3 4 5 6 7 8 9 10

"Justice is a big rug. When you pull it out from under one man, a lot of others fall too."

—DOROTHY KILGALLEN

"The dead cannot cry out for justice. It is a duty of the living to do so for them."

—LOIS McMASTER BUJOLD

Dedicated to my parents,
Vera and Marvin Shaw
and to my loving wife,
Wen-ying Lu

INTRODUCTION

No praise was ever more deserved than when the *New York Post*, during the early 1960s, called Pulitzer Prize–nominated journalist and media icon Dorothy Kilgallen "the most powerful female voice in America." To that article was another adding, "Wherever Dorothy Kilgallen goes fame precedes her, envy follows her and a crowd looks on. She is one of the communication marvels of the age."

As good fortune would have it, this remarkable woman inspired me to write not only a book specifically about the JFK assassination entitled *The Poison Patriarch* but three books touching on Dorothy's life and times and her mysterious death including the bestselling *The Reporter Who Knew Too Much*, as well as *Denial of Justice* and *Collateral Damage*. Doing so, along with additional books I had published and other matters of interest including fifteen years' worth of research materials, caused my alma mater, Purdue University, to decide to archive my body of work. A portion of the October 2020 announcement read:

> **Purdue University Acquires Alumnus and Bestselling Author Mark Shaw's Body of Work Complementing the Existing Archives of Amelia Earhart and Neil Armstrong**
>
> We are delighted that Mark Shaw has chosen Purdue Archives and Special Collections as the home for this impressive collection," said Beth McNeil, Dean of Libraries. "Shaw's work touches on some of the most interesting and impactful events and individuals of the 20th century. In this respect, the collection beautifully complements others at Purdue, like the Amelia

Earhart and Neil Armstrong papers. All provide a rich, primary account of 20th-century American history.

Such recognition for a small-town Indiana, near college dropout with, at best, average intelligence who did not publish a book until age forty-seven has been exhilarating as well as humbling. In many of the thirty-plus books I've written with very little, if any, training to do so, there is a common theme: taking up the fight for justice banner in the spirit of acclaimed novelist Lois McMaster Bujold's words of wisdom: "The dead cannot cry out for justice. It is a duty of the living to do so for them."

Accepting this responsibility in my books, one I could have never imagined, in some ways "defending" those denied justice as I had done during my years as a noted criminal defense attorney in the Midwest, became the bedrock of my body of work. During the journey, I learned about Dorothy Kilgallen and used her as a role model so as to aspire to be a man of the truth as Dorothy was a woman of the truth, challenging distortions of history at every turn.

As thousands of readers of my books and those who have known me since childhood have asked: How did you become what may be termed a "voice" for justice, and most especially a "voice" for three twentieth-century luminaries who tragically died at an early age—Marilyn in 1962 at age thirty-six, JFK in 1963 at age forty-six, and Dorothy in 1965 at age fifty-two?

The answer necessitates several chapters in the beginning of this book touching on life experiences before I became an author in an autobiographical sense so as to better understand how I would later substantiate credentials as a bona fide historian to anyone who doubted the accuracy of my writings. These life experiences, as will be explained, combined to mold and then strengthen my character so that I could challenge through my words the disdain for the rule of law. The transformation has permitted my holding accountable one of the most powerful families in history, the Kennedys, specifically Joseph, the patriarch, and son Robert.

As you will learn, I now take on two more powerful men, FBI director J. Edgar Hoover and President Lyndon Baines Johnson, both of whom were responsible for the granddaddy of all distortions of history, the bogus Warren

Commission conclusion that Lee Harvey Oswald acted alone during the assassination of President John F. Kennedy. How I landed on the motherload of all assassination breakthroughs by exposing for the first time the corrupt inner-workings of that commission through the account of a "whistleblower" of sorts provides the crowning jewel during my many years of research, ones that have exposed government corruption at the highest levels.

As will be explained, my contributions to history in these arenas of interest only became possible when I began to learn more about Dorothy, a woman of great integrity who, in effect, became my "copilot" for the research journey I conducted on a daily basis. Before my discovery of the revered journalist, the media icon, my early years of defending women's rights, first in the courtroom and then with my early books, initiated me into dogged research methods resembling her own. Becoming something one might call a protégé of hers opened a window leading to the truth about what happened to JFK in 1963 and eventually to the discovery of the suspicious nature of Dorothy's death in 1965 and then Marilyn's in 1962. Investigating them in that order, even though Marilyn died first, has resulted in resolving three true-crime murder mysteries that were not, in fact, mysteries at all if they would have been properly investigated at the time.

As new evidence appeared on the horizon, much of it from highly credible sources, I would ask, during my improbable journey, "Well, what would Dorothy do with this evidence?" Other times, I wondered how she would follow up, how I could use information provided from a reader tip, missed or ignored government documents, or a new, credible source that landed on my doorstep. Being smart enough to realize Dorothy was smarter than me, I began utilizing what I called "The Dorothy Method," akin to how a prosecutor gathers evidence for a trial so as to examine witnesses and present both opening statements and final arguments to uncover important historical data based on solid, primary-source evidence.

Dorothy thus became a central part of my life even though she had died decades earlier, and as time passed, I began to realize that by following her path to the truth about matters of historical significance I could become a budding historian and compile a worthy list of my own contributions to history. This involved combining Dorothy's research with my own and adding to the equation what I had learned through many valuable life experiences that I came to realize were indeed "defining moments" in my life. As you will read, connecting what I had learned during those moments in time to my own research methods became quite relevant to my discovery of new evidence. As an example, shortly after *Collateral Damage* was published in 2021, a slew of that new evidence came floating into my life and I felt the need to share it with you, the reader.

That is the intent of this book: to add more of my contributions to history while at the same time honoring Dorothy for her contributions, ones that have been, thus far, the trigger point for nearly *seven million* YouTube views of presentations and interviews for my last few books, *The Reporter Who Knew Too Much*, *Denial of Justice*, and *Collateral Damage*. During each one, I took the viewer on my research journey with me, and that is the intention of this book as well: to share the research strategy I utilized from the moment I began to investigate Jack Ruby's attorney Melvin Belli for his role in defending Ruby, culminating in the 2007 biography *King of the Courtroom*. Doing so, I am proud to say, has been possible by my having established the reputation as a man of the truth leading to the best, most credible sources contacting me, as happened to Dorothy based on her stellar reputation, with never-before-published evidence contributing to such revelations as the first exposure of the Jack Ruby trial transcripts in *Denial of Justice*.

The result is *Fighting for Justice*, a blending of evidence included in previous books for clarity and context purposes with shocking new evidence pointing to cover-ups existing since the early 1960s. This evidence includes: 1) FBI director J. Edgar Hoover's obsession with Dorothy and her life and times for years on end beginning in the 1950s, 2) the eyewitness account never presented before exposing for the first time the disturbing inner workings of the Warren Commission controlled by LBJ and J. Edgar Hoover to guarantee an "Oswald Alone" conclusion, and 3) insight into a condition known as "neurosis" affecting the Kennedy family men, especially Joseph, John, and Robert, causing each to become sexual predators. Also included are a compendium of disturbing revelations about Frank Sinatra's illicit life and times, two new credible accounts of how Marilyn Monroe died, and critical information adding to the proof that Dorothy Kilgallen was murdered in 1965. In each case, there is no predisposed agenda on my part permitting independent evaluation of the facts collected, just the opposite of many author's intentions resulting in books packed with distortions of history.

As you will read, the journey to my exposing the cover-ups of the truth about Dorothy's and Marilyn's deaths and the JFK assassination traces a long and winding and in many cases serendipitous road, but one that involves an immense amount of evidence for those who have read any of the previous books and those who have not read any of them. It is also a book that is a call to action, a call to fight for justice, a demand for immediate, proper, and thorough independent investigations into JFK's, Dorothy's, and Marilyn's tragic endings to their lives so that each is provided that justice sooner rather than later. Although it has been too long already since justice was denied them, it is never too long to fight for the truth, especially regarding historical figures involved in key events of the last half of the twentieth century, events that crucially shaped many of the challenges American politics and government face today.

—*Mark Shaw*
(www.markshawbooks.com)

CHAPTER 1

In 2006, while researching a proposed book on the life and times of famous San Francisco attorney Melvin Belli, I came across the following comments about him made during his representation of Lee Harvey Oswald's assassin Jack Ruby in 1964:

> *Washington Post* reporter Bill Flynn focused on the overall "Belli look." He described the lawyer's fondness for "Saville Row suits, handmade shirts with diamond studs, flowing Byronesque ties, starched cuffs, and polished high-heeled black boots."
>
> Famed reporter Dorothy Kilgallen, a steady lunch partner of Belli's during the Ruby trial who later mysteriously died of a drug overdose, observed, "The Carl Sandburgs of the future will spend whole lifetimes trying to analyze the drama of this week and this scene." She described Belli's demeanor as "Chesterfieldian."

Due to a lack of compelling interest in Jack Ruby, Lee Oswald, or even the JFK assassination, I paid little attention to either quote. Certainly I had no interest in Belli's wardrobe choices, so Flynn's description never made much of an impression on me. And the information about Dorothy Kilgallen barely registered since all I knew about her at the time was that she had been a panelist on one of my parents' favorite CBS television shows when I was growing up. It was called *What's My Line?* and the idea, as I recalled, was for the panelists to guess someone's unusual occupation.

What did catch my eye was that the latter quote was apparently intended to indicate that, for whatever reason, Kilgallen was at the Ruby trial. This made little sense since she was just one of the stars of a quiz show. Even the part of the quote relating to her having "mysteriously died of a drug overdose" did not resonate and neither did her claim that the "drama of this week," a reference to the Ruby trial, would be analyzed by me in the future.

Little did I realize, however, that what might be called my "introduction" to Ms. Kilgallen would trigger more than fifteen years of research about matters touching on the assassination. As noted in the introduction, she would become my inspiration for being able to contribute to history in ways I could have never imagined by exposing the truth about how President John F. Kennedy, Marilyn Monroe, and Dorothy herself had been murdered— why and how that happened and by whom.

* * *

To better understand the essence of the improbable journey leading to this book and others I've written since age forty-seven, a compendium of details regarding my background is necessary. Any accomplishments early on are not intended at all to be boastful but only to provide context for what happened in the future when I probed the JFK assassination and the deaths of Marilyn and Dorothy.

While my mother Vera and father Marvin were the finest parents a youngster could ever wish for (my dad taught me that if one wasn't the smartest person around, she or he just needed to work harder than anyone else), lessons learned regarding how to deal with failure began when I entered Purdue University located in West Lafayette, Indiana, in 1963 at age eighteen. That was the year civil rights chaos happened in the Deep South; Martin Luther King Jr. was arrested and President John F. Kennedy was assassinated. Every freshman like me who lived in a dorm (Cary Hall) had to wear a little green beanie, but I discarded mine shortly after I received it. Playing by the rules was never a focus of mine; a rebel attitude against authority became a given when I felt the rules were unfair. That aspect of my character would carry through to current times.

Like most everyone, I recall exactly where I was when the president was assassinated. All male students entering Purdue were required to take two years of ROTC (Reserve Officer Training Corps) classes, and I chose air force instead of either navy or army. On the twenty-second of November, 1963, as I dressed in my spiffy blue uniform, the news about the assassination blared on a roommate's radio, and I recall sitting on my dorm room bunk stunned at the news with tears quickly streaming down my cheeks. I never made it to that class or any other for the next day or so, but as time passed, I merely moved along, never paying much attention to why, how, or by whom the president had been killed. Little did I know that more than fifty years later, I would write and publish six, yes, six books, including this one, touching on JFK's assassination.

Despite studying hard for a Physics 152 exam since it was required in the field of Electrical Engineering, I received a score of five out of one hundred (yes, a *five*), more than qualifying me for an F. Despondent, I decided to drop out of the university, having been overwhelmed as a small-town kid amongst thousands of students. Fortunately, in a life-changing moment, the physics professor took me aside and said, "Mark, if you quit now, you will be a quitter all of your life." Bless him for his words of wisdom, since the "never give up" attitude I subsequently adopted, including when I nearly gave up while investigating JFK's, Marilyn's, and Dorothy's deaths due to the complicated nature of the evidence, may be directly attributed to the professor's sound advice to a young man who needed that advice at the time.

While at Purdue, I became a member of the Beta Theta Pi fraternity. A close look at the "pledge class" photo indicates an independent streak, which

would follow through the years. Notice that I am, for whatever reason, sitting alone in front sporting a nerdy haircut and horn-rimmed glasses. That independent attitude would bode me well later on when I tackled significant historical matters on my own and would be criticized for doing so.

Like millions of young men my age, when college days were about to end, I was eligible to be drafted into the armed services as the Vietnam War escalated to new heights on a daily basis. Viewing body bags on television frightened all of us, and many, to avoid the draft, went to great lengths, including shooting themselves in the foot, to keep from being called to duty.

I never thought of such things, since my father had taught me the great life lesson to never shirk my duty, and I appeared for a physical examination in Indianapolis at the proper time. In what surely is the most important defining moment of my life, I somehow, despite never having had problems before, flunked the hearing test, *twice*.

After the second time, a tough-talking sergeant took one look at me in my snazzy orange boxer shorts and barked words I will never forget: "Mr. Shaw, you cannot be drafted, you cannot enlist, now get the f___ out of here." I limped out of the building wondering what had happened, but that improbable rejection permitted me to continue on with my life instead of risking it on the battlefields of Vietnam where I could have been killed. To this day, I feel guilty that I did not serve, and I recall deciding that I would try to do my best to make a difference in the world since I had been spared by whatever spirit was guiding that life of mine at the time.

The Purdue years were a "growing up" experience for me as I was on my own for the first time. I relished the educational opportunities, socializing, and meeting new people, and fraternity life taught me the special meaning of friendship. Some folks make fun of Midwesterners, but most are honest, trustworthy, and dependable, with their word being their bond.

* * *

Nearly *six years* later, having heeded the sound advice provided by the physics professor to stay at Purdue, I had graduated with my mother and father alongside. I recall them both taking a deep breath while saying to themselves, "Thank you, Lord, Mark finally graduated."

Dad, Mom, and me celebrating Purdue graduation

This said, now it was time to head out into the big, bad world and discover what new adventures lay dead ahead. No stretch of the imagination could have prepared me for how life would unfold, including my becoming a lightning rod for controversy despite my attempts to avoid such things.

Following the graduation in 1968 (age twenty-four) with a degree in industrial management, a catch-all area of interest at the time, I was fired from my first job, one that had taken me to Minneapolis as a salesman for a chemical company. The job was boring, and I failed miserably at it, but after I ridiculed management for its shoddy treatment of a disabled young woman who was the victim of sexual harassment, dismissal was inevitable: the result of my standing up for the woman who needed someone on her side. Taking on such wrongful conduct ended up being a precursor to later defending those, especially women, who were treated unjustly.

Disappointed but not dejected, and with the determination to take a negative and turn it into a positive based on lessons learned thus far in life, I moved to Chicago, where I had lived with some college buddies one summer, and quickly landed a job as a bartender at a bar near Rush Street called The Depot owned by some Indiana buddies, Pete Johnson and Art LeFleur. One necessary part of my duties was to help pay off the Chicago beat cops each week so they wouldn't hassle underage customers with ID checks. A brown sack full of cash (at least $100 as I recall) was passed to the men in blue when they stopped by on a regular basis. I hated doing it and it soured my belief in law enforcement. I finally refused to hand over the cash; just a matter of principle which would lead to many such instances in the future where if I knew something was wrong, I couldn't reconcile or rationalize doing it regardless of orders from those who demanded that I do so.

Exactly why I wanted to be a lawyer still remains a mystery, but like how I would feel about many future adventures that headed me down a different road, it just seemed like the right thing to do. While pouring beer at The Depot, guys and gals would stroll in and talk about law school and becoming a lawyer. I had never thought of such a thing, but my saying, "Yes, I'll be going to law school," sounded good to the chicks, and so I began to see what might be possible and where. Of course, since my college grades were dismal (C minus), chances of getting into any law school of renown were dismal. Ever the optimist, ever the one who thought anything was possible despite the odds, I began to investigate what law school might be crazy enough to accept me.

In yet another defining moment, Indiana University Law School in Indianapolis (now Indiana University McKinney Law School), the "practical law" partner to the theory-driven campus in Bloomington, had a well-respected night division. The powers-that-be there decided in 1969 to create a day division, and when I researched their plan, it seemed clear that they were looking for bodies whether or not a brain was attached, which was perfect for me because my marks on the Law School Admission Test (LSAT) were mediocre at best.

Combined with bad grades at Purdue, chances of being accepted were slim, but calls to the admissions dean at the law school in Indianapolis, bless him, resulted in an acceptance. On the day I received that news, I marched over to the Oak Street Beach and screamed in delight, scaring those in the sunbathing mode.

CHAPTER 2

Without question, law school (average grades at best) provided me the skills that would be highly beneficial in the future, especially when I dealt with the JFK assassination and my "representation" of Dorothy Kilgallen and Marilyn Monroe and their having been denied justice. One course, Evidence, instructed by Professor William Harvey, a true man of integrity, taught me the importance of honesty in the courtroom and how to build a case for the prosecution or defense. When I later laid out the evidence in books like a prosecutor would do at trial, I often thought of the lessons learned in Professor Harvey's class.

As the prelude to yet another defining moment in my life, this one hard to believe by anyone with a sane mind, I reconnected in 1972 with my friend Larry Wallace, a public defender (PD) whom I had interned for when I was a law student. He was a free spirit like me, never afraid to try new things even though it meant taking risks that others never even considered.

Larry, a jovial fellow and a partner at a prestigious Indianapolis law firm, had decided to enter the world of politics and thus became a candidate for the state legislature. When we met at a downtown tavern after my adventurous spirit led me to visit England, France, Italy, and Germany, where I planned to practice law despite no knowledge of the language (dumb idea), he told me that if he won, he would have to resign from his part-time position as a public defender in the criminal courts. "And if I do win," he said, "I might be able to convince the judge in Criminal Court Number Three, a good friend of mine, to appoint you to take the position if you're interested."

"Uh, Larry, that's nice of you," I replied, "but I don't have any experience with criminal matters, let alone with even practicing law." He smiled and said something that would truly define how I handled any possible excursion into the unknown in the future, job or otherwise: "Oh, Mark, c'mon, you could just wing it," reminding me of previous experiences in my youth where I had done the same thing.

Larry won the legislative seat and Judge Harold Kohlmeyer hesitantly agreed to appoint me a PD. On a Friday afternoon in early 1973 I was unemployed at age twenty-eight, and the following Monday I was standing in court before a jury wearing an ill-fitting tan seersucker suit defending James Jethroe, a man in his mid-thirties charged with shooting his girlfriend with a twelve-gauge shotgun from six feet away in front of her three kids! Yes, that's right, a first-degree murder case, not a parking ticket or DUI case or anything like that—first-degree murder.

When I had wandered into the Marion County Jail, where I'd never been before, to meet with my new client early on a day when rain poured down from the heavens, James asked the obvious question: "Mr. Shaw, you seem pretty young. How many cases like mine have you tried—I mean, to a jury?"

I replied, "Well, uh, James, uh, none, but I studied criminal law in law school and, uh, I'm sure I can handle, uh, your case. Now tell me what happened here?"

James looked at me like I was from Mars, hesitated, and then said, "Well, Mr. Shaw, I just wanted to scare my wife Olivia by shooting over her head and I missed. Too much booze. I did love that woman so."

Right then, I learned the first lesson of a good defense attorney, one that would be a building block for future days in the legal arena: that no matter the story your client tells you, no matter how strange or unbelievable it sounds, you owe her or him the best defense possible. And you never consider whether your client may be guilty. That's not your job but that of the judge or the jury, and if you even start thinking about that potential, you should resign immediately because that client is counting on you as their last bastion of hope of not losing their freedom, let alone their life.

When I stood with James, who had never been in trouble before and whom I felt some sympathy for despite his evil deed, in the courtroom for the first time, my knees were shaking, but as the trial proceeded, I just "winged it" as Larry Wallace suggested and started to feel the excitement of every aspect of the criminal court process. During jury selection, I put on my best "Perry Mason" face (I actually watched some episodes of that show to learn how to act in the courtroom, how to question potential jurors, handle cross-examination, and so on) and tried to ask questions I thought he would ask without making a fool of myself. Every once in a while, I would glance at the judge, and two or three times he nodded at me with a bit of a smile. During a break, he even gave me a couple of pointers such as not standing too close to the jury box and making sure I stood up when the jury walked into the courtroom.

As the trial continued in a rather surreal atmosphere, I thought, "Am I really doing this?" Adrenalin took over when I cross-examined the detective assigned to the case. The Q&A seemed to make sense, and I could feel my heart pumping at full throttle. James wanted to take the stand and testify, and while I wasn't certain that was the best thing to do, he convinced me it was, and I guided him through that testimony during several practice sessions at the jail.

After James testified, and the state wrapped up its case, I gave the first final argument of my life akin, it would strike me later, to when I would write books "arguing" that Marilyn Monroe, JFK, and Dorothy Kilgallen had been denied justice. In James's case, somehow, my ability to converse with the jury didn't scare me at all even though a man's freedom was at stake. I emphasized James's remorse over what happened and how too much alcohol had clouded his judgment when he fired the shotgun. I asked the jury to consider his mental state and take that into consideration when deciding his fate.

Somehow the idea came to me to humanize James but while doing so, ask the jurors not to consider the act of murder in their own terms, in the context of their daily lives, but rather in his terms. This would help, I argued, to avoid judgment based on what they might have done in the situation he found himself in where James suspected, as he testified, that his wife was cheating on him. Thus, I said, "Put yourself in Mr. Jethroe's position: jealous, drunk, and thus unable to stop from killing the woman he loved." Noticing a few nodding heads, I actually believed I might have swayed some of the juror's minds and while I knew a guilty verdict was to be anticipated, I hoped it might be for a lesser offense, perhaps second-degree murder or even manslaughter. If so, prison time would be cut considerably.

When the jury retired to decide its verdict, Judge Kohlmeyer (bless him for giving me a chance as a PD) asked where the prosecutor and I could be located when the jurors were ready to announce its decision. Armed with the belief that I might have swayed the twelve men and women to take their time making a decision, I told the judge that I would be across the street at my law office. Before I could take a step in that direction, he replied, "Oh, Mr. Shaw, why don't you just stick around for a short while."

Suddenly, I realized what everyone in the courtroom knew: that despite my arguments to the contrary, James was a goner. Sure enough, after about fifteen minutes, the bailiff told us the verdict was in. When I stood beside my client with my hand on his shoulder, a move I'd seen Perry Mason do in court to show a bond between him and his client, the jury foreman announced, "We, the jury, find the defendant guilty of first-degree murder," not the last time I would hear those dreadful words during my years as a PD.

Needless to say, I was crushed, but in a moment I will never forget, James turned to me, extended his hand to shake mine, and said, "Mr. Shaw, thank you for doing your best." At that moment, I realized that doing my best would be my credo from then on, that despite my inexperience, clients could be certain I'd defend them to the best of my ability with justice as the earmark of every case I tried. And I promised myself I would just work harder than any other lawyer, sixteen hours a day if necessary, when defending the little guy or gal, the downtrodden, those who could not defend themselves.

Later, at The Cozy, a downtown locals' pub near the courthouse, the judge, the bailiff, and several attorneys patted me on the back, even bought me a beer or two or three. I had been christened under fire with the realization that I might make a decent defense attorney if I worked at it.

Best of all, seasoned lawyers Owen Mullin, John "Kit" Carson, and P. K. Ward (Mullin was the finest trial lawyer I ever knew; his imagination in the courtroom legendary) took me under their wing and made sure I followed orders when I began to represent private clients as well. At one point, they were watching while I represented what we called "a lady of the evening," a nice term for a prostitute, in front of a stern municipal court judge who found 95 percent of those charged with crimes guilty despite lack of evidence. Using what I called "my lawyer voice," a bit louder than usual, and referring to three or four law books I'd brought to show the judge how smart I was as I stood before him, I argued for a good twenty minutes or so. The moment I closed my mouth, the judge uttered, "Guilty as charged," and my client was sent to jail.

When I walked into the adjacent hall bent over in defeat, there was Owen waiting to speak to me as Kit and P. K. looked on. "Okay, Mark," Owen, aka "Owenie," said, "First rule of practicing criminal defense law: it has nothing to do with the law!" I gulped at those words and then the four of us headed for The Cozy where they educated me regarding the fact that being a criminal defense lawyer was, yes, all about the nuances of the law but more about the human side of the law, permitting judges or juries to become involved in the defendant's life and times and getting them to understand that the strict rule of law wasn't always the standard regarding guilt or innocence. That day, like them, I became a "seat-of-the-pants" lawyer by learning to meander through the court system using my street smarts as a guidepost. Once again, this experience would be a precursor to the days when I'd "defend" those denied justice like JFK, Dorothy Kilgallen, and Marilyn Monroe using street smarts and common sense instead of paying attention to wild theories that were true distortions of history.

Although I had no experience when I began my days as a criminal defense lawyer, cases came my way with ease since I had a reputation of going to the mat for my clients and doing the extra work necessary to make certain they received a proper defense. Many criminal defense lawyers were actually afraid to go to trial and thus became what I would call "plea bargain" attorneys, which reduced their effectiveness since prosecutors knew they feared appearing before juries or even judges in court.

My daily regimen consisted of 6:00 a.m. visits to the county jail to meet with the alleged lawbreakers I represented. Such discipline boded me well for my later becoming an author since I'd begin writing during the early hours (most days 5:00 a.m.) when I was working on a new book.

Up next during my daily routine were morning and afternoon court sessions either appearing for clients or defending them in jury trials before spending evenings investigating my cases. This "training" would continue when I investigated the trials and tribulations of the potential subjects of my books using the same methods employed, for instance, of organizing evidence I planned to rely on to "defend" the rights of those denied justice.

Regarding the PD investigations, I did not, as many lawyers did, hire private investigators to do the legwork. I wanted to locate and question witnesses firsthand, watch their facial expressions, and decide for myself whether they were telling the truth or not. Doing so permitted me, when I faced them on the witness stand, to ask the hard questions, to probe their credibility. One matter of interest I learned from Perry Mason was to watch closely when a witness began answering a question, "Let me be perfectly honest with you." In my experience, 95 percent of those who said that were dead-solid liars.

Again, looking back at the research, the investigations I would later conduct as an investigative reporter, I would shun for the most part second-hand observations, ones that were speculative in nature, and instead focus on primary-source accounts and documents that were credible in nature. Certainly, this attitude carried on when I began to investigate the JFK assassination and the life and times of Dorothy and Marilyn.

One light moment occurred during an aggravated-assault case where my opposing attorney was an assistant prosecutor named Donald Duck. One may only imagine the snickers when I rose to say, "Ladies and gentlemen of the jury, can you really believe Mr. Duck?" His parents should have been indicted for their name choice.

Never known for being much of a fashion plate (a reputation continuing to this day—Goodwill is still my favorite shopping choice), I had but two suits, both cotton, one a light blue and another khaki, that I wore on alternate days. The ensemble normally included a blue cotton button-down shirt and a colorful tie. But my trademark was wearing a khaki trench coat similar to the one actor Peter Falk wore on the hit TV show *Columbo*. Some lawyers liked to dress up with outfits straight from Saks Fifth Avenue, but I wanted to be a "regular Joe" when addressing jurors. That way I could better identify with the regular citizens who were going to decide my client's fate.

This tactic would be repeated during YouTube videotaped interviews and presentations regarding my future books since, again, I wanted readers to identify with the "regular Joe" aspect of my personality, not some fancy dandy dresser trying to impress them. [Author's note: A common criticism of me on those videos resulted in many viewers making this strong suggestion: quit wearing the same damn brown corduroy coat and get a haircut.]

While it normally takes years to build up a successful private law practice, I did so in a matter of months by gaining a reputation as a defense lawyer who sought the truth and fought for justice for the accused at every turn. Based on a solid reputation, referrals came my way even from police officers, prosecutors, and bail bondsmen who admired a solid work ethic.

In addition, unlike many defense attorneys, during examination of witnesses, I did not have a prepared script for asking questions but instead listened very carefully to what the witness was saying. This permitted meaningful follow-up questions instead of just following the script, which would have caused a disconnect in the continuing dialogue between the witness and me.

These lessons learned, though I didn't realize it at the time, would prove most valuable when I was investigating subjects I covered in my books and needed to question those who had primary-source information about what had happened. Little by little, although I did not realize it at the time, my character was being molded into the type of person I wanted to be: a ferocious advocate for the truth.

At one point, when my status increased as a noted defense attorney, I celebrated with my colleagues at the smoke-infested Cozy on a regular basis since I was now one of the "guys," which made me feel proud. My name seemed to be in the media on a regular basis, and to that end the *Indianapolis Star* published an article about my exploits in the courtroom comparing me to Tony Petrocelli, star of the 1974 hit TV series *Petrocelli*. Most of what the reporter wrote was true, and the free publicity brought a bevy of clients to my doorstep. This said, most also agreed, as did friends and family, that the mustache I grew never lived up to expectations.

13

The article began, "A rumpled trench coat is his trademark. His office looks like a teenager's bedroom, with clothes and pop bottles stuffed in the corners." Larry Wallace was then quoted as calling me "odd," arguably a compliment, before writer Grace Hanley quoted me as saying, "I have found that I myself can't get wrapped up in a robbery or rape case and I usually don't take them. I have never taken a child molesting case and I never will." That certainly was true although at one point I had defended a thirty-five-year-old black man who had been accused of rape based on the alleged victim identifying him through "smell" and no other evidence. Her explanation of how she did so appeared to be racial in nature and the judge handling the charges agreed—case dismissed.

CHAPTER 3

One highly publicized case made me not only feel like the dumbest person in the world but also the most embarrassed, even though my intentions were good. When an African American fellow named Ricky Lee Vaughn was suspected of killing a white policeman, a manhunt began like none before in Indianapolis. No other lawyer would take the explosive case, but I could not turn down Ricky's mother when she contacted me. Soon thereafter, the police chief and I appeared on television where Ricky's mother, tears rolling down her face, begged her son to turn himself in before a trigger-happy policeman, bent on revenge, killed Ricky.

Death threats came my way for taking the case, but nevertheless, to make it easy for Ricky to surrender, the police chief suggested that he and I appear on a street corner in a rather crime-ridden neighborhood at 9:00 p.m. one evening. The chief said he would be unarmed and no police would try to harm Ricky. True to this promise, the two of us stood on that street corner, but while we waited, we agreed that this was just about the craziest thing either one of us had

Ricky Vaughn's mother, Police Chief Hale, and me

TEARFULLY BEGS HIM FOR FATHER'S SAKE

'Give Up,' Suspect's Mom Pleads

REPORTED NEAR BORDER

Patty, Harrises In Canada,
Ex-Mobster Cohen Claims

Cherub Of Skid Row   *Tells Him*
                      He Won't
                      Be Hurt

Boycott Boosting Lawyer

ever done since anyone considered armed and dangerous might decide to shoot us both.

As it neared nine o'clock and darkness prevailed, we were ready for Ricky to show up. Then fire truck sirens wailed in the background headed for a nearby fire. Frightened that it was a setup, Ricky never showed and a few weeks later was captured in Ohio. When he returned and was charged with first-degree murder, which carried the death penalty, I represented him in a packed courtroom. A few weeks later, as I was making a passionate argument on his behalf, Ricky stood up, addressed Judge John Tranberg, a good man and a very fair judge, and screamed, "I don't want Mr. Shaw as my lawyer. I want to fire him." Embarrassed by the sudden turn of events, I crept out the side door of the courtroom hoping nobody would see me. Ricky's mother was upset, but he wouldn't listen to her when she told him he had made a mistake.

With another lawyer by his side, Vaughn was convicted and received the death penalty. Even though I never learned why Ricky fired me, I always felt that I had somehow let him down. Years later, I heard he had been stabbed to death while in prison.

Despite that setback, my robust practice would culminate in my becoming involved in nearly every significant criminal case that came along as I became the fashionable, "go-to" lawyer in Indianapolis. I liked to think that it was the trust factor making a difference, that people knew my word was my bond. The practice of being trustworthy was a goal that I would seek when I became an author.

When people lose hope, that's when they lose their dignity, their will to live, and I did my best to stand up for those who were depressed, especially when they had entered the world of the criminal and wondered if there was any way out. This set of values would come in handy when several of my published books, despite good marks for the most part, were panned by critics or assaulted by those with an agenda based on political beliefs or jealousy. In each case, I cast a deaf ear toward them and moved on.

While I would become an accidental author in the future, I had really become an accidental defense attorney since there was never any intention to spend the rest of my life in the trenches of the court system with those accused of crimes, small and large, each day. This said, there was one particular case where I believed justice certainly prevailed, although it wasn't the kind people regularly hear about.

The instance of justice being served in an unusual manner occurred when I defended Harriet, a mild-mannered African American woman who had killed her husband by shooting him *five times* in his back in front of a packed courtroom as he stood in front of a judge with a pistol she had carried in her purse for thirty blocks in freezing weather. Harriet was headed straight for prison until I learned that her husband Walter had stomped her eighty-five-year-old father to death during a drunken rage in front of Harriet and her children the night before her courtroom escapade.

Behind the scenes, I convinced the prosecutor of Harriet's "sudden impulse" to drill Walter based on an understandable motive to kill the bastard. Together, he and I visited the chambers of criminal court judge John Wilson and told him we'd like to "bury" the case for a few months so it would fall from the front pages of the *Indianapolis Star*. The judge agreed, and when we finally brought the case before him in an empty courtroom, he agreed with our plea bargain and Harriet was granted probation and sent home to her children. The unusual result gave all of us involved a sense that justice had prevailed despite, in this case, it being a sort of vigilante justice. Made sense to me.

Days later, while celebrating a courtroom victory with a bottle of Boone's Farm Strawberry Hill wine, my favorite, and a group of rowdy friends in a home I had purchased alongside a bubbling brook, the phone rang. "Is this Mark Shaw?" the man asked in a deep voice.

"Yes, it certainly is," I bellowed in my inebriated state, "It certainly is."

"Well, this is F. Lee Bailey," the caller said.

I quickly quipped, "Yeah, sure, hey, c'mon over and have some fun with us," while banging down the receiver believing it was one of my prankster friends.

F. Lee Bailey

Before I could move into the next room, the phone rang again. I picked up the receiver intending to bark at the caller, but before I could, he said, in a strong voice, "Listen, this *is* F. Lee Bailey, and if you hang up, it will be the dumbest thing you have ever done."

Fortunately, I listened, and Lee, famous at the time because of the Boston Strangler, Dr. Sam Sheppard, and Patty Hearst cases, requested that I accept an offer to become co-counsel with him during the representation of a seedy doctor named John Lind in Anderson, a city near Indianapolis. This was certainly another defining moment in my life since the fact that Bailey, licensed in Massachusetts, had chosen me to be his Indiana co-counsel over every other defense lawyer in the state provided additional credibility as a bona fide criminal defense attorney. I recall sitting in my house completely amazed at how far I had come from the days of the James Jethroe murder case, and a sense of satisfaction certainly set in along another "Why me?" moment among literally hundreds during a life packed with excitement and wonder.

Dr. Lind had been charged with "surgically removing" the head of an undercover DEA agent who suspected the physician of drug trafficking, and then tying the headless torso to a cement block that bobbed up in a shocked farmer's pond one sunny day. Predictably, the newspapers referred to it as "The Headless Torso Case."

Headless Torso

★ Continued From Page 1

"brains" behind both the explosion and the slaying, there is no way all the pieces of the murder puzzle can be put together.

Meanwhile, terror-stricken Anderson residents wonder what is going on. Among them are more than 100 persons who have given statements or signed affidavits.

IN ADDITION, The Star has learned that the son of a man who already has testified before the Federal grand jury was the target of a shooting within hours after his father's testimony.

The youth was not injured, leading probers to believe the blast was just another warning designed to discourage further testimony.

And the principal suspect in the murder and bombing has retained an Indianapolis attorney, Mark W. Shaw, it was learned.

Shaw verified to a reporter he has been retained by an Anderson man "when and if any charges are filed."

After speaking to Dr. Lind from a public telephone booth in Anderson, which he insisted on doing, we arranged for him to visit my Indianapolis office on a Saturday morning. While checking some trial notes, I looked up from my desk to see the beady-eyed, dark-haired doctor wearing an ill-fitting suit standing beside a tiny woman, whom I believed to be his wife, at the entryway. To my amazement, both were adorned in socks while holding their shoes in the air beside them.

Before I could speak, Dr. Lind put a finger across his mouth and whispered, "Our shoes are bugged." I didn't reply, but nodded toward a small, checkered couch in the corner of the office. There the three of us sat with me in between the two of them, no space in view.

While still whispering, Dr. Lind, his voice a bit squeaky, presented me with some questions about his case that he had written on the back of a grocery store receipt. After answering them, I walked to my desk while telling him not to keep that receipt on him since the police could confiscate his notes and use them against him in court if he was arrested.

I then leaned down to get a business card, and when I looked up, the doctor had a big bulge in his right cheek. To my bewilderment, he had *eaten the notes*. I didn't react and nor did his wife, but afterwards I referred to the dandy couple as Dr. and Mrs. Strange. Soon after, the police served a search warrant on Dr. Lind's home and, when they found a machine gun in his basement, arrested him for not only the firearms violation but the murder of the DEA agent.

Also key to Dr. Lind being nabbed was the testimony of two young Anderson convicted felons who, after being arrested on a burglary charge, told police the doctor had hired them to dynamite Plumb-Rite Supply, a local hardware store. As difficult as this was to believe, investigators learned that Lind was upset with the owner of the store who sent him a bill ever so slightly exceeding the amount previously quoted for an order of lead for the doctor's X-ray machine. Believing he had been overcharged, Lind had, according to the two men, ordered the dynamiting to get even with the proprietor. If you can figure that logic, you're smarter than I was.

Soon after Dr. Lind was arrested, Lee Bailey, with prissy wife Linda in tow, arrived at the Indianapolis airport in a private plane that Bailey, an experienced pilot, had flown from San Francisco, where he had blown the Patty Hearst case by permitting a military man to be on the jury. This was a mistake for sure since even a novice criminal defense attorney like me knew you didn't want any authoritative person like that on the jury since there is a danger that they will take over the deliberation and, if they believe the client is guilty, attempt to sway the other jurors toward conviction.

Hiring Bailey could have backfired on Dr. Lind, since throwing a famous lawyer from far away into the mix normally offends jurors who have less trust in that sort of attorney than a local lawyer with whom they are acquainted. There is also the potential to believe that the accused must be guilty or else he or she would have selected the local lawyer.

Nevertheless, with Bailey and me at his side, the firearms

Doctor Seeks New Judge

Charging that Federal Judge Cale Holder "would be unable to act as a fair and impartial arbiter," Anderson physician John Lind filed a motion for a new judge yesterday.

Lind, indicted by a Federal grand jury on charges stemming from the Sept. 28 bombing of Plumb-Rite Supply Co. in Anderson, asked through his attorneys, F. Lee Bailey and Mark Shaw, to have the case moved from the Southern District of the Federal Court.

The motion criticized Holder for releasing an entry at a bond hearing April 22 that indicated government agents are investigating Lind in connection with attempts on the lives of two Anderson physicians; the death of Gary Lake, whose body was found in a pond near Pendleton last November; arson; burglaries, and vandalism.

Lind's motion said the entry contained "hearsay" evidence prejudicial to his case.

The motion also sought to have Lind's case severed from that of Max Howard. Howard, an Anderson attorney, was indicted on charges of perjury when Lind was indicted.

Bailey and Shaw asked Holder to provide them with transcripts of the grand jury testimony and to have the government furnish information concerning any inducements, rewards or bargains being made with potential witnesses.

violation and the dynamiting—but not the murder charges, which the prosecution could not prove—would be judged by a jury not in Indianapolis, due to pretrial publicity problems, but in downstate Evansville. Cale Holder, a stern, no-nonsense federal judge, presided, and I watched as Bailey did his best to untangle the web of mystery as to why a distinguished physician had motive to own a machine gun and order a hardware store to be blown up.

I chipped in by cross-examining some of the witnesses, but we never made a dent in the prosecution's case.

Predictably, the jury convicted Dr. Lind, and while Bailey, who had shared part of the $100,000 attorney's fee with me, flew off into the sunset for another high-profile case, I stood with Dr. Lind before Judge Holder for sentencing. Before doing so, the judge made it clear he believed Lind

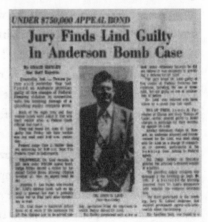

UNDER $750,000 APPEAL BOND

Jury Finds Lind Guilty In Anderson Bomb Case

was responsible for the DEA agent's death and, with that in mind, said, "I am sentencing you to nine years in prison, which is the maximum for the charges the jury convicted you of. I wish it could be more."

Watching Lee Bailey in action taught me some good courtroom strategy, but he wasn't at his best. Losing the Patty Hearst case devastated his ego, and he was never the same again, to the extent that years later he was disbarred in both Massachusetts and Florida. Before he died in June 2021 of what I believed was a broken heart since he loved the law so much and couldn't practice anymore, Lee lived in the northeast and operated an investigative organization, a true waste of a once-brilliant legal mind. We had kept in touch following the Lind case, and as will be explained, he played a big part in my entrance into the television arena shortly after Dr. Lind was sent to prison.

* * *

Despite a solid reputation as a defense lawyer for the poor and down-trodden with headline-making cases that kept me in the limelight, I first became disillusioned with my new profession when a young fellow charged with theft left my office and, upon exiting, stole my secretary Kathy's purse. While I raced after him down a main street in Indianapolis, like some sort of Keystone Cop, a thought occurred to me: "Hey, maybe it's time for a change."

During the next few days, as I questioned whether the profession as a criminal defense lawyer really suited me in the long run, I learned of a most disturbing case. A young man we will call Stephen had been charged with kidnapping a young woman and driving around with her tied up in his car trunk. After a court hearing where I attempted to lower the man's bond, the kidnapped woman's mother spit in my face while screaming at me for being a worthless derelict. I slithered out of the packed courtroom while wiping my face, but I felt like a true lowlife even though I was doing "my duty" as Stephen's attorney.

Stephen's case, which led to several sleepless nights, was the latest in a long line of my representing young people who had gone astray. When I stood in front of a judge with one such youngster, no more than fifteen or sixteen, who had been transferred to adult court because of the severity of his crime, the youngster actually said "thank you" when the judge imposed a heavy sentence. This kid was so naïve, so oblivious to what was occurring that it startled me, made me realize that this child, one with no mother or father to guide his path, was headed to prison where older inmates would tear him apart.

Time and time again, I saw that with each senseless crime, lives were destroyed; everyone lost—the victims, of course, but also the ones inflicting the harm. For all practicable purposes everyone, including juvenile delinquents, who entered the prison system were goners, especially considering the penal system's de-emphasis on rehabilitation. Many times I sat alone on a courtroom bench or at a tavern and simply shook my head. Parenting was the real issue; the majority of the kids I represented had never been parented, especially by fathers who had either abandoned them or were in prison themselves. These kids were lost, and most quit school and drifted into the crime world.

The confused state of affairs rolling around in my mind intensified after I won an acquittal for a client we will call Clarence, a skinny sixteen-year-old charged as an adult with the senseless murder of a young social worker on the northside of Indianapolis.

Clarence, his grandmother, and me in court

During his trial, the prosecutor made a strong case, and thus my goal was to force the jury to consider strong inconsistencies in the evidence against my client. Several times I found myself nearly crossing the boundaries of ethical conduct especially regarding the whereabouts of the murder weapon that had never been located.

Once the jury returned with a verdict of not guilty after I'd done my job creating reasonable doubt as to Clarence's guilt, an *Indianapolis Star* reporter named Carolyn Pickering, a woman of the truth in the ilk of Dorothy Kilgallen, walked up to me at the counsel table and said, "What do you think of the verdict, Mark?"

I looked at her and replied, "That's it. I quit. I'm done. Enough of this. I'm moving to Colorado." Shocked, Carolyn told me she would print the news in the Sunday paper if I did not get in touch with her, and after I didn't do so on purpose, Carolyn wrote her article including a cartoon of my skiing off to Colorado alongside a caricature of Lee Bailey in a garbage can.

Young Criminal Lawyer Shaw 'Retiring'

Part of the article read:

> One of the biggest surprises to hit the legal fraternity here in many a moon was the announcement last week by young criminal lawyer Mark W. Shaw that he's shucking it all and moving to Colorado soon after Christmas.

Shock waves hit the legal community based on my "retiring" since I had been successful in garnering several "not guilty" verdicts in a row, each of them dealing with murder allegations, but I knew if I continued on I might end up like many other criminal defense lawyers—a drunk, a drug addict, a mental patient, perhaps disbarred due to legal ethics violations since the stress involved with defending those charged with violations of the law takes a great toll on the soul. Nothing beats the courtroom for drama (later I would learn of Dorothy Kilgallen's fascination with trials), but one must constantly be dealing with people from the seedy world of crime who are destroying their lives and the lives of others.

Also, I was disenchanted with the legal system, believing it certainly favored the rich instead of giving the poor a fair shake in addition to causing most defense attorneys to realize they had to prove their clients innocent instead of the prosecution proving them guilty. Of concern were police officers, not all of them for sure, who were pressured into fabricating evidence and prosecutors who followed that line of thinking to protect their jobs.

In addition, there were racial issues in Indianapolis at the time, ones lurking beneath the surface that would escalate as the years passed. Frustrated,

I lashed out, and the article in the *Star* that appeared did not go over well with many of my legal colleagues and judges since I called for public defenders to be full-time and paid more, that two more criminal courts be added since the four current ones were overcrowded, that the prosecutor should be required to appoint a special prosecutor when there were conflicts of interest, and that attorneys needed to specialize if they were going to defend those accused of a crime.

Attorney Calls Law Enforcement 'Sham'

By JOE JARVIS

Attorney Mark Shaw will quit his specialized practice of criminal law Friday afternoon in Indianapolis, because, in his opinion, law enforcement here has become a sham.

He claims to hold this opinion without bitterness or prejudice against any individual.

With Shaw, the problem is the environment in which he has been practicing for four years.

"It's no longer any fun," he explains, blaming much of what appears to annoy him on prosecutors and judges.

Shaw, 31, is a native of Auburn, Ind., and has been in Indianapolis since 1969 when he entered Indiana University Law School. He said he has no motive for speaking out at this time beyond

Giving Up Practice
—Shaw

3 Marion County should have two more criminal courts (there are now four) to end the use of pro tempore judges and special judges because of crowded calendars; the public is not getting the justice it should from the use of pro tems and specials.

Article in *Indianapolis Star*

I had the mindset necessary for challenging the establishment, in this case the entire Marion County criminal court system, for which there was significant backlash. It wouldn't be the last time I'd challenge authority, those in power, especially when I began writing books. In fact, at times my attempts to change things for the better would backfire. But things don't change if nobody cares, and looking back, part of my destiny was to be embroiled in controversy, to speak up and risk the consequences especially when false facts and conclusions tarnish or destroy someone's reputation as would be the case when Marilyn and Dorothy died.

This all said, it is difficult to believe I actually "retired," left the practice of criminal defense law as abruptly as I did. Carolyn Pickering was correct when she wrote that my decision was "one of the biggest surprises to hit the legal fraternity," and many friends and colleagues thought it was the dumbest decision they had ever heard about. I had some second thoughts, but while I loved the action of the courtroom and all that went with it, it was time to move on especially so I would never have to, I hoped, view another autopsy report or visit a morgue to view the remains of a shooting victim, with those images then keeping me from a sound night's sleep.

This said, little did I know that one day in the future my knowledge of autopsies during my many murder cases, what to look for when determining the true cause of death, would be most helpful when I investigated the deaths of JFK, Dorothy, and Marilyn. In fact, as will be explained, their autopsies would become a major factor in learning the truth about what happened when they died since that truth had been covered up by powerful men threatened with accountability for their murders.

CHAPTER 4

While continuing to build the credentials that would serve me well when I began to investigate high-profile cases for the books I'd write, and despite the risk of not having any apparent means of earning a living, I moved to Aspen, Colorado, in 1977 to escape the images of dead bodies and career criminals. Why Aspen? Because I felt that the tranquility of the Rockies offered the prospect of a fresh start at age thirty-two during a time when the world was focused on Jimmy Carter's presidency and entertained by such classic motion pictures such as *Annie Hall*, *Rocky*, and *Star Wars*.

Before I left Indianapolis, we had a wingding "going away" party at the house, and I was flattered that so many friends, fellow attorneys, judges, and even a detective or two showed up. Boone's Farm wine flowed, along with better wine and beer, and it was a jolly time for all of us including Owen Mullin, P. K. Ward, and John "Kit" Carson, the three seasoned attorneys who had taken me under their wing when I first began practicing law as a public defender. To show them how much I treasured their advice and friendship, I bought each one a trench coat, as noted, one of my trademarks, and we laughed until midnight and beyond. Then tears flowed as I said "so long" to so many of those who had been so important in my life for years on end.

P. K. Ward, John "Kit" Carson, Owen Mullin, and me

At the time I moved to Aspen, John Denver, the singer/songwriter of "Rocky

Mountain High" fame along with many other hit songs, lived there. Since I had the round wire-rimmed glasses (before he did, I swear), and our face shapes and hair color matched (I had let mine grow), he looked a lot like me and I looked a *lot* like him. At the urging of friends, I began leveraging the resemblance to impress the fair sex until I was forced to sing "Rocky Mountain High" in public. My rendition caused coyotes in the nearby hills to howl.

My look-alike John Denver

When I met John on the slopes of Aspen Mountain in late 1977, thanks to my good friend Mike Hundert, the "Rocky Mountain High" singer asked, "Haven't I seen you in the mirror?" due to the similarities in our appearances—facial features, reddish/blond hair, wire-rimmed oval glasses, and all. Later, when I became an author and my mug was featured on the inside back flap of a book or I'd give interviews and presentations, one of the first comments was always: "Mark, you really *do* look like John Denver." I took that as a compliment.

In another of the totally unexpected events punctuating my life, one where once again I would be in the right place at the right time, ABC's *Good Morning America* (*GMA*) hired me as a legal analyst at the recommendation of F. Lee Bailey to cover the Aspen trial of Andy Williams's ex-wife, singer Claudine Longet. Bailey was *GMA*'s legal expert and he was supposed to cover the Longet case, but trial commitments caused him to suggest me as a replacement. His doing so meant a great deal to me—that Lee respected my abilities in the courtroom based on the Lind case.

Being in Aspen at the outset of the trial for Longet allegedly killing her boyfriend, famed skier Spider Sabich, a US Olympic team member and pro skiing champion in 1971 and '72, at his home, was certainly serendipitous since anyone interested in a television career normally starts at the bottom with a local station. Due to this unusual situation, I actually started at the top with a network program, not the first time unforeseen experiences like this came my way.

Despite no experience as a television commentator, I handled being on camera as if I was talking to a jury instead of a national audience. This sort of experience, especially talking to juries, would become so beneficial when I began to "talk" to readers through my published books by being, in effect, a storyteller.

In addition, although I did not realize it at the time, my analyzing Claudine's trial was preparation for doing so with certain cases in the future such as those involving JFK, Dorothy, and Marilyn. In effect, I was banking information about how to analyze a high-profile case, being "educated" in a sense, in addition to what I had learned during my criminal defense days for use when the time was right to investigate the mysterious deaths of the three twentieth-century luminaries.

Following the trial, one where I sat in the front row proudly wearing my ABC media badge, Claudine gave me the only interview she ever permitted at that time based on her trusting me to give her a fair shake. In that soft, French voice of hers, Claudine showed me how she held the gun in front of him so he could teach her how to use the safety. She then explained that the gun discharged accidentally. Regardless, I firmly believed that she shot Sabich in cold blood and would have been convicted of murder and sent to prison instead of receiving a light sentence for negligent homicide if not for police misconduct and prosecutor ineptness.

Not long after the Longet trial, where I told viewers Sabich had been denied justice when he died, the producers of *GMA* hired me as the program's roving "on the road" correspondent. Despite being claustrophobic and afraid of heights, I accepted the risk of an assignment to fly in an F-4 fighter jet during air force war games at Nellis Air Force Base in Nevada, whereupon, from a tiny seat directly behind his in the cockpit, I threw up all over the pilot when he swerved that plane in a pretzel-like formation scaring the bejesus out of me.

In another assignment, *GMA* asked me to interview young Travis Walton—the man who swore "little green men" aliens captured him in an Arizona forest and held him hostage in a spaceship for five days. I did so and found myself believing every word of Walton's story as he chronicled in the book *Fire in the Sky: The Walton Experience*. This caused many viewers to call me a "kook"—not the first time that happened. Regardless, the experience of being open to matters of the mystical would significantly affect future books to be published, especially regarding Dorothy Kilgallen's belief in UFOs.

Keeping an open mind came in handy when F. Lee Bailey asked me to travel to Cripple Creek, Colorado, to chat with *Sun Signs* author Linda Goodman, a famous American astrologer. Her daughter had been, she alleged, kidnapped, and she wanted Bailey's help but he was tied up in a trial. Thus, I traveled to see Linda and when I arrived she was sitting in a huge chair surrounded by, at the least, twenty purring cats.

Linda and I chatted about her daughter (I never found out what happened to her) and my life adventures to that point. When the next edition of Linda's book was published, I was surprised that she included me in her writing to the extent of predicting "wild adventures" in my life, ones "unpredictable" in nature. Boy, was Linda right about that happening.

With a flashy cigarette holder dangling from one corner of his mouth to the other, and a stiff drink, usually Chivas Regal or Wild Turkey, being sipped at breakneck speed, "Gonzo" journalist Hunter S. Thompson was quite the celebrity (author of *Fear and Loathing in Las Vegas*) and a good friend of the owner of Aspen's Hotel Jerome bar. One evening, the three of us engaged in useless banter about Hunter's desire to raise wild turkeys and ostriches on his nearby ranch or some gibberish like that. At the end of the discussion, the owner, who I'd prepped to do so, asked "Mr. Gonzo" if I could interview him on camera for *Good Morning America*. He agreed, but the next evening when the ABC camera crew and I waited for Hunter, he never showed up, even though we waited until 4:00 a.m. just in case the drug-crazed Gonzo-man wandered in the bar. Such an experience made me realize that dealing with celebrities, as would happen in the

Gonzo journalist Hunter S. Thompson

future when I tackled cases such as those involving Marilyn and Dorothy, required a special acumen.

A few years later, I attended one of Hunter's book signings at the Aspen Institute and chatted with him for a few minutes as he signed the book *Hey Rube*. In a true "Hunterism," he asked me, "Hey, Mark, when are we going to do that *Today* show interview?"

What was the effect on my psyche during these delightful days in Aspen? As time passed, my brain had been rescued from representing folks, rich, poor (I accepted many cases pro-bono), and in-between who had destroyed their lives and those of others through criminal conduct. Instead, my new life was all about enjoying each day while counting the blessings of one fascinating experience after the other. And the fascinating experiences taught me that when taking a chance the results may quite often be beyond belief.

* * *

Dealing with the law came next as fascinating experiences, one after the next at age thirty-three, rolled into the strange scene that had become my life. Following the airing of my well-received interview on *GMA* with Philadelphia Mafia kingpin Angelo Bruno's attorney—who violated the underworld's Omertà credo by talking to me about the mob's interest in Atlantic City gambling—I called the lawyer's office to seek a second interview. The weeping secretary said, "Mr. Shaw, I guess you don't know—my boss started his car this morning and it blew up, killing him." Afraid I might be next to die, I left Philly in a hurry despite the temptation to investigate his tragic death.

As was apparently meant to be, my experience with the attorney being "eliminated" by those in the underworld would come into play in the future when I dealt with the JFK assassination. I had learned that if one crosses the Mafia, one must realize there is a significant price to pay since these dangerous men play by their own rules, as will become apparent.

If not enough blessings had come my way, yet another came along one day when I visited the smallest network TV station in America, located in Miles City, Montana, on assignment for *GMA*. Owned by a mom and pop who acted as anchor and sports reporter, these senior citizens of the airwaves based much of their news on the local newspaper, the *Miles City Daily News*.

Captivated by this idea, I returned to Aspen and, some time later, cofounded and became a columnist for the *Aspen Daily News*, still in print today. This was the first time I was published (1978), and once again, attempting a new occupation despite the risk was certainly worth the effort, one based on a confident attitude that had been injected into my DNA early on in life.

Shortly after the paper hit the stands, my fantasy world turned upside down upon learning that *GMA* producers decided they wanted a "bigger name" to be their roving correspondent and cut me from the show. I tried to hide my

Phyllis George and me—
CBS *People* program

disappointment, but before long, the departure led to a new adventure and yet another amazing defining moment. This happened when I was chosen in 1980 to cohost the *People* prime-time program on CBS with former Miss America Phyllis George.

The show was patterned after the celebrity-driven magazine of the same name. I moved to New York City, where the studios were located near Times Square.

Those who knew me before this happened were shocked at my good fortune since this was Network Prime Time TV, no less. I couldn't believe it either. A real plum of an assignment occurred when the producers asked me to interview Academy Award–winning actor and race car fanatic Paul Newman. I ended up riding with the film legend as his car raced around Watkins Glen racetrack at breakneck speed, with him telling me, "Hold onto your balls, Mark, there's no room for a sissy on my watch." I did so as he zoomed around tight corners shifting gears with the hand-eye coordination of a man in his twenties.

Paul Newman—film legend and race car driver

Newman agreeing to the interview was based on his doing some homework to the effect that I had the guts to take a ride in the F-4 fighter jet. Our jaunt around Watkins Glen was breathtaking and afterwards I had to pinch myself to realize the man sitting before me sipping a Budweiser was none other than Butch Cassidy.

For whatever reason, Phyllis George was mercilessly attacked in the media as being too silly and not a serious reporter, just one that could cover fluff stories. To the contrary, everywhere I went, during every interview, I defended her. She was not just a pretty face but highly intelligent. As if it was meant to be, the experience of witnessing how Phyllis's beauty actually played against her caused me to recall what happened then to Marilyn Monroe when I began to learn about her life and times. Marilyn wasn't taken seriously despite, as will be explained, her being quite intelligent as well.

Since CBS had scheduled its *People* program against *Monday Night Football*, the die was cast for failure, and just six weeks after the premiere, the show was abruptly cancelled. I was greatly upset and even embarrassed over this bad turn of events. But, again, I decided to make a positive out of a negative. Instead of returning to Aspen, I drove cross-country to California even though, as would happen many times in my life, I wasn't exactly sure of the reasons for doing so other than I had a gut feeling that the sunshine and the Pacific Ocean would soothe my soul after being a TV network celebrity one day and out of work the next.

Ready to practice law again, I passed the bar exam on a fluke (I believe they mixed me up with another Mark Shaw when the results were posted) and, in another of those inexplicable defining moments, shortly thereafter became a Hollywood entertainment attorney representing, among others, United British Artists actors Maggie Smith, John Hurt, and Ben Kingsley. The latter I met during a London lunch just after he played Mohandas Gandhi in the film *Gandhi*. While he enjoyed a delicious dish of tandoori chicken, I felt as if I were talking to the famous Indian freedom fighter, a man of honor, a great role model for someone like me.

Donna Rice and Gary Hart exposed

One sunny Beverly Hills afternoon, I met the infamous Donna Rice. Her sexual escapade with the presidential hopeful, US senator Gary Hart, aboard the yacht *Monkey Business*, wearing a T-shirt with those words emblazoned on it, doomed his chances for higher office. As tears rolled down her face, she asked me to represent her so she could resume her career, but I had to tell Donna that nothing short of a miracle could overcome the terrible reputation she had with the big shots in Hollywood.

Later on, when I considered writing a book about Marilyn Monroe, Donna came into my mind since, like the famous movie star, I knew Donna had not been treated fairly by the media. There are certainly blessings and curses to being a celebrity, and both women endured hard times from reporters bent on crucifying them in the press.

Meanwhile, after reading in the Hollywood "trades" that several recent novels had been adapted into screenplays, I thought, "What the heck, I can write a novel based on my legal experiences." It was called *Professional Courtesy* and featured an off-beat lawyer like I had once been who struggles with the ethical standards just like I did. The storyline even included the three mentors who helped me learn the ropes, and in the end, the lawyer quits the business when he is burned out and needs a change of scenery to save his soul. Sound familiar?

Once the manuscript was in good shape, I sent it to a literary agent I'd met during an encounter with one of his clients at a Hollywood party. To my shock, he called the writing "sophomoric," a dagger to any creative heart, for sure. He was probably right since it was my first try, but to my later regret, I gave up on that book, one of the few times in life rejection made me surrender, at least for the time being.

CHAPTER 5

An urge to once again enter the legal arena in some fashion triggered my desire in 1981 to produce a syndicated television program (yet another "career choice"). The show focused on the world of law, presenting updates on various national trials of interest, offering advice for everyday legal issues, highlighting personalities in the legal field, and answering questions sent in to the "legal mailbag." My sidekick for what I called "Trials and Tribulations" was a loveable dog, the "Legal Beagle," who could bark on cue.

The "Legal Beagle" and me

Even though the show was a precursor to *Court TV*, famous *American Bandstand* host and ABC television personality Dick Clark, who loved the program idea, and his production company cohorts couldn't find a syndication company willing to air the show. This was a great disappointment since I wanted once again to help people through my knowledge of the law.

Just when I thought my television days were over and I'd have to get a "real job," up popped another program during my magical mystery ride through the TV world. I became a host, along with actor James MacArthur (*Hawaii Five-O* fame), of sixty-five segments as "Mr. Science" on the Disney Channel series *The Scheme of Things*. This was so ironic because I was the same guy who flunked physics and barely passed chemistry at Purdue. Some of the filming was set at the Epcot Center in Florida, where we unlocked the mysteries of the world through science. It covered a wide array of natural and man-made phenomena, including robots, pyrotechnics, energy farms, and foods of the future. https://dcba.fandom.com/wiki/The_Scheme_of_Things

My skeleton friend "Luther" and me on Disney's *Scheme of Things*

Searching for spiritual guidance as to where my life should head, I began attending the Beverly Hills Presbyterian Church on Rodeo Drive. And presto, as if it was meant to be in another defining moment too difficult even for me to believe, I was very blessed to notice film icon James Stewart at the church in 1987 as I approached forty-two years old.

I didn't attend church on a regular basis but when present, there would be Mr. Stewart sitting in a pew a few rows back from the front. One holiday season, he read *The Story of Christmas* and I felt like God himself was doing so. A few days later, in a rather strange experience, I awoke one morning with the idea to research the songs of Christmas and where they had originated. What I discovered was quite amazing and suddenly I had the idea for a television program featuring those songs and their origins.

And there was more. As if touched by a saintly hand, the next evening an even more bizarre idea entered my head: perhaps Mr. Stewart might host the program. Never averse to trying something new despite the risk of failure, a few days later I took my idea for a musical tribute to the songs of Christmas to be hosted by Mr. Stewart to the minister and requested a meeting with the film legend.

Nervous to the point of stuttering during our meeting, I told Mr. Stewart my idea. To my surprise, he quickly uttered, "Why, sure!" in that unforgettable *It's a Wonderful Life* voice of his.

With his magic name to draw other celebrities to the show, the program also starred Burt Reynolds, George Burns, and Lucille Ball, whom I spoke with prior to the filming since she was worried about close-ups revealing her advanced age. She said Mr. Stewart told her that if I promised to prevent close-ups, it would happen, and I certainly kept that promise.

In a heaven-like moment, Mr. Stewart and Ms. Ball together read *The Story of Christmas*, and *A Beverly Hills Christmas with James Stewart* aired to significant response on television in 1987. https://www.youtube.com/watch?v=_cASOTJ5d-0

James Stewart, Burt Reynolds, and me

Following the production of the program, Mr. Stewart, a role model akin to my father, invited me to his Beverly Hills office several times, one being on the day of his eightieth birthday. Listening to his stories, I was captivated with his zest for life, his love for film, and his down-home nature. Having him as a friend was as difficult to imagine as many other bigger-than-life experiences, such as interviewing Paul Newman, so I cherished every moment spent in Mr. Stewart's presence. He later sent me a birthday card, which I still have today, and the whole experience bolstered my confidence to the extent that I began writing, "Keep the Faith. You never know when there is a miracle right around the corner," on a notepad I kept in my back pocket. It is now written on a notecard by my computer.

Mr. Stewart, young singer Alisan Porter, and me

Despite the good fortune, by this time I had become disgruntled with the whole Hollywood scene even when I became a talent manager for an agency owned by a true entrepreneur, Larry Thompson. He procured me an invite to the Golden Globe Awards where small-town Indiana Mark mixed with celebrities such as Diane Keaton and Jack Nicholson, who was so stoned one night at the Hotel Jerome in Aspen that my friends and I watched him repeat his Academy Award–winning performance in *Five Easy Pieces*, specifically the hilarious scene with the waitress from hell.

Among those I worked with at the agency were Jamie Farr (*M*A*S*H*) and actresses Charlene Tilton (*Dallas*) and Donna Mills (*Knots Landing*). Once again I noticed the difficulties of being a show-biz personality, a star, especially for women whose beauty at times was an impediment to them being treated fairly by the male big shots in Hollywood.

Uplifted over the success of the Christmas program but discouraged with continually knocking on doors trying to make a living, I took a long walk along the Santa Monica Beach and tried to be realistic as to what might lie ahead. The bottom line of that realism landed on the fact that I was nearly broke. Several potential television appearances and production deals had fallen through. More to the point, I didn't have my heart in practicing entertainment law, and small-town Mark felt quite alone in the magical world of Hollywood.

What to do, I asked myself? Stick it out in LA and hope for the best? Move to San Francisco, which had always been a great city for me to live and work in? Move to Mars, and figure out what to do there? All of these options and jests filled my mind, but I decided that the one that made the most sense was to move back to Indiana near my family and true friends. It would be a step backwards professionally, but I was homesick for what I called "real people," for those who could be counted on through good and bad times, those who were straight shooters, those who, when they made a promise, kept it.

Throughout my up-and-down television career, people who knew me wondered how I had been so blessed. On the surface, I appeared to have it made, but there was a void inside me that could not be filled. I truly missed genuine, caring people, most of whom gathered in the heartland of America, or the mountains of Colorado. The experiences I had on the West Coast and beyond were ones I would never forget, but I needed some fresh air far from the Hollywood craziness. Those who learned of my decision to leave California for Indiana thought I was as confused and mixed-up as when I had left Indiana for Colorado years earlier.

* * *

With a swift kick, the fast-track rollercoaster ride through the Hollywood lifestyle came to an end. Dreams of grandeur needed to be put aside, as least for the time being, so that I could breathe again in the atmosphere of the Midwest, where I had lived for the first thirty-plus years of my life.

Back in Indiana, it was time to swallow my pride, since I was returning with the intention of practicing law after having quit in the mid-1970s when I was disgruntled with the legal profession for moral and ethical reasons. Now here I was, with no car, no place to live, no sense of what might happen to me, no clothes other than a suitcase or two full of them. For the first couple of weeks, I avoided going out in public since I was embarrassed that, for all practical purposes, despite some success in the entertainment field, I was a failure. At least that's how I felt.

Interestingly enough, when I finally came out of my shell and ran into people I had known years earlier, they didn't give a damn about any failures but instead congratulated me on how I had the guts to quit the legal profession, take on new challenges, and succeed beyond their wildest expectations. I recall walking into a bar in the tony Broad Ripple area, and damned if some folks didn't stand up and cheer. Hoosier hospitality warmed my heart, and I blended back into the community as if I had never left. I knew that my departing from a fantasy world and moving back home was the right decision for me.

Slowly, through referrals, I began to put together a few legal clients. When a couple called me about how the arrest of their son for rape was a true injustice since he had a solid alibi, I contacted Owen Mullin and we were able to get the charges dismissed. Doing so helped me feel good about myself as I had resumed my fighting for justice, but I was still eager to see if there wasn't another way to make a living.

Several months passed and then another "defining moment" happened that would further prepare me for my investigations into the JFK assassination and Marilyn and Dorothy's cases. In 1992, the year Bill Clinton replaced George H. W. Bush as president of the United States, former heavyweight boxing champion Mike Tyson was indicted for allegedly raping Desiree Washington, a young beauty queen contestant in Indianapolis.

Interested in the trial as a potential journalist at age forty-seven, I wrote to Patricia Gifford, the trial judge whom I knew from my days when she was a prosecutor and I was her adversary in Indianapolis during the early 1970s. After Pat granted me access to the trial, she asked me to handle the media for the case. I not only did so but also became a legal analyst for several networks including ABC, CNN, British Channel 4, and ESPN while writing a column for *USA Today* and correctly predicting Tyson would be convicted despite the sketchy evidence.

Mike Tyson

From the start, I knew the champion was doomed. Instead of his manager, Don King, hiring a local trial lawyer with courtroom experience in a rape case, he decided that a Washington, DC, corporate attorney named Vincent Fuller, who had won a tax-evasion case for King, was the perfect choice. Go figure. Alongside him, King at least brought local attorney Jim Voyles into the mix as co-counsel but Voyles was more of a "fixer," a plea-bargain expert rather than a seasoned trial lawyer.

Before the trial testimony even began, Fuller made an unforgiveable mistake since the first words out of his mouth to the jury during his opening statement caused me to gulp and nearly stand and shout, "Mike, quick, get another lawyer." Why? Because I knew Fuller had backed himself, and worse, Tyson, into a corner when he told those jurors, "You will hear from Mike Tyson…." Any defense lawyer worth her or his salt never makes that commitment since if the evidence presented points strongly toward acquittal, the defendant may not need to testify. But Fuller, as incompetent an attorney as I ever met, had guaranteed that Tyson would testify, a promise that would backfire big time later in the trial.

Little did I know that after I took notes day after day at the trial, what I had seen and heard from my front-row seat would stir my emotions enough to do something I had never considered to that point in my life. Despite no training, no writing classes, no fancy University of Iowa writing workshops and so forth, I decided to write a book, one that I would call *Down for the*

Count: The Shocking Truth behind the Mike Tyson Rape Trial—the full story of the champ's clash with the American legal system.

As I wrote in the book, the Mike Tyson trial permitted me to examine the legal process up close and personal as a legal analyst, just as I had done with the Claudine Longet case. I told my ESPN, ABC, and *USA Today* audience that the most devastating clue to my realizing the former heavyweight champion of the world was most certainly headed for prison came when the Fuller legal team decided this was their main defense to the charges: "Mike Tyson is so dangerous, so violent, so abusive, and so much a menace to society that Washington should have never gone to his hotel room in the first place." Yes, that's right. That's actually what was said. Consequently, the nearly all-white jury kept watching for evidence about Tyson's violent tendencies in and out of the ring and slowly, began to believe that the defense team was right, that the boxer was dangerous to the extent that he ought to be thrown into state prison.

As this was occurring, I wanted to scream from my front-row seat and try to save the poor guy being denied justice. The worst cross examination I have ever seen happened when Washington, whom Tyson had met during a visit to the beauty pageant, took the stand. Her testimony made it clear all he was interested in was sex and nothing more. Fuller, as cold a fish as ever entered a courtroom, one who never showed any sort of companionship with Tyson, never patted him on the back or sat close to him, asked the most superficial questions imaginable and neglected to secure specifics about what really happened in that hotel room. Washington thus escaped unscathed when even a superficial cross would have indicated she knew exactly what Tyson wanted when he asked her to the hotel room and did not object to his sexual advances there.

If the incompetent examination of Washington wasn't enough, against any sort of common sense, Fuller decided to let Tyson testify. I wanted to yell, "No. No. Don't do it," since I knew this ill-prepared boxer's testimony would be a disaster. And it was, as I informed the ESPN viewers when I appeared with Charley Steiner, a prominent ESPN reporter.

Where had Tyson's lawyers been while he awaited his fate while sitting alone in the courtroom? Drinking champagne and eating a tasty steak dinner at a fancy nearby restaurant. Finally,

Tyson escorted by sheriff's deputies

the lawyers rejoined him, but when Tyson first heard the word "guilty" spoken by Judge Gifford, I watched from my courtroom seat as his head cocked to the

side like he had been hit with a thunderous right cross. He whispered, "Oh, man," and slumped down in his seat.

Quickly the news spread to the world as Tyson was led out of the courtroom in handcuffs. From the top of the mountain to the bottom, he was now a convicted rapist.

Once the Tyson trial came to an end, I learned even more reasons why a true injustice had occurred, and what I discovered made me want to throw up. During the proceedings, the

Tyson during jury verdict announcement

prosecutors, led by Greg Garrison and Barb Trathen, swore that Desiree Washington had not pursued possible television and film avenues with her story and thus any attempts to do so were kept from the jury. To the contrary, evidence surfaced that she had hired an attorney to do just that, and it was clear that the prosecution team had hidden the truth.

To my way of thinking, both Garrison and Trathen and their boss Jeff Modisett should have been disbarred for their misconduct. Several

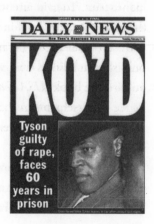

DAILY NEWS

KO'D

Tyson guilty of rape, faces 60 years in prison

jurors posttrial, as I revealed in *Down for the Count,* were quite upset with the prosecution, including Juror Number Ten, Dave Vahle. He told a Philadelphia radio host, "I cannot see Desiree as a credible witness from what I know now. We [the jurors] felt that man raped a woman. In hindsight, it looks like a woman raped a man. [And] I would sign an affidavit that if we had known about the money, I wouldn't have voted to convict him. Mike Tyson deserves a new trial."

Juror Number Eight, Rose Pride, said, "I would have been more skeptical of Washington's testimony if I had known about the alleged movie and book deals." Despite these and other jurors and the furor over Garrison and Trathen's misleading behavior, the appellate courts did not reverse the jury decision and no misconduct charges were ever brought against the prosecution team. A sad state of affairs for sure, and ultimately Tyson spent less than three years of a six-year sentence in prison. He should never have spent one day there.

Becoming an author was purely accidental, since I had never intended to write anything longform. Other than the few short columns I'd written for the *Aspen Daily News,* all I had written approaching what I was about to attempt was a long appeal brief or two when I was a public defender, and that was just legal jargon.

When the manuscript was in good order, I began to seek a publisher with hopes of getting just one book published with no consideration of a career as an author. Having no idea how to do so, I consulted a reference book, discovered a few possibilities, and started sending out letters and the manuscript. To gain attention to the package, I bought a rubber stamp with the image of a dog on it in red font and peppered the priority mail envelopes with several of them. Lo and behold, after getting several rejection letters, a publisher in Illinois who was a dog lover liked my ingenuity and agreed to publish the book. *USA Today* reporter Jon Saraceno, among others, gave me a nice endorsement on the back cover: "Shaw's blow-by-blow legal account gives you a ringside center seat to the most dramatic knockout of a major sports figure ever."

When that publisher decided to release the book, I added another profession to my resume: author. Holding the book in my hands was a very special moment in time. For days, I kept looking at the cover.

Most book reviews across the country were terrific, but one Indianapolis reviewer lambasted it under the headline, "Shaw's book on Tyson worthless." Well-reviewed books received five stars, but this reviewer granted me none. Later, I found out he was upset that I hadn't used a quote of his he gave me for the book.

Publishing the book about the Tyson trial, as I would later understand, set the stage for future books dealing with injustice. To this point in life, I'd experienced numerous lessons-learned moments strengthening my character and my investigative skills, and when the time came to first deal with the JFK assassination, I would be ready to do so.

CHAPTER 6

When ESPN asked me to comment on the O. J. Simpson case the day he was driving around LA's freeways on June 17, 1994, evading the police, I appeared via satellite on the Jim Rome television program and described how Simpson's fleeing would inhibit his defense at trial. While doing so, I recalled a party in LA where I had met O. J. and his wife Nicole when she walked into the room and appeared as if she had the moon shining on her beauty. Later I commentated on the trial itself.

When it came time for the jury to reach a verdict, my prediction that he would be acquitted was met with skepticism, but experience as a defense trial lawyer told me the prosecution's performance was less than effective. When Johnnie Cochran said, "If the glove doesn't fit, you must acquit," as corny as that sounded, he gave the jury its peg to do just that, acquit, to the dismay of most of the planet. Seeking that "peg," one critical piece of evidence any jury may use to convince friends and the public they made the right decision, I would discover, would translate to my investigations of the JFK, Marilyn Monroe and Dorothy Kilgallen deaths where one key piece of evidence would prove worthy to my theories regarding the truth about what happened to each of them.

Based on the success of *Down for the Count*, books published from the point on before I hit some hard times included *Larry Legend* (1998) about Boston Celtics star Larry Bird and his first year of coaching the Indiana Pacers.

The hard edge to Bird's story that I wrote became quite controversial. Despite his glorious career as an NBA legend, Larry had failed miserably

during the most important day of his life. This
happened when he failed to acknowledge the birth
of a child who was his daughter while a student at
Indiana State and thus abandoned her at birth. I
held him accountable in *Larry Legend*, and Larry,
even though I noted in the book that at some point
the daughter and he had something of a reunion,
threatened to sue me. Regardless, I was proud of
my calling him out despite his badmouthing me
to anyone who would listen. Writing the truth
triggers consequences, especially when famous,

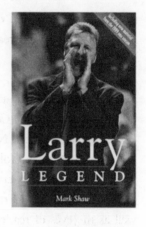

powerful men are involved. Down the line, I would learn about those consequences when I took on the Kennedy family.

As my books became popular, I realized they were like children in some
ways, an extension of myself, since they came straight from my heart and my
brain onto the book page. I was educating, entertaining, and making people
stop and think about the life and times of well-known figures or historical
matters. Each book was special, like a newborn. I didn't try to inflate my ego
by dwelling on any great impact I'd made on society through my stories but
an author may make a difference in people's lives, although many times the
exact impact is never known.

While researching the lives of others was of interest to me, the writing,
especially the first draft, was the most amazing part of the publishing process. Why? Because, like an artist who has no images on the canvas when she
or he begins, I started with no words on the page and then there was one
word, and two, and a hundred and then a thousand and so forth. In 2021,
I would write *Collateral Damage*, the longest book of my career, spanning
nearly 185,000 words, but I had started it, yes, with only one word.

During the writing process, I also relished the way my brain worked,
how words flew into my mind, some of which I had never used before, as is
happening right now as I add word after word to this book. Down the line,
folks would say my books were easily read and that I was a prolific author.
True, and yet the reason the books were easily read, a compliment for
sure, is because, as somewhat of a small-town Indiana yokel, I don't have a

highbrow vocabulary. I thus have never attempted to try to impress the reader with big words most people can't decipher.

During this time, the first book where I became the "voice" for a woman happened when I published *Testament to Courage*, exposing the injustices at Ravensbrück, a Nazi prison camp solely for women, based on a Holocaust journal by Cecelia Rexin—a Christian German woman, a true angel of mercy. That story brought tears to my eyes as well as the eyes of readers. This courageous woman risked her life to save the life of a Russian child about to be gassed at the camp by befriending a German prison guard, an action that caused readers to chastise her for doing so. Of all the books I've written, I'm most proud of bringing Cecelia's story to print to the extent of defending her using the enemy, the guard, to save a life.[1]

Due to my accidental entry into the world of writing and publishing books, words had become my tool for reflecting on the world and the people in it. Most all of my books were, and are, historical in nature, providing an opportunity to make a contribution to important events that were happening or had happened in the world.

The accidental author at work

* * *

During the fall of 2000, as George W. Bush and Albert Gore readied themselves for the presidential election, I was completing a biography of Jonathan Pollard, the American navy intelligence specialist who had spied for the Israelis. I had heard of his case when his father, Dr. Morris Pollard, was a

---

1 In 2018, I told this story again with some fictionalized material added based on a viable account where Cecelia, the little girl, and the prison guard meet after the war. Keeping Cecelia's "voice" alive per the Holocaust journal, the book is entitled *Courage in the Face of Evil.*

guest on the southern Indiana radio show I hosted. I had believed Jonathan was the traitor the government portrayed in court filings and that the life imprisonment sentence was justifiable.

This said, when Dr. Pollard, a revered professor at Notre Dame, spoke of the *why* behind the reason his son had leaked US government secrets to our ally Israel, I began to understand the motive. Jonathan, in his capacity as an intelligence specialist, had discovered the government was hiding critical intelligence data from the Israel intelligence community.

A devout Zionist, Jonathan finally decided to cross the line and become a spy. Perhaps if he hadn't been paid for doing so, the treatment given him on judgment day wouldn't have been so harsh. But this treatment should not have been harsh anyway, as I discovered since Caspar Weinberger, the secretary of defense, double-crossed Pollard by requesting the long sentence instead of a much shorter one promised if Jonathan pleaded guilty. The result of my investigation to expose injustice by exposing the truth was the book, *Miscarriage of Justice: The Jonathan Pollard Story*, published in 2001.

Heavy criticism followed. Going against the grain, confident I was doing what *was* right even though others did not agree or approve, resulted in my being a magnet for controversy, including my being called a traitor. Justice had not prevailed, and I wanted readers to stop and think about whether the life sentence was commensurate with those imposed on others guilty of spying against the United States. One review caused some satisfaction for my taking on the case. It happened when Morton A. Kaplan, professor emeritus of political science, of the University of Chicago, wrote, "*Miscarriage of Justice: The Jonathan Pollard Story* by Mark Shaw is a gripping account of an infamous prosecution by a vindictive government…The life sentence not only reneged on promises that had been made for confession but were entirely out of proportion to the offense…."

The miscarriage of justice inflicted on Pollard lasted until the end of 2020. After being released from prison and being on parole for five years

48

while forced to wear a monitor on his ankle (as if he could be dangerous), he was finally free of any government interference with his life. He moved to Israel, where he was treated with respect.

While I was on top of the world with my published books, the ESPN exposure, and even the radio program I hosted, difficult times suddenly appeared as problems with my private life surfaced. This was partially my fault as my ego had gotten to be the size of Texas, and I didn't handle the celebrity status as well as I should have.

When there is a "defining moment" that shakes your confidence and causes you to conduct an inner probe of the type of person you have become, soul searching enters in. Consistent with my love for books, I found comfort in one of them when I entered a Barnes & Noble bookstore in Indianapolis and was drawn to a table stacked with new releases. On the top of one pile I saw Pastor Rick Warren's bestselling book, *The Purpose Driven Life*.

Believing that this was somehow meant to be, I bought the book and read it that evening cover to cover. Warren's message, especially his writing, "It's not about you," which resonated with my over-the-top ego, presented a roadmap for a mystical journey of sorts, including a daily meditation schedule and practical steps that could help me quit feeling sorry for myself and decide life changes were necessary.

To be certain, not everything of a conservative nature Pastor Warren included in the book resonated with my beliefs, but there were certainly kernels of wisdom I took to heart. One passage involved the need to apologize to those who may have been wronged by certain actions even where the need to apologize may not be deemed necessary. I took this advice seriously and mended some wounds to others so I could move forward.

Despite the criticism, the publication of *Miscarriage of Justice* and my reading *The Purpose Driven Life* brought back my enthusiasm for moving ahead. I decided, as I had before, to make things happen by packing my loving dog, Black Sox, in my truck and driving back to Colorado.

The basis for doing so was because in the town of Eagle on the western slope of Colorado, LA Lakers superstar Kobe Bryant had been charged in 2003 with rape. ESPN obtained a media pass for me that reserved a front-row seat when the hearings began, and Bryant sat, not more than fifteen feet from me, with a smirk on his face as if he were the victim. In my live reports for ESPN and *USA Today* as their legal analyst,[2] I ridiculed the defense lawyers for unethical conduct when they violated a court order by exposing the name of the rape victim. This led to her reputation being destroyed and a forced monetary settlement of the case. To this day, I believe Bryant was guilty of rape. The woman involved had been denied justice, and if a jury could have heard the evidence, justice would have prevailed, and the basketball icon would have been convicted and sent to prison based on the evidence. (Later, when both Marilyn Monroe and Dorothy Kilgallen's reputations were destroyed due to wrongful conclusions about their deaths aired in the media, I thought about the victim in the Bryant case.)

With some regret, I had decided it was time to leave Indiana for greener pastures, and while I was in Eagle covering the Bryant case, I drove to Aspen, where friends of mine still lived. Walking through the village, I realized that being in Colorado again was meant to be, and two weeks later Black Sox and I moved to Aspen. While walking along the Roaring Fork River one day, just after having met Pastor Warren when he spoke at the Hotel Jerome, a flash of an idea hit me based on a book I was reading that dealt with spiritual transformation being possible through seminary experience.

Armed with this idea at the age of sixty in 2005, I researched alternatives and landed on San Francisco Theological Seminary located in San Anselmo in Marin County. I called and asked, "Do you let old people in with bad grades?"

The woman laughed and said, "Well, we might."

A month later I was attending classes with the eventual outcome that I spent nearly three years earning a master's degree in theological studies. To my surprise, I received the best grades of my life since, for once, I

Black Sox digging at the beach near the seminary

---

2 Time and time again, having the law degree I earned at the Indiana University School of Law in "my back pocket," so to speak, opened doors to exciting opportunities I could have never imagined. These included not only practicing law in both Indiana and California and becoming a network TV legal analyst, but possessing the skills to become a competent investigative reporter.

really enjoyed the learning process with Black Sox alongside as my study companion.

While at seminary and re-acquainting myself with the man I wanted to be, I attended a class called "Spiritual Direction" and learned about the revered American Trappist monk Thomas Merton, writer (author of nearly sixty books), theologian, mystic, poet, social activist and scholar of comparative religion. His book, *New Seeds of Contemplation*, immediately resonated with me, especially when he wrote:

> We are at liberty to be real, or to be unreal. We may be true or false, the choice is ours. We may wear now one mask and now another, and never, if we so desire, appear with our own true face. But we cannot make these choices with impunity. Causes have effects, and if we lie to ourselves and to others, then we cannot expect to find truth and reality whenever we happen to want them.

Suddenly, I realized that for many years, I had chosen to wear a mask, to be the big-shot TV celebrity and so forth when that was not really my true identity. From my twenties, I had been a seeker of justice, a man who defended those denied justice, and that identity had somehow disappeared from view. To change my behavior, I needed to try to find the "old Mark Shaw," to appreciate that I could change and return to those elements of the kind of spirit I wanted leading my way. This meant "unmasking" and returning to the values I cherished when I was a youngster and then as a criminal defense attorney. That profession had been my chosen destiny, but I had lost my way and, based on the literary journey I had begun, there was now a chance to regain my "spiritual balance" and become a "new and better Mark Shaw."

As I considered this potential, I learned of Merton's love affair with Margie, a student nurse half his age. But I was surprised that no one had wanted to talk about this human side of the man who had sought love all of his life. Immediately, I understood Merton deserved a type of "justice." Instead of the Catholic Church portrayal of him, which excluded the affair, I was in a position to give the public an inside view of the "real" Merton based on a journal he kept about the love affair. The result was a book entitled

Beneath the Mask of Holiness: Thomas Merton and the Love Affair That Set Him Free.

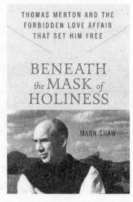

Immediately upon release, the book was promptly condemned by Merton's followers because the book publicly exposed for the first time his "human side." The famous singer, Joan Baez, confirmed his love for Margie when I interviewed her for the book. She told me she wasn't surprised when learning about the affair because she knew he was in love. She concluded "that watching him drinking and in love showed how the greats are human too."

While many praised this book for its honest perspective of Merton, Merton's Catholic loyalists ripped it with nasty Amazon reviews, many critics calling me "anti-Catholic." My dedication to telling the truth despite the criticism necessitated learning to deflect such criticisms by developing a thick skin.

Merton's inspiring words continued to impact my soul when I learned more about his conversion process. There was a more human side to him than most people knew about, and his struggles with pre-monastic sinful conduct, including alcoholism and adultery, made me realize that even, or perhaps especially, saint-like people have dark sides too. Merton has traveled with me as a spiritual companion ever since.

Learning the truth about the spiritual guru had an upside, however, since it provided me with many words of wisdom to live by through his bestselling book, *New Seeds of Contemplation.* Through Merton's guidelines and contemplative thought on my own, I was now the Mark Shaw I wanted to be, one worthy of marrying a beautiful and gracious Taiwanese woman named Wen-ying Lu, a catalog librarian at Michigan State University.

Lu, Black Sox, and me after the wedding

52

Lu brought love and stability into my life when I needed it most. We were married in 2008 on a small ship in the waters near Alcatraz shortly after graduation at age sixty-two from SFTS with Black Sox smiling all the way.

At the time, my love for books had translated into my purchasing a small (very small) bookstore in Sausalito that I called "Cricket's Books and Gifts." Our specialty was vintage books, and volunteers helped me run the store when I had seminary classes. One point of interest; notice the life-size cutout of a famous actress we positioned outside that store. Meant to be?

What a blessed man I was, one whose mind had been cleared of the "noise," as Thomas Merton called it, in the world that had allowed me to continue my literary journey. His influence along with Pastor Rick Warren's words of wisdom, especially "it's not about you," and Lu's loving ways had prepared me to write a book of historical importance so as to hopefully make, as I had promised myself when I was spared serving in Vietnam, a difference in the world. The result was publishing *Stations Along the Way*, a chronicle of young German woman Ursula Martens's worship of Adolf Hitler and her learning the truth about Hitler through a spiritual transformation when she left Germany for the US. In the book, I defended her having joined the Hitler Youth since, like so many young people at the time, she had been brainwashed by the Nazis.

Graduating from San Francisco Theological Seminary

My Sausalito bookstore

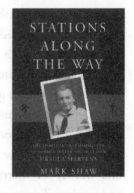

Standing up for Ursula caused me to feel good about myself, and I was now full of energy, ready to take on new challenges. Telling her story was in line with having fought for justice during the days when I was a criminal defense attorney defending Ricky Lee Vaughn, the alleged cop killer; Harriet, whom I had saved from being imprisoned for shooting her husband after he killed her father; and helping the man wrongfully accused of raping a woman based on his body odor. My books had included shining a light on Cecelia Rexin, the "angel of mercy" during the Holocaust, and standing up for Jonathan Pollard, whose life sentence was the result of a double cross.

Fully energized by this limited body of work, I was ready for new challenges, ready to focus on any opportunities to fight for justice and to correct distortions of history by using the skills I had learned as a man of words, one whose legal acumen permitted a unique perspective of the world I lived in. Little did I know that whatever spirit was guiding my life had in mind a research and writing adventure/journey that in hindsight would seem too amazing for even me to believe. My learning about a remarkable woman—a skilled journalist, one who would become the inspiration for not one, not two, not three, but including this one, four of the six books touching on the JFK assassination—was about to change everything.

CHAPTER 7

As mentioned in this book's introduction, the early chapters have provided insight as to how certain life experiences through 2007 prepared me to tackle matters of historical importance involved with the JFK assassination and the life and times and deaths of Dorothy Kilgallen and Marilyn Monroe. My investigations of these three twentieth century luminaries could not have been predicted by me or anyone who knew me, but all at once, as will be explained, I would begin an improbable journey exposing cover-ups of the truth about what happened to them based on the credentials earned as a former criminal defense attorney, investigative reporter, and established author.

In logical fashion, we may now turn to the true crime aspects of this book. Like most Americans, I presumed that the Warren Commission had nailed it when the members concluded a "nut" named Lee Harvey Oswald was the lone assassin of President John F. Kennedy. This said, the long and winding journey to unraveling the truth, to the extent of completely destroying any credibility of the Warren Commission report through the explosive new evidence to follow, began when I researched and then published *Melvin Belli: King of the Courtroom* in 2007. He was the legendary San Francisco attorney whom I had briefly practiced law with in the mid-1980s.

We became friends to the extent of dining together and my producing a series of "The World According to Belli" segments for television in 1984 where the loquacious lawyer espoused his views on the state of the legal profession. We also attended the Major League Baseball All-Star game when Belli took me there in his gold Rolls-Royce.

Belli, while being married six times, represented famous personalities such as actors Errol Flynn, Lana Turner, Mae West, and boxers George Foreman and Muhammad Ali. Other clients included the Rolling Stones and comedian Lenny Bruce, which, it will be revealed, connected, as I came to learn, with Dorothy Kilgallen's defense of Bruce's outlandish stage performances in 1964.

During my initial inspection of Belli's life and times, curiosity piqued when I learned he had also represented Jack Ruby, who shot Lee Harvey Oswald, the alleged assassin of JFK. Within a year's period of time, my research, honed during my years as a criminal defense attorney, provided revelations included in the book.

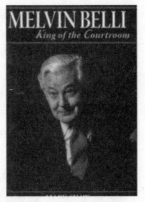

Since no one had written a biography of the loquacious lawyer, what I exposed startled many unfamiliar with his career. Belli was a civil attorney famous for winning multi-million-dollar verdicts against many pharmaceutical companies. He was dubbed "The King of Torts" by *Life Magazine* but had tried very few criminal cases and none dealing with the death penalty, which made him an illogical choice to represent Ruby. He was also a Mafia "groupie" of sorts, known to only a few people, since his main client and close friend, I learned, was LA gangster Mickey Cohen, described in a 1957 FBI file as "THIS MAN IS EXTREMELY DANGEROUS. A COLD BLOODED KILLER."

Melvin Belli had provided several conflicting versions as to how he became Ruby's attorney. One version has it that Earl

Mickey Cohen and Melvin Belli with unidentified man in 1955 when Cohen was charged with a deadly assault in Los Angeles

56

Ruby, Jack's brother, had watched Belli during an LA trial and then hired him. To the contrary, my interview of Seymour Ellison, one of Belli's law partners, revealed this explanation: "It was not Earl Ruby who hired Mel. It was someone connected with what I called the 'gaming industry' in Las Vegas. That name was on a memorandum in the Ruby files that Mel brought back from the Ruby trial. There were five or six boxes stuffed with them and unfortunately they were destroyed later on."

I also interviewed J. Kelly Farris, a close friend of Belli's. He described what happened during a lunch with the attorney at Fisherman's Wharf in San Francisco on November 24, 1963, two days after JFK was assassinated. Farris recalled: "A waiter walked up and said, 'You won't believe it, some guy named Ruby just shot Oswald.'" Farris then added, "Moments later, Mel's face was all flushed and he said, 'Well, now I'll have to represent Ruby.'" Belli's statement, as I discovered through further research, implied his prior knowledge of JFK's assassination as he had apparently been "on call" to become involved in any possible assassination cover-up.

Melvin Belli and J. Kelly Farris

With every book I've written, there is an "ah-hah" moment that propels me into full investigative mode, just as had always occurred when I was handling a high-profile trial or covering one for the networks. This time it happened when I interviewed another primary-source witness, Milton Hunt, Belli's chauffeur who was in Dallas with Belli during the Ruby trial. He told me, "At one point, Mel admitted, 'We're just going through the motions; the trial's a whitewash,'" causing me to wonder whether Belli had been ordered to make certain Ruby was convicted.

Due to these revelations from Ellison, Farris, and Hunt, further researching Belli's underworld leanings was a must. Milton Hunt described for me his boss's office in 1964 as being that of a "Mafia

Jack Ruby and Melvin Belli

wannabe who held court in his San Francisco lair like he was a Mafia king-pin. The whole office was like something out of Chicago gangster movies." From my days of having a small upstairs office above Belli's show-stopping San Francisco headquarters (the Gray Line Bus Tour stopped there), I knew Hunt was correct. There indeed was a *Godfather* movie-like dark atmo-sphere present in many ways, with Belli even posturing himself like Don Corleone behind a huge oak desk that he had raised so he could look down on visitors.[3]

Milton Hunt also told me Belli was "enamored" by the mob and other corrupt individuals. This comment echoed another by a Belli associate who stated, "Mel was intoxicated with the Mafia. He loved the power, the money, the irreverence they had for authority just like he did." At one point I learned that Belli told anyone who would listen that he was a member of the "San Mateo Mafia," a band of thugs from south of San Francisco.

Simply put, as Seymour Ellison told me, "Mel loved the Mafia and they loved him, and he traveled many times a year to Vegas to just buddy-up to mobsters so others would think he was one too."

This primary-source evidence collection, with no speculation permitted, would become the mode of operation for my research journey about the JFK assassination. That Belli had employed the ludicrous psychomotor epilepsy insanity defense on behalf of Ruby caused further suspicions on my part about Belli's involvement in the Ruby case. Those suspicions led to my questioning whether Belli, due to his Mafia affiliations, had been ordered to represent Ruby by Mafia figures who may have been involved in JFK's assassination. The goal: to make Ruby look crazy and keep him from testifying, which is exactly what happened despite Ruby's demands to the contrary.

Among many revelations in the Belli book, a single reference to Dorothy Kilgallen stood out as was previously cited in the first chapter of this book. It read:

---

3 Belli was quite the actor himself. As described in a *Variety* article, in episode sixty of the October 11, 1968, television program, *Star Trek*, the publicity release for "And the Children Shall Lead," read, "An evil superbeing disguised as an Angel has taken over Triacus and persuaded the children to kill adults. Only the crew of the Enterprise can stop him from invading the galaxy. Friendly Angel is played by the high-profile lawyer Melvin Belli whose son Caesar plays carrot-topped kid Steve O'Connell." https://www.youtube.com/watch?v=chAcEYLTZ3U.

Washington Post reporter Bill Flynn focused on the overall "Belli look." He described the lawyer's fondness for "Saville Row suits, handmade shirts with diamond studs, flowing Byronesque ties, starched cuffs, and polished high-heeled black boots."

In the article, famed reporter Dorothy Kilgallen, a steady lunch partner of Belli's during the Ruby trial who later mysteriously died of a drug overdose, observed, "The Carl Sandburg of the future will spend whole lifetimes trying to analyze the drama of this week and this scene." She described Belli's demeanor as "Chesterfieldian."

Beyond the relevance of Kilgallen's comment about Belli's demeanor, it was surprising that Dorothy, only known to me as a panelist on the *What's My Line?* TV show, not only had been at the Ruby trial but was no less than "a steady lunch partner of Belli's." Despite the Sandburg reference and the comment about "the drama of this week" calling out for analysis, my investigative-reporter instincts did not kick in. Even learning that Kilgallen had "later mysteriously died of a drug overdose" did not prompt me to investigate her death since I was focused on Belli, his mob ties, and his absurd defense of Ruby.

In fact, in my haste to move forward with my investigation of Belli's conduct, I ignored a startling quote from Dr. Martin Schorr, a physician friend of Belli's, about Kilgallen's death. At that point I had no idea who she really was and why I needed to learn more, much more, about Dorothy Kilgallen.

* * *

Despite six years having passed after I published the Belli book, what I had learned never left my mind. Little did I know that my literary journey would connect that book to the next one of interest and so forth, leading to the writing of this very book.

This said, further research surrounding Belli's Mafia connections, especially his close friendship with mobster Mickey Cohen, and previous knowledge that Joseph Kennedy had Mafia connections early in his business career, bolstered the belief that underworld figures could have been responsible for JFK's death. These suspicions would lead to my publishing a second book touching on the assassination, *The Poison Patriarch: How the Betrayals of Joseph P. Kennedy Caused the Assassination of JFK*, released in 2013.

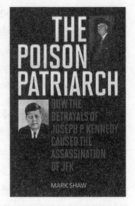

Curiosity piqued, I discovered that Joe, upon realizing that JFK was going to lose the 1960 election if he did not win West Virginia and Illinois, had secured, through Kennedy family friend Frank Sinatra (more to follow), the assistance of certain underworld figures to help JFK win those electoral votes. In effect, to do so, Joe made a "deal with the devil" by assuring the mafiosi if they came through and JFK won, the Kennedy administration would not pursue prosecution against them for any illegal dealings. This evidence was nothing too startling since other authors had discovered it, but as will be seen, evidence from my later books would provide a new context for what I included in *The Poison Patriarch*.[4]

When victory was assured and JFK was catapulted into the White House, the mafiosi Joe had enlisted through Sinatra to help win the election, among them Chicago-based Sam Giancana, New Orleans-based don Carlos Marcello, Tampa, Florida's Santo Trafficante, and the like felt secure. Little did they know that the Kennedy patriarch was hell-bent on double-crossing them by positioning none other than Robert F. Kennedy as attorney general.

How this came to light, as also noted in later books, was a primary-source interview with Kennedy family confidant John Seigenthaler, an eyewitness to history. He confirmed that RFK told him Joe was insistent on Bobby becoming attorney general.

Seigenthaler said he was present during the two days in 1960 when JFK made his decision. "The president first floated the balloon about Bobby

---

4 Interestingly enough, in early 2022, I discovered through a valuable source, James Hart Long Jr., an ignored *Time* magazine article published December 2, 1957, that showcased how popular JFK had been at least among those in the Democratic party. Entitled "DEMOCRATS: Man Out Front," the article also delved into the Kennedy clan providing insights into Papa Joe and mother Rose even to the extent of what it may have been like to be invited to dinner at the Kennedy home including "Excerpts from Rules for Visiting the Kennedys." Reading this article is valuable with regard to understanding the political landscape as JFK readies himself for a shot at the presidency. http://content.time.com/time/subscriber/article/0,33009,825326,00.html

becoming the attorney general during a Florida golf match with Bill Lawrence of the *New York Times*," Seigenthaler recalled. "Bobby told me 'that's dad,'" meaning Joe was insisting on the appointment and that Joe gave the tip to Lawrence that JFK was considering the appointment of RFK as attorney general.

"JFK was running the idea up the flagpole to see what kind of reaction he would get," Seigenthaler said. "And there was sharp criticism right away since Bobby was aligned with Joe McCarthy (Communist "Red Scare") and had been on the McClellan Committee. But Joe was pushing the issue and so I drove Bobby around to various people so he could see what they thought. We went to the Mayflower [hotel] to see [former president] Harry Truman, and Bobby had coffee with him and came back dejected."

Seigenthaler then told this author, "We went to see Bill Douglas [Supreme Court justice], J. Edgar Hoover, and others, including Senator William Fulbright. I used to accuse Bobby of having a 'cross face' when he was pissed off, and after all of these meetings that was how he looked, since nearly all of them told him not to take the job as AG. In fact, Truman told him to get as far away as possible; he was really plain spoken and didn't like Bobby anyway."

Regarding Hoover, future fireworks between RFK and him were predictable, as Curt Gentry noted in his excellent book, *J. Edgar Hoover: The Man and His Secrets*. He quoted Bobby as telling Seigenthaler, "Hoover had not been straightforward [during their chat]. It was clear, at least to Robert, that the wary bureaucrat did not want him to accept the nomination."

That evening, Seigenthaler recalled, he ate dinner with RFK and Ethel at their Hickory Hill home. "They talked about how RFK could teach, write, and travel and what a great career he had in front of him. Bobby wasn't going to take the job, and he said, 'This will kill dad,' a reference to disappointing Joe." But the next morning, during breakfast with JFK at his Georgetown flat, Seigenthaler said the president responded to Bobby's initiating words, telling him, "There is no one around I really know. I need someone who will be interested in my interests, and I need you." During the seven-to-ten-minute monologue, Seigenthaler told this author, "JFK made his case, brief and concise, by saying that Bobby was best qualified to handle organized crime and so forth. JFK then poured them both some coffee before Bobby said, 'Well, I have some points to make.' But Jack had made up his mind and he said, 'Let's just grab our balls and go.'"[5]

While several books have been written about how RFK became attorney general, Seigenthaler's eyewitness account, an example of the best, most reliable sources coming my way even during the early stages of my JFK assassination investigation, is the most plausible. And, as my later research journey would indicate, the course of history changed the moment Bobby accepted JFK's offer. His doing so, as will be explained, directly or indirectly cost three twentieth-century luminaries their lives—JFK, Marilyn Monroe, and Dorothy Kilgallen.

Following up, I read the late 1979 House of Representatives Select Committee on Assassinations Report (HSCA). It was apparent in the report that among the plethora of Mafia figures who had incurred RFK's wrath, New Orleans Mafia kingpin Carlos Marcello was number one on the list. Even before he became attorney general, the report concluded, Kennedy was priming his plan to deport the mafioso. Under the banner, "Marcello: A Kennedy Administration Target," the report stated that RFK "ordered the Justice Department to focus on him, along with other figures such as Teamsters president Hoffa, and Chicago Mafia leader Sam Giancana."

Marcello's attempt to make peace with the Kennedys was not widely known at the time or since. The HSCA report detailed efforts by Santo Trafficante to intercede on Marcello's behalf through singer Frank Sinatra, the friend of the Kennedys and Trafficante. A wiretap conversation between Philadelphia mobster Angelo Bruno[6] and Russell Bufalino, an underboss in Pennsylvania, disclosed that Sinatra discussed Marcello with RFK. The effort backfired, and Robert Kennedy intensified his efforts to nab Marcello.

True to his word, on April 4, 1961, the report stated, RFK had over-seen/orchestrated the illegal abduction of Marcello, in New Orleans. When

---

5 JFK stating that "Bobby was best qualified to handle organized crime" suggests that the president was aware that the justice department, with RFK at the helm, would need to deal with certain underworld figures once JFK took office. Whether he was aware of Joe's "deal with the devil" has always been debated, but Seigenthaler's account makes it appear JFK may not have known of his father's "promises."

6 Recall my experience when I interviewed Bruno's attorney for ABC's *Good Morning America* after which his car was blown up the next morning following the interview being aired.

the unsuspecting don walked into the Immigration and Nationalization Office (INS) to report as an alien (the legal term for non-citizens used then), agents arrested and handcuffed him, whisked the angry Mafia boss off to a waiting plane, and dumped him unceremoniously in Guatemala City. The next

Carlos Marcello in custody at immigration office in New Orleans, April 1961, while being illegally deported to Guatemala

day, a smiling RFK took credit for the deportation while Marcello and powerful allies of his vowed revenge, dubbing the incident nothing less than a "kidnapping," as it was described in a *New York Times* article.

On June 5, 1961, the report noted, Marcello, seething over the actions of his mortal enemy RFK, was smuggled back into the country. Within two years, the report noted, the government struck back, filing charges alleging conspiracy in falsifying a Guatemalan passport and perjury as well as hitting Marcello with an $835,000 tax-evasion indictment (a huge sum in those days).

The HSCA report noted Marcello's threats against the Kennedys. Among them was a credible account noted in an FBI report to the effect that when Robert Kennedy's name was mentioned, Marcello, upset that RFK was still hounding him, "shrilled the Mafia cry of revenge: '*Livarsi na petra di la scarpa*,' meaning 'Take the stone out of my shoe.'" This was the same Marcello of whom acclaimed author Nick Pileggi (*Wise Guy: Life in a Mafia Family*) told this author, "He was Sicilian, but born in Tunisia and grew up with both Sicilian and Arabic vendetta. He was not a turn-the-other-cheek kind of guy. Fury and revenge were his credo."

According to the report, verified by Ed Reid, author of *The Grim Reapers: The Anatomy of Organized Crime in America* (1970), Marcello added, "Don't worry about that little Bobby son of a bitch. He's going to be taken care of." Reid then related that Becker told him Marcello "knew that to rid himself of Robert Kennedy, he would first have to remove the president.

Any killer of the attorney general would be hunted down by his brother; the death of the president would seal the fate of the attorney general."

In the paragraphs under "Analyzing the Evidence," the HSCA denounced the FBI for failing to properly investigate the allegations, one of a number of times J. Edgar Hoover played deaf and dumb to any acknowledgment that the Mafia even existed. Regardless, the report did not discount the statements alleging Carlos Marcello threatened to have the president killed.

Regarding the president's death, it was apparent that the key, as this author suddenly realized, was asking not why JFK *was* killed, but why Bobby Kennedy *was not* killed. This focus on RFK instead of on JFK became more credible during my interview with Jack Ruby prosecutor Bill Alexander, who told me, "Bobby had many more enemies than JFK," and thus he expected RFK to be killed instead of JFK.

When Alexander uttered this valuable information, another "ah-hah" moment occurred as it had in many of the criminal cases I had handled, telling me yes, an important part of the story remained to be told, one of great historical significance since, at that point in time, researchers had not challenged the distortion of history, that of leaving RFK out of the story. This new perspective changed everything, and by researching Marcello's mindset, it was clear he realized that if he had RFK eliminated, then the president would come after him with every government force possible. But if Marcello could successfully orchestrate the death of JFK, then Bobby *would be powerless, which is exactly what happened.* The proof: Marcello and his Mafia friends were never bothered again, even during the remainder of Bobby's reign as attorney general.

Based on all of this research, only possible since I had known Belli and could use that experience as a starting point, a distinct advantage over previous authors examining the JFK assassination, I had figured out the key to how, and by whom, JFK had been murdered was focusing on RFK not JFK. With this in mind, I suddenly, one morning, realized what had happened—I had come full circle by once again becoming the man I had respected, the one who made me feel good about myself, the one who had been a criminal defense lawyer in the 1970s, the one who had battled for justice at every turn. And now, my "client" was none other than President

John F. Kennedy, who, I began to realize, had not been assassinated by one man, Oswald, but instead through a well-planned plot to kill him. (With few exceptions, I avoid use of the word "conspiracy" in my books since it has a very derogatory connotation to it and immediately triggers doubt about any conclusions reached.)

In essence, as I researched and wrote *The Poison Patriarch*, I had become JFK's advocate, his paladin, in some ways his "voice." Based on what I had learned, the president needed someone to fight for the justice denied when he died since the truth had been covered up. As my research journey continued, I would seek that truth.

* * *

Regarding Marcello's "no alternative" decision to eliminate RFK from hounding him, research indicated that as 1963 came to a close, the Mafia don's back was to the wall based on a one-two punch from the attorney general. The first punch was Bobby's intention to deport Marcello again, and the second, RFK's having indicted Marcello, whose multi-million-dollar empire stretched to Dallas, for racketeering, one that carried a lengthy prison sentence if a conviction resulted. Actually Marcello was on trial in a New Orleans courtroom at the very moment JFK was shot. His empire at stake, the mafioso had little choice. Bobby had to go, and through his Dallas underlings, Joseph Civello and Joe Campisi, Marcello, based on motive, orchestrated JFK's assassination.

Confirmation of what had happened, according to my theory of focusing on why RFK wasn't killed instead of why JFK was, became a focal point when I further read the HSCA's 1979 comprehensive report. For years on end the Committee had labored through secret sessions inspecting evidence and listening to witness after witness describe every nuance of the JFK and Oswald killings. [Author's note: To my strong disappointment, when I began investigating Dorothy Kilgallen's death, HSCA chief counsel Robert Blakey would tell me: "Our look [into Kilgallen's death] was not substantial. In any event, we thought it was 'fishy.' But we were not able to solve it and do the JFK and Martin Luther King assassinations investigation at the same time."]

The result of the HSCA probe was an unanticipated bombshell: members determined that there *was* a conspiracy to assassinate JFK. Some specifics were left to the imagination of the public, but there was little doubt "lone assassination" theories regarding the killing had been debunked.

The Committee concluded "a high probability" existed that at least two gunmen fired a total of three shots at the president, with the second and third striking him and the third being fatal. The Committee further believed that Kennedy "was probably assassinated as a result of a conspiracy" but was "unable to identify the other gunmen or the extent of the conspiracy." It discounted involvement in the conspiracy by the Soviet government, the Cuban government, including anti-Castro groups and the Secret Service, FBI, and CIA.

The Select Committee also raised new questions concerning Jack Ruby, and answering these questions became important to understanding the historical events in Dallas. Determining that more mystery surrounded Ruby, the Committee investigated him thoroughly. A foreword to volume nine of their report read: "Early in its investigation, as soon as it was realized that a plot of elements of organized crime in the United States to assassinate President John F. Kennedy warranted serious consideration, the committee decided to assemble the most reliable information available on the subject. The focus was to be primarily on the history of organized crime; the impact of the Kennedy administration's campaign against it…possible links of Lee Harvey Oswald and Jack Ruby with underworld figures; and the development of new evidence or leads." A few lines later they added, "*A major reason for suspecting conspiracy was Oswald's murder by Jack Ruby* [emphasis added]."

By 1960, the report said, organized crime was flourishing. JFK and RFK attempted to combat its influence. Allegations were made that they did so, the report concluded, to "get even" for mobsters having impinged on the success of their father, Joseph Kennedy. Much of his fortune, the report stated, stemmed from bootlegging, but mob boss Frank Costello's operation cut into Kennedy's share of the profits. Now it was payback time, the report concluded, time for the Kennedy brothers to attack organized crime with a vengeance. To do so, the report noted that when RFK became attorney general, "as a first step, [he] dramatically expanded the number of attorneys in the Organized Crime and Racketeering Section of the Justice Department." He also, the report stated, "put together a list of 40 organized crime figures who were targeted for investigation." At the top of that list was New Orleans don Carlos Marcello.

Melvin Belli escaped mention in any part of the report. Like when the Warren Commission was convened, the HSCA missed a golden opportunity to learn more about the assassinations by excluding Jack Ruby's lawyer from their investigation.

An FBI internal memorandum, included in the report, indicated how dangerous the underworld was as of May 1963, six months before the JFK assassination. It stated, "The Mafia [La Cosa Nostra] represents one of the most ruthless, pernicious, and enduring forms of criminality ever to exist in the United States. The viciousness and the effectiveness of the Mafia stems from its conspiratorial groups of Sicilian-Italian hoodlums, its adherence to a code of secrecy and silence, and its use of intimidation, violence, vengeance, and murder."

Under the banner, "Attitude toward the Kennedys: Before and After," the report analyzed mob disapproval of the famous brothers. Typical threats against the Kennedys included an associate of Philadelphia crime boss Angelo Bruno: "See what Kennedy [JFK] done. With Kennedy, a guy should take a knife, like one of them other guys, and stab and kill the [obscenity] where he is now…I mean it. This is true. Honest to God…I hope I get a week's notice. I'll kill him. Right in the [obscenity] in the White House. Somebody's got to get rid of this [obscenity]."

Bruno's threats against JFK were certainly lethal in nature, but it was Bobby whose actions against Marcello triggered the president's death.

Regardless, the HSCA investigation was certainly a milestone regarding the search for the truth about what happened to President Kennedy. Based on the disturbing new evidence revealed later in this book about the inner workings of the Warren Commission, it is unfortunate that those who worked so diligently on the HSCA were not privy to this evidence.

As will be seen, if they had been, the Committee might very well have reached alternate conclusions and thus would have been much more valuable as an historical research tool than it was at the time or since then.

CHAPTER 8

When Jack Ruby suddenly died in 1967, Melvin Belli did not appear to be surprised. Carol Anna Lind, his office manager at the time, told this author Belli, after learning of the death, said, "Something's not right. Maybe *they* injected Ruby with cancer cells."

Others, including Belli's partner Seymour Ellison, who explained that Belli told him the same thing "many times," all wondered what Ruby's lawyer knew that no one else did. Who were "they," and was it true that Ruby had been murdered? Belli never expanded on his comments, never offered any explanations, leading one to wonder whether the "they" Belli spoke of were the same "they" Bobby Kennedy had referenced when he told Justice Department spokesman Ed Guthman shortly after learning of JFK's death: "There's so much bitterness, I thought *they* would get one of us…I thought it would be me."[7]

Common sense indicates the plausibility that the "they" both men mentioned, those who hated Bobby and those who had hired/ordered Belli to defend Ruby, were one and the same. If this is true, then Belli must have suspected that "they" had shut Ruby up for good by injecting him with cancer cells, farfetched perhaps, but certainly possible by those who were expert at such diabolical schemes when a cover-up is in progress.

---

7 RFK's statement is only one of several where he admitted belief that it was his enemies who killed JFK to the extent that the "they" he mentioned revolved around the "New Orleans don" Carlos Marcello. In future years, Bobby Kennedy Jr. would confirm during public appearances including one at the Commonwealth Club of San Francisco that his father indicated Marcello was the one who ordered JFK's death.

Having provided solid research dealing with the JFK assassination for readers to consider, I turned my attention to Dorothy Kilgallen by returning to the days when I was researching Belli's life and times for *King of the Courtroom*. While doing so, there had been a statement made by one of his friends that I could not get out of my mind.

The statement to me was made by Dr. Martin Schorr, a San Diego-based forensic scientist later to become involved in the Sirhan Sirhan/Robert Kennedy murder case. Shortly after Dorothy died on November 8, 1965, Belli asked Dr. Schorr for his medical opinion about Jack Ruby, and what I recalled when I checked my notes was one portion of the interview I had paid little attention to during my research journey. Little did I know at the time that what Belli had said would motivate my writing several books about the assassination based on certain instincts learned when I was a criminal defense attorney.

While interviewing Dr. Schorr in 2012, he had calmly told me, "You know, Mel knew Dorothy Kilgallen."

I then asked, "Do you mean he was a guest on *What's My Line?*"

The respected physician, a very reliable source, replied, "No, Mark, you don't know anything about her. She was a top-notch reporter for a main New York City newspaper syndicated to two hundred newspapers across the country. She also covered the Dr. Sam Sheppard murder trial and the Lindbergh baby kidnapping case. Dorothy cohosted a radio show listened to by a million people in that city all while raising three children. And of course, besides her *What's My Line?* celebrity status, she was at the Jack Ruby trial."

Arlene Francis, Bennett Cerf, Dorothy Kilgallen, and host John Daly on *What's My Line?*

The last comment confirmed what I had learned during my early research of Belli's life and times. And then Dr. Schorr stunned me when he said, "And when Dorothy died, Mark, Mel said to me, 'They've killed Dorothy. Now they'll go after Jack Ruby.'"

Despite my further questioning, Dr. Schorr could not provide any additional information as to what Belli meant by the quote. But that didn't matter, for it appeared to me very likely that Kilgallen's life and times and the "mysterious death" I had learned about before needed to be the object of an intensive investigation. Because of my experience with such matters when I was investigating a criminal case or preparing to cover a high-profile case for the TV networks, I was prepared to do so.

As I began to work out a strategy, I was shocked that despite Kilgallen's impressive body of work, her apparent celebrity status, and so on, there was very little media attention about her following her death. Why that happened would become clear later, but after she died in 1965, Dorothy was a forgotten woman, eliminated from any discussion, any mention of her, as if she had never existed despite her death being dubbed "mysterious."

In effect, I was starting with a blank slate, but like JFK before her, I felt that Kilgallen was now my client, that I could be her "voice," and if nothing more, shed light on what had happened to her when she died. Suddenly, one day, it all made sense: the amazing journey during my life from the struggling days at Purdue on through the criminal defense years, the improbable television career escapades and even my experiencing the tough times leading me to the seminary years and into a literary journey of sorts. In some ways, I now possessed the credentials to tackle a case where I represented a woman's potential denial of justice just as I had done by standing up and fighting for justice when Harriet Jones, who had killed her husband after he beat her father to death, was headed for prison. Women's rights had always been an issue of interest to me and to that end I had "defended" Ursula Martens when she was chastised for being a member of the Hitler Youth even after conversion and Cecelia Rexin's actions when she befriended a German prison guard at Ravensbrück who then helped her save the life of an orphaned Russian little girl.

With this in mind, my first interest in Dorothy's life and times began with her childhood, since any investigation of her "mysterious death" had to start where a crack detective would start—with a background check of the deceased. Learning about Kilgallen's roots and the part they played in her ascendance to celebrity status was essential, I believed, to learning the truth about how she died.

Kilgallen was born on July 3, 1913. Her family lived in a low-rent apartment at Garfield Boulevard and Morgan Street in Chicago. Father Jim, a slim man also called "Jimmy" or "Kil," was a Hearst newspaper chain reporter. He met Dorothy's mother Mae, whom he described as "a stunning redhead, five feet two inches tall," when he heard her sing at the Tabor Grand Opera House in Denver. Mae's father was American born; her mother moved from Ireland to the US in 1879. The couple was married at Mae's Catholic church in Denver.

The knowledge of the "Ireland connection" did not resonate at the time but later I would discover Dorothy's Irish heritage, with her great grandparents having settled in the Sraheens/Bohola area of County Mayo located a four-hour drive west of Dublin. An 1850s photograph obtained by this author from Kilgallen's second cousin depicts her great grandfather, Andrew Kilgallen, alongside her great grandmother, Mary Hyland. She is donning what was known as a "Mayo shawl."

Kilgallen's great-grandparents

For a reason unknown even through in-depth research, Kilgallen's parents chose the name Dorothy. It meant "gift from heaven," and no truer selection could have made since in the future, as I'd learn, she would gift so many blessings to the world through her sparkling personality, dogged work ethic, and impressive contributions to history.

Despite an early interest in the theater, by the time she turned eight, Kilgallen yearned to be a reporter like her father. She admired his growing reputation as a tenacious journalist. Jim's editor said, "When he got hold of a story, Jim was just like a bulldog—he'd get his teeth in it and never let go."

Al Capone and Thomas Edison (deaf at the time) were among the celebrities Jim interviewed. He also covered the Rosenberg spy case, the

McCarthy hearings, and most importantly, as a correspondent during World War II, exposed existence of the Dachau prison camp in Germany. Each of these achievements, especially the latter, where Dorothy's father risked his life to report the truth, served as the perfect role model for his daughter.

One exploit Dorothy listened to day and night was when Jim accepted an assignment to pursue an American fugitive named Sam Insull around the globe. He was a utilities baron who had attempted to escape deportation when he was indicted for fraud. To get the story, Jim paid money from his own pocket to hire an amphibious airplane. One cloudy day, with him on board, the plane floated out of the sky and landed next to Insull's freighter.

Startled at the reporter's ingenuity and panache, Insull nevertheless gave Jim an exclusive interview as he joined the fugitive on the ship's trip to the US. A star reporter had been born that day.

Irene Corbally Kuhn, a fellow reporter at the time, had this to say about her rival:

> He was just a lovely, simple man, not very well-educated, but with a kind
> of Irish quality that just unfolded people. Another reporter Jim Farley, had
> it, Jimmy developed it. Hearst always nurtured people like that when they
> had qualities that enabled them to get close to people of importance.

Predictably, based on her admiration for her father, it's no wonder Kilgallen argued with her mother when Dorothy insisted on becoming a reporter instead of obeying Mae's wish that she pursue a career as an English teacher. Mae pushed that career because of the good hours and summer vacation time. Dorothy's stubbornness led to several shouting matches.

Interestingly enough, during these "growing-up" years, Dorothy impressed her family much more than she did those outside the family. The first significant defining moments in Kilgallen's life happened when Jim had moved the family to the Flatbush section of Brooklyn, New York. Dorothy started school in a red brick building, PS 119, located one block from their home. She was an average student, and teachers who had been interviewed during the years about her did not recall any outstanding traits Dorothy possessed. To them, she was a bit shy, kept to herself, and did not participate in many school activities.

St. Elizabeth's Catholic Church, near the Kilgallen home, provided religious instruction. The family then began to regularly attend St. Thomas Aquinas Church on Sunday mornings.

Kilgallen enjoyed friendships with several schoolmates, but some were harsh. When she learned one girl called her "stuck up and not even good looking," Kilgallen boasted, "I'll show you. Someday I'll be very famous and all of you will read about me."

To that end, her father told the story that "Dorothy used to sit on the front stoop of our home and tell her little pals and her younger sister, Eleanor, how someday she would amount to something—be a big star and go to faraway places she had read about." As will be learned, that prediction was an understatement.

The "not even good looking" comment may have been true at the time. Those who knew Kilgallen said she was of medium height and skinny like her father. She parted her dark hair in the middle. She did not have full, attractive lips. One friend called her a "sweet" girl, but another said she was "mousy."

In Dorothy's graduation photo from Brooklyn's Erasmus High School in 1930, she is second from right, row three. She doesn't stand out and there is a very serious look on her face. In a rather odd interview by a national newspaper years later, a girl who swore she was one of  Kilgallen's closest friends told a reporter Dorothy "used to dream of tiny, tiny pussycats and miniscule cookies only to wake up and be confused at the actual size."

As fate would have it, at her father's urging, the twelve-year-old Kilgallen began writing letters to newspapers. One she wrote to the editor of the *Brooklyn Eagle* was so special it became her first published work. This happened after a reader criticized Ramon Novarro, a Mexican-born silent screen legend at the time. Defending her idol, Kilgallen fired off a letter. The writing was professional enough that an *Eagle* editor thought an adult had sent it. Instead of using her own name, Kilgallen signed the letter "Dorothy Laurington."

When the letter appeared in the newspaper, Kilgallen made copies and gave them to all her friends. Her father passed the newspaper around his office. When she visited the next day, there was a round of applause. She liked the attention. She liked being special.

Kilgallen kept sending letters to the editor, but despite her predictions of becoming famous, she gave no hint of stardom, at least through academic achievements. At one point later on, Jim, during an interview, boasted that "Dorothy was so bright that the high school decided to test her IQ." Grades she received were average at best and her having failed French and Latin do not back up a father's love for his daughter. Even Dorothy's marks in spelling were suspect, a surprise since Kilgallen would become one of the finest wordsmiths journalism has ever known.

Writing was a different matter. She excelled enough to become associate editor of *The Erasmian*, her high school's literary magazine. When writing did not consume her time, Kilgallen took the job as associate editor seriously. Her schoolmate Bernard Malamud, later to win both the National Book Award and the Pulitzer Prize for Fiction, described her as "unique, tall, animated, immaculately dressed woman without a chin, very careful about her physical appearance." He added, "She had a sense of her own importance." When Malamud submitted a novella to Kilgallen, he said, she rejected his story as being "too depressing."

Armed with the mindset of the reporter she would become in the future, Dorothy visited her father's office regularly and enjoyed the daily chatter of reporters sharing stories with her. When she asked Jim, later described by revered writer Damon Runyon as "an editor's dream of a reporter," what the most important characteristic of a journalist should be, he said, "Nothing is more important than the truth." Of anything Jim ever told her, these few words *were* the most important, since from the first day she became a journalist to her last breath on the face of the earth, Dorothy had the reputation as a woman of the truth.

When Kilgallen celebrated her sixteenth birthday with a modest party, she invited friends whose families were suffering hard times during the Depression. One girlfriend later said Kilgallen was "the best friend I ever had. She gave me a dollar her dad had given her for her birthday."

In 1930, at age seventeen, and despite an urge to join Jim's world of journalism, Kilgallen entered the College of New Rochelle, located twenty-five miles from Brooklyn. Ursuline nuns were the educators. Kilgallen lived on campus and visited her parents on weekends. George Kuittinen, whom she dated, later described her as having "fine and Irish skin—flawless porcelain; her eyes very large and blue. Though she was thin, her breasts were well-developed and her legs excellent." Hearing of Kuittmen's comments about her physical attributes later caused Dorothy to call him a "punk."

Although Kilgallen's intentions toward a college education were sound, she became restless and wanted something more. On a momentous day in June 1931, Amster Spiro, the *New York Evening Journal*'s city editor, provided the temptation. He agreed, as a favor to Jim, to give his eighteen-year-old daughter a two-week trial as a reporter. "I was still at college [but when] it came time to send a check for the next semester," Kilgallen said later, "I told my parents, 'I don't want to go back. I want to be a reporter.'" Her mother objected, Dorothy recalled, "because her idea of a female reporter was someone who drank whiskey straight, sat on desktops, swore, and had more mannish haircuts and clothes."

Regardless, Kilgallen had become a college dropout, one of the first similarities I noticed between us—she dropped out and I almost dropped out of Purdue with each of us poor-to-average students for sure. Even her poor marks in English matched mine, although I would pale in comparison to Dorothy's becoming a gifted wordsmith. Nevertheless, the more I learned about her early years, the more I felt a kinship with her.

That two-week trial run at the newspaper—Kilgallen said later, "My dad never suggested that I follow in his footsteps but the footsteps were there, and what other way could I have gone?"—turned into decades at the newspaper. From day one, Kilgallen immersed herself in the world of journalism. When possible, she accompanied reporters covering social and political events. However, the world of law most fascinated her. On a daily basis, she roamed the criminal courts, captivated by the human drama of trials where freedom and even life or death were on the line. Based on my experiences and love for the law, another bond existed with Dorothy.

Kilgallen begged for assignments to important stories like her father covered. However, the newsroom was definitely a man's world, and women were supposed to stay in the background and let the men undertake the crucial stories. Besides, Dorothy was still a teenager, even though she was more mature than her age indicated.

Kilgallen's entry into a "man's world" startled the veteran *Evening Journal* reporters. On her first day on the job, she arrived wearing a white organdy dress carrying an opera bag of some sort with drawstrings attached. Marjorie Hall, then a seasoned journalist, did a double take right away since women normally did not dress, as she later told a reporter, "like they were on the way to a school prom."

To gently introduce the youngster to the fast world of journalism, Amster Spiro told an assistant city editor, "You've got Kil's kid. Go easy on her. She's just out of the convent." [Author's note: This comment, based on Kilgallen having no experience, caused me to admire her savvy, her willingness to take chances, to risk failure, to, in some ways, "wing it," as I did many times during my career.]

Later, in a stunning example of her courage, she would stand outside Sing Sing prison in New York City and while walking down the steps, be confronted by a man upset with an article she had written about his sister. Before Dorothy could pass, he stuffed a gun in her face but somehow by her not screaming or moving away, the man lowered the gun and fled. Later, she told a *Daily News* colleague, "I fully expected to die and I couldn't move 'cause I was too scared to do so."

To her good fortune, the newspaper editors became obsessed with front-page murder case headlines. Kilgallen leaped with joy when one of the editors assigned Dorothy her first murder trial. It involved the beating death of a girl her own age. When she handed in the story, the editor rejected it. She re-wrote it and submitted it again. He rejected it again. Five re-writes later, the story was published, a preview of the tenacity Dorothy showed in improving her writing skills year by year.

Those who underestimated Kilgallen's prowess as a competent reporter paid the price. She was tough handed despite her young age. Building a reputation, she wrote sharp-edged, detailed, primary-source stories including a headline-maker about a sensational Bronx case. It involved a woman charged with killing her philandering husband by lacing his chocolate pudding with arsenic. At the courtroom entrance, Kilgallen proudly displayed the New York Police Press Card she had earned.

Dorothy, the cub reporter

Proof that Kilgallen had arrived as a newspaperwoman of stature despite her young age was an *Evening Journal* three-quarter page promotion:

> To read one of Dorothy Kilgallen's brilliantly written stories—it might be an interview with a famous politician or a gangster, it might be the current day by day reporting of a famous murder trial—one would immediately infer: Here is the writing of a veteran newspaper woman with a lifetime of experience in reporting.
>
> She is a modern up-to-the-minute woman reporter. With her versatile, sparkling writing and her far-beyond-her-years perception and power of observation, she can cover everything from a baby shower to a sensational police court trial.

At age twenty-one in 1934, Dorothy Kilgallen covered the infamous Anna Antonio murder-for-hire trial. Prosecutors said the slight Italian woman paid drug dealers $800 to kill her husband, Salvatore. Motive: a $5,300 life-insurance policy.

Kilgallen's front-page story announced the guilty verdict. She included quotes from those upset when the jury pronounced a death sentence for "Little Anna." Last-minute appeals to save her proved fruitless. Kilgallen reported the gory details of the Sing Sing prison electrocution, proving she went wherever the story took her and printed the truth without holding back.

Up front, despite her youth and inexperience, *Evening Journal* editors praised Kilgallen's articles since she had a knack for understanding the legal system like a seasoned lawyer. Her storytelling acumen and talent for focusing on critical aspects of trials set her apart from other reporters. It caused those in the newsroom to realize Jim Kilgallen's daughter had a bright future.

As a slight to this female who was gaining way too much attention, the assistant editor assigned Kilgallen to the city morgue, telling her, "Get accustomed to the sight of death if you are going to be of any use to the paper." To that end, she had to view the dead bodies, the ones

Dorothy and her sister Eleanor on CBS radio

where suicide was involved. They were on display so friends or relatives could visit the morgue and identify their loved ones.

Though Dorothy accepted the assignment with vigor, on her first day covering the morgue and also examining autopsy reports packed with horrid photographs, a medical examiner noticed she was about to faint since her facial features were as pallid as a nearby corpse. To the rescue came a stick of gum, and apparently the sugar intake saved Dorothy from hitting the cement floor face first.[8]

As 1935 dawned with a frigid winter storm, Kilgallen got her big break when she was assigned to cover a murder case dubbed by the media, "The Trial of the Century." Prosecutors charged German-born Bruno Hauptmann with kidnapping and killing famed aviator Charles Lindbergh's son. Kilgallen sat directly behind the defendant during one court session. After prosecutors entered into evidence the ladder used during the kidnapping, the baby-faced Kilgallen tapped Hauptmann on the shoulder. She asked him about the

---

8 Dorothy's reaction reminded me of a similar one I experienced when reading autopsy reports early on in my legal career. Having to view even photos of dead bodies kept me awake at night and became one of the factors in my finally leaving the defense attorney arena.

ladder. Despite being impressed with her gumption, he told her his lawyers forbid him to talk to the press. No matter; father Jim later bragged that his daughter was the first to "interview" Hauptmann.

As would be the case later, when she was front and center at the Jack Ruby trial, heavy competition for "getting the story" was no impediment during the Hauptmann trial. There, she competed with famed reporters of the day including Damon Runyon, Walter Winchell, Edna

Bruno Hauptmann

Ferber, Ford Madox Ford, and her chief rival, Adela Rogers St. Johns. Despite the competition, Dorothy was chosen as one of the reporters to "babysit" Anna Hauptmann, Bruno's wife, both in the courtroom and beyond.

When St. Johns, due to her fame, began to obtain every exclusive interview with those surrounding the case, Kilgallen was upset. But, like a team player, since St. Johns was a Hearst reporter like her (Hearst owned the *Evening Journal*), she took a back seat while swearing to never do so again.

Realizing that Kilgallen "covered" high-profile cases like this one resonated when I recalled my having also done so with the Claudine Longet, Mike Tyson, O. J. Simpson, and Kobe Bryant cases. To that end, I was becoming even more aware of how her career and mine, though down different paths, coincided.

* * *

One day during this time, Kilgallen made good on a promise, the one where she had told childhood schoolmates she would one day be famous. This happened when she was permitted to be a contestant in what was heralded as the "Race around the World." Competitors were required to employ commercial methods of transportation only available to the public during the globetrotting excursion.

As noted in *Collateral Damage*, Kilgallen's competitors were two New York newspaper reporters, Bud Ekins of the *World Telegram* and Leo Kieran of the *New York Times*. Once she was chosen, Kilgallen obtained sixteen visas and a passport in *two days*. Her only baggage: a battered typewriter and a converted tweed hatbox.

During the October 1936 race, Kilgallen, who finished second to Ekins based on traveling issues including an unexpected typhoon, noted references to her as a "modern-day Nellie

Dorothy Kilgallen, Bud Ekins, and Leo Kieran entering the "Race around the World"

Bly," the pen name for Elizabeth Cochrane Seaman, famous for an 1889 record-breaking trip around the world in seventy-two days, in emulation of Jules Verne's fictional character Phileas Fogg in the classic novel *Around the World in Eighty Days*. Humbled by the comparison, Kilgallen wrote, "I'm supposed to be a 1936 Nellie Bly. I feel like Bly, a female Gulliver and Columbus all rolled into one. I can't discover a new world but I can discover the fastest way around it." She then added, "Nellie Bly, watch over me. You may be astonished at what you see—but, watch anyway."

Kilgallen also wrote of the challenge: "I'll circle the globe by plane, blimp, motor, train and bus, perhaps even by camel or bicycle if they'll get me where I want to go."

In the book (*Girl Around the World*) Dorothy wrote about the adventure, she trumpeted her willingness to take chances. She said, "I'm off on a race around the world—a race against time and two men. I know I can beat time. I hope to beat the men." Kilgallen also included words that would define her career until she died twenty-nine years later, "I'm a reporter who likes danger and excitement," while adding, "This assignment has been much easier than covering murder trials, and much prettier," while admitting to being a bit scared in Calcutta "when a lizard crawled in bed with me" but enthused when the "guys learned I could shoot dice."

Kilgallen's itinerary included hurried flights on the German dirigible *Hindenburg* with Nazi swastikas visible on its sides, Pan America's famed *China Clipper*, and several other airlines. Scurrying about with little time for rest permitted her to make the trip in twenty-four days, thirteen hours, and fifty-one minutes. Among the countries she visited were China, the Philippines, Germany, England, France, Italy, Greece, Egypt, Iraq, and India.

Dorothy, the globetrotter, in 1936

Weather conditions varied from good to bad to worse as the fall temperatures dipped from highs in the eighties to lows in the thirties with wind gusts an obstacle on many flights. Crouched in her seat, Kilgallen braced herself for hard landings while at times eating day-old food as the airplanes bounced around in the clouds, many times with rain pelting the wings.

Newspapers heralded the young daredevil as the first woman to travel around the world on commercial airlines. In addition to her feat of crossing the Pacific, the fearless Kilgallen set a record for the fastest five-thousand-mile span ever flown, Hawaii to New York City. Providing her readers with a chronicle of the adventure, Kilgallen wrote, "Dawn found us sailing serenely northward—over French Indo Chinese jungles where tigers and great constrictor snakes lie in wait for little girls...Bump! Bump! Splash! We thumped down in the middle of a rice field...Appearing like gnomes from the ground, about 600 chattering natives, nearly naked, surrounded the plane. They spoke no English, of course, and we could not understand Siamese."

October 1936 newspaper article

Dignitaries including First Lady Eleanor Roosevelt congratulated Kilgallen on her achievement. Famed aviator Amelia Earhart was also among the women who cheered the young reporter's feat. Kilgallen was famous at last, just as promised early on, with several newspapers lauding her willingness to carry the banner for women's rights by challenging the two men. Her doing so was a prelude to Kilgallen becoming a true advocate for her gender, though she may have never realized the accomplishment at the time.

When Kilgallen returned home from the "Race around the World" amongst family, friends, and neighbors who flew the American flag on their front porches, greeting her was her beloved cat, Cotton. She had somehow taken charge of the little fuzzy friend during the Hauptmann trial. Research as to how this happened has not proven fruitful.

While a special moment occurred when Dorothy's grandmother, Delia Ahern, phoned congratulations from Denver, what must have meant most to Dorothy was the tribute her father wrote after she had safely come home to Brooklyn. It read:

Dorothy and her cat
Cotton, 1936

> You took your round-the-world assignment casually—on a few hours' notice. You made good with a bang. You proved you had what Damon Runyon termed "moxie"—COURAGE—to say nothing of the other traits necessary to deliver 100%.
>
> And so I say I am proud of you Dorothy. Proud of you as a daughter and as a newspaper woman but more than anything else I am proud because success and the blast of fane have not changed you a bit. You are same girl "the working press" in New York has known—and liked—for the past five years or more.
>
> I salute you as a credit to your newspaper, to your family and to your craft.

While doing so, she became the first female to fly across the Pacific Ocean. Marguerite Mooers Marshall, a noted writer at the time, said, "[Dorothy] is the most daisy-fresh globe-girdler I ever hope to see—and so much prettier than even the best pictures of her printed in the *Evening Journal*. Her little features are cut with cameo delicacy, her skin has the lucent pallor of white lilac, her Irish eyes are not only smiling, but sea-blue and black-lashed, her dark hair, parted in the middle, is arranged in a most artful series of curls and purrs—not a hair out of place."

Not yet twenty-four, the Chicago-born little girl who was interested in acting was now a household name. Louis Sobol, a fellow reporter at the *Evening Journal*, wrote of Kilgallen's world at the time: "This slender, wide-eyed, deceivingly naïve in attitude and soft-spoken mannerisms female reporter was to herself mingling with a new set of characters—racket guys, grafters, phonies, creep janes, society fops, chorus girls, pimps, overdressed jezebels and their rent payers."

Dorothy very stylish in 1942

Sobel, commenting on Kilgallen's appearance at a theater opening, wrote, "Out of a streamlined, shiny chariot stepped a fragile, raven-haired honey…A thinnish youth with bat-ears and pop-eyes and a Tenth Avenue subdeb fought each other to be at her side. 'Willya sign this, Miss Kilgallen?' pleaded the boy thrusting out his soiled autograph album…." Sobel added, "She still goes to church on Sundays, blushes when profanity is set loose within her hearing, and walks away from obscene stories."

In a tribute to Kilgallen's father, Jim, William Randolph Hearst Jr. said of him, "I am sure no journalist in history was more devoted to his profession." In fact, when Hearst chose the *New York Journal-American*'s ten most memorable men and women reporters for his book, *The Hearsts: Father and Son*, at the top of the list were "Jimmy and his daughter Dorothy." His reasoning: "Jimmy because he saw and covered so much of America and the world. Dorothy because much of her career, and her life and death, were so dramatic."

CHAPTER 9

Meanwhile, Kilgallen's column, "Hollywood Scene as Seen by Dorothy Kilgallen," (later changed to "As Seen in Hollywood by Dorothy Kilgallen") appeared in the *Evening Journal* and then in the *New York Journal-American* when the *Evening Journal* and the *New York American* merged in 1937. Kilgallen felt honored when she was given the prize assignment to cover the wedding of FDR Jr. to Ethel du Pont. Even more prestigious was her traveling to England to attend the coronation of George VI. Her debut in London society at various high-profile events provided more media exposure for the fast-rising star of the Fourth Estate.

During the Christmas holidays in 1938, a surprise announcement appeared in Hearst newspapers across the country:

> The first and only Woman Columnist Dorothy Kilgallen's *Voice of Broadway*
> Column Starts Monday. A Man's Job. Beginning Monday in the *New York*
> *Journal-American*, Dorothy Kilgallen will Report Daily on the Deeds and
> Misdeeds of Broadway. A Man's Job. But Dorothy has been doing a Man's
> Job and Doing It Better.

The Voice of Broadway column was created to deal with the news and gossip of the day, theater, politics, and crime. Kilgallen's main competition were all men—Walter Winchell, Ed Sullivan, Lucius Beebe, and Leonard Lyons.

At the height of its popularity, the column appeared in every Hearst syndicated newspaper nationwide, small towns and large cities, two hundred and counting. At twenty-five, she was the only prominent female Broadway columnist. An entertainment magazine called her an "authentic celebrity."

Despite Kilgallen's sudden rise to stardom, she displayed a humble attitude. When a snowstorm hit New York City and the *Journal-American*'s electricity faltered, she retired to a local pub with male colleagues she called "the guys" and downed a few beers with them. Kilgallen even picked up a pool cue. There was laughter when a ball she hit too hard bounced off the table and hit a startled reporter squarely in his private parts.

Kilgallen, circa 1939

* * *

During this time, Kilgallen had been truly worthy of the *New York Post* calling her, as noted in the introduction, "the most powerful female voice in America" as well as a journalist there proclaiming, "Wherever Dorothy Kilgallen goes fame precedes her, envy follows her and a crowd looks on. She is one of the communication marvels of the age." Ernest Hemingway, a close friend of the reporter's, called her, "She's one of the greatest woman writers in the world," a comment Dorothy would have appreciated while being upset at the same time since the comment was sexist.

Dorothy and Hemingway at the Stork Club

In essence, Kilgallen was on top of the world, celebrated, respected, a role model for every woman in America. If any case symbolizes Kilgallen's courage, her bravery, her integrity, and her willingness to fight for the rights of others, it happened when NYC detectives arrested comedian Lenny Bruce. The controversial comedian, who first gained fame on the Arthur Godfrey television program, was the Richard Pryor of his day, delighting some members of his audiences while insulting others with his off-color material. He was arrested when he used the "F word" and too many other obscenities during a performance in Greenwich Village (Bruce's act may be seen in this rare footage: https://tinyurl.com/y4lp77tb).

To his defense rose Kilgallen despite the risk to her reputation for doing so. Other celebrities like Paul Newman and Bob Dylan also appeared, but Dorothy had the most to lose due to Bruce's filthy language.

At trial, Kilgallen was the star defense witness in a packed courtroom. Asked about the artistic merit of Bruce's, she told the jury, "I think Lenny Bruce is a brilliant satirist—perhaps the most brilliant I have ever seen—and I think his social commentary, whether I agree with it or not, is extremely valid and important."

Despite her words of wisdom, the jury convicted Bruce, but the decision was overturned by an appellate court. The result caused Bruce's trial counsel to applaud Dorothy's power at the time, telling the *New York Times*, "I have to think [Kilgallen] had a lot to do with the ultimate result of the case. The briefs that were filed placed an enormous reliance on her, again because of what she is and what she stands for."

Kilgallen's view of Bruce was in line with that of Melvin Belli who represented the comedian when he was arrested in San Francisco on bogus drug charges. One must wonder whether Belli having respect for Dorothy's defense of Bruce contributed to his permitting her, as will be explained, to interview Jack Ruby at his trial.

How popular was Kilgallen at this time? Not only was she featured in *Mad Magazine* but also as a character in the long-running cartoon *Flintstones* series television program as "Daisy Kilgranite" at the *Bedrock Chronicle*. Further, a street artist captured Dorothy's essence, especially her smile in this caricature likeness:

DOROTHY

Another indication of Kilgallen's stature had occurred on June 12, 1953, when Kilgallen attended Queen Elizabeth II's coronation.

Wearing a tiara, Kilgallen had looked stunning in a silver gown with ten thousand embroidered jewels and pearls encrusted at the scalloped neckline. A white mink cape lined with silver lamé completed an outfit truly fit for a media queen.

While in England, Dorothy achieved a "scoop" when she somehow learned that the queen experienced her first hair "permanent" and then let her worldwide newspaper audience know the details. Dubbed in the column "the plucky, globe-trotting girl reporter," she let readers known the inside story, that "the royal head was tied up in clamps and pads for some two hours at the palace as beauticians at Emile's, the royal hair-drummer, worked nervously in preparation for the coronation."

Notice of Kilgallen's appearance at Queen Elizabeth's coronation, June 1953

Kilgallen's gaining access to the "exclusive" is an indication of the stellar reputation she had at the time, that those close to the queen trusted her with the inside story. And no evidence exists that what she wrote had to be "approved" by Her Majesty.

Dorothy's coverage of the coronation had earned her a Pulitzer Prize nomination, surprisingly the only one she received during her long and illustrious journalistic career. Of course, if she had lived to write her book about the JFK assassination so as to expose who planned it and who covered it up, as will be explained, no doubt a Pulitzer would have come her way.

When the queen visited Williamsburg, Virginia, in 1957, "a press plane carrying reporters that had been following her Canadian tour taxied up to the airport terminal" according to a *New York Post* account. "As the door of the plane opened," the report stated, "some of the most bedraggled ill-use, sagging newspaperwomen in America hustled down the ramp loaded down under typewriters, portfolios, attaché cases, etc.

Kilgallen at the queen's coronation

Last of all came Dorothy Kilgallen, slim, poster perfect, smiling, daintily toeing her way downward, unwrinkled, unruffled, fresh-faced, in a brown suit with a chinchilla beret, carrying a makeup case and little else."

Later, in 1960, Kilgallen secured another scoop when she wrote of Princess Margaret's wedding "inside Westminster Abbey." At age twenty-nine, the princess married photographer Antony Armstrong-Jones.

All the while, Kilgallen continued to write front-page stories featuring her favorite subjects: crime and criminal trials. To that end, the headline-making case Kilgallen had tackled involved the 1954 Cleveland murder trial of Dr. Sam Sheppard, on trial for killing his wife.

He swore he was innocent and that a "bushy-haired, one-armed man" whom he had confronted in their home struck Mrs. Sheppard with a sharp metal object twenty-seven times. How she handled the Dr. Sam Sheppard case before, during, and after his infamous trial was the crowning moment in her life, one where she stood tall and proud with both her journalistic and investigative reporter skills.

In both *The Reporter Who Knew Too Much* and the follow-up book, *Denial of Justice*, I chronicled how Kilgallen had singlehandedly overturned the guilty verdict handed down to Dr. Sheppard when the case reached the Supreme Court.

Dorothy Kilgallen at the Dr. Sam Sheppard trial surrounded by admiring fellow reporters

Prior to jury instructions, Sheppard trial judge Edward Blythin had asked to meet Kilgallen privately. The two posed for photos while chatting. Later, Bob Considine, writing for the Hearst syndicate, described Kilgallen's star power: "Dorothy's daily arrivals at the little courtroom in Cleveland where Sam Sheppard was on trial were not unlike the arrival at home plate of Mickey Mantle with the bases filled. All the girl wanted was to get on with the story, do her job, but the jury, judge, defense attorney, prosecution and warring families of the accused murderer and the deceased all seemed straining to get her autograph."

More fully documenting Kilgallen's appearance at the Sam Sheppard trial was a November 13, 1954, *TV Guide* article entitled, "Dorothy Kilgallen: Girl Reporter." The article, written under the byline "A Television Star Covers Cleveland's Sheppard Trial," confirmed Kilgallen as the most famous reporter of her time. I included it in *Denial of Justice*.

One example of her prowess as a reporter was Kilgallen's updating coverage of the Sheppard case and then condemning the verdict. She wrote: "There were a number of reasons for my startled reaction to the jury's verdict. Basically, the state had failed to present…anything resembling a conclusive case that established 'beyond a reasonable doubt' the doctor's guilt." She added, "I could not have convicted him of anything except possibly negligence in locking his back door. So I was aghast at the verdict."

In 1964, Kilgallen was responsible for the US District Court overturning Sheppard's conviction based on her exposing Edward Blythin, the trial judge, for bias. Before the trial, he had told her in confidence his opinion of Sheppard's conduct, but she kept silent until the judge died, showing another instance of the integrity she possessed as a journalist. [Author's note: The District Court decision was affirmed by the Supreme Court in 1966.]

Kilgallen and Judge Edward Blythin

True to her upholding a strong sense of integrity, Kilgallen, as noted, had not divulged any portion of what she considered a private conversation with Judge Blythin, but when he died, Kilgallen felt it was her duty to do so. In the affidavit she provided F. Lee Bailey, Sheppard's appellate counsel, Kilgallen said the judge summoned her to his chambers due to her celebrity status. He then told her, "I am very glad to see you, Miss Kilgallen. I watch

89

you on television very frequently and enjoy the [*What's My Line?*] program. But what brings you to Cleveland?"

Kilgallen said she replied, "Well, [the case] has all the ingredients of what in the newspaper business we call a good murder. It has a very attractive victim, who was pregnant, and the accused was an important member of the community, a respectable, very attractive man. Then, added to that, you have the fact that it is a mystery as to who did it."

Judge Blythin, Kilgallen told Bailey, replied, "Mystery? It's an open and shut case."

"Well, what do you mean, Judge?" Kilgallen asked.

"Well, he's guilty as hell. There's no question about it," the judge proclaimed. Friends of his later disputed what he told Kilgallen, arguing the judge never used swear words like "hell."

Regardless, Kilgallen's disclosure impacted Bailey like a bullet train, and he quickly was able to confirm the judge's bias since a court clerk had heard a similar remark. These disclosures became the hallmark of Bailey's appeal to the district court and, ultimately, the Supreme Court decision to overturn the jury verdict and order a new trial.

```
        And I said, "Then added to that, you have the
fact that it is a mystery as to who did it."

        And Judge Blythin said, "Mystery? It's an
open and shut case."

        And I said, "Well, what do you mean, Judge Blythin?"
I was a little taken aback because usually, I have talked
to many judges in their chambers, but usually they
don't give me an opinion on a case before it's over.

        And so I said, "What do you mean, Judge Blythin?"

        And he said, "Well, he is guilty as hell. There
is no question about it."
```

Kilgallen deposition testimony, Sheppard case

Bailey acknowledged Kilgallen's part in securing justice for the doctor. He also said of her: "She was a very bright and very good reporter of criminal cases. The best there was."

To Kilgallen's relief, a subsequent jury acquitted Dr. Sheppard. Years later, DNA tests confirmed the verdict. The television series *The Fugitive* starring David Janssen as Dr. Richard Kimble was a huge success, leading to a film of the same name starring Harrison Ford. The death of Marilyn Sheppard remains unsolved.

My version of Kilgallen's appearance at the trial stands true, but in 2001, James Neff, an award-winning author and chairman of Investigative Reporters and Editors, a prestigious nonprofit organization that trains journalists nationwide, published a must-read book entitled *The Wrong Man: The Final Verdict on the Dr. Sam Sheppard Case*. He wrote, "Many high-profile journalists were assigned to [the Sheppard case]." Neff then listed some of them including "Robert Fabian, a famous Scotland Yard detective, now retired, who worked for Scripps Howard at the time" as well as Kilgallen's adversaries Bob Considine and Walter Winchell.

Regarding Kilgallen, Neff added, "These reporters paled in celebrity power to Dorothy Kilgallen, the queen of all media. [She] starred on the popular TV quiz show *What's My Line?* wrote a syndicated newspaper column called 'The Voice of Broadway.' She covered the occasional big story for Hearst's International News Service, hosted a morning radio talk show in New York City, and found time to swirl through New York's social scene in ermine and pearls."

By showcasing Kilgallen as one of the most skilled wordsmiths in journalistic history, Nell then observed, "Like most of her colleagues, [Kilgallen] came to town assuming Dr. Sam was guilty. Kilgallen, a quick study, soon fell under the spell of the Sheppard case." During the first week of the trial, Neff quoted one of her columns reading, "The fact that at this stage it is equally possible for the rational mind to find him innocent or guilty is what may make the Sheppard trial a celebrated cause to rank with the still unsolved Hall-Mills case or the classic puzzle of Lizzie Borden. Furthermore, with Susan Hayes cast as the other woman, 'the case gets its final element—sex guaranteed from the start.'"

While later in his book detailing Kilgallen's saving Sheppard from a life sentence through his excellent reporting, Neff's portrayal of Dorothy during the trial provides a true insight into the type of journalist she was at the time. Neff wrote, "[Kilgallen] tried to be one of the gang, going for lunch with lowly paid reporters at the Express Grill, a smoke-filled greasy spoon next to the courthouse where hamburgers were forty cents and the jukebox played polkas. Most of the reporters respected her skill and speed and work ethic but they resented the fanfare she created by simply appearing in public."

In a tribute to Kilgallen regarding her keeping silent about what Judge Blythin had told her—"He's guilty as hell"—Neff wrote, "despite her sympathy for Dr. Sheppard, the woman who could outwrite and out ruse a pack of journalists never did write a new story exposing Judge Blythin." Such the character of the reporter who had integrity oozing out of her very being.

Reporting such hard-edge news caused the elite of the New York City reporting world to take special notice of Kilgallen. The legendary Damon Runyon, impressed with Kilgallen's exploits, wrote of her:

> She has soft, dark hair, and huge, appealing eyes that gaze at you with an expression of infinite innocence buried in their azure depths. She looks so young and helpless that you say to yourself, "My goodness, I must assist this poor child in her work. I must have shied her from the rough edges of life…" Then you turn your watchfulness to the hard-eyed members of the sterner sex, and you are positively shocked when you pick up the Journal the next day and discover that the little girl with the eyes of a gazelle has scooped your eyes off. Ah yes, that Kilgallen girl.

Asked at the time why Kilgallen had become so successful as a reporter, her father, Jim, told the *New York Post*, "This is the greatest working newspaperwoman alive. She's friendly with everyone she works with but first of all she is a newspaperwoman. She'll be sitting in court and suddenly have an angle in the testimony and bang, she is out like a dart dictating to her office." (This skill would come in handy later when Kilgallen covered the Jack Ruby trial.)

Jim added, "Some people have criticized her for this, but hell, she's a newspaperwoman first. Hell, she's even done that to me. First, you think, 'That little brat, my own daughter!' Then you start to think, 'Why didn't

I think of that?' and you realize and respect her for what she is—one hell of a newspaper gal."

Jim was correct and one only has to read the hundreds of Kilgallen's columns to understand the diversity of the subjects she chose to write about. In April 2022, Paul Chimera, an avid reader of my books, sent me the copy of a column with the unlikely title of "Unwelcome . . . . ." The heretofore never published column appeared in the December 19, 1958, edition of the *Cincinnati Enquirer*, a Hearst-owned newspaper, on page 26.

Having never been aware of this type of column before, I found it is interesting that Dorothy wrote about a restaurant hangout for "theatrical celebrities" where the ownership "would be pleased if the sultry Diana Barrymore (American actress – daughter of renowned actor John Barrymore) took her business elsewhere since "she talks too loudly" (apparently the reason for the "Unwelcome" headline) as well as news that actor Ernie Kovacs "is set to star in four TV spectaculars." Marlon Brando and Debbie Reynolds were also featured in the column as was celebrated artist Salvador Dali who shocked guests at a dinner he hosted by "placing an enormous rhino horn on the table."

CHAPTER 10

Of most interest as my research journey continued was discovering that Kilgallen had launched an obsessive eighteen-month investigation of the JFK assassination, which included the attendance at the Jack Ruby trial in March 1964.

Why? Because I learned that Kilgallen was a close friend of the president's and more so, that he had fussed over her young son Kerry when both were invited to the White House. After JFK was killed, she wrote, "The picture that stays in my mind is the one of this tall young man bending over a small boy, carefully scrutinizing envelopes until he came to the name 'Kerry Ardan Kollmar—Grade 3B.' This is the man who was assassinated in Dallas."

I also learned that Kilgallen had been described by highly respected author and "Oswald Alone" skeptic Mark Lane as the "only serious journalist in America who was concerned with who killed John Kennedy and getting all the facts about the assassination." An AP photograph captured Kilgallen and Ruby trial co-counsel Joe Tonahill during a serious conversation.

At this point in time, I realized that since I had not been present in Dallas when JFK was assassinated, or at the Ruby trial, and Dorothy had

Joe Tonahill and Dorothy

been,[9] I needed to in some ways "step aside" and let her tell this part of her one-of-a-kind coverage of the assassination. My job thus became to discover everything I could that she said and wrote about the events in Dallas and, as accurately as possible, provide them to the public through my books.

Even before the trial, Kilgallen had become suspicious of whether the federal government was being forthright concerning disclosure of important documents regarding the JFK and Oswald assassinations. To that end, she wrote a biting column that included facts from a ten-page letter Tonahill had written to J. Edgar Hoover requesting the documents. Hoover declined the request. Kilgallen wrote, "It appears that Washington knows or suspects something about Lee Harvey Oswald that it does not want Dallas and the rest of the world to know." She added, "Why is Oswald being kept in the shadows, as dim a figure as they can make him...?"

Remaining skeptical of the "official" versions of what happened, including J. Edgar Hoover's shouting "Oswald Alone" to the world and telling his agents and the Justice Department that no sense of any "conspiracy" was even remotely possible, Kilgallen, unlike any of the other four hundred reporters at the trial, published columns denouncing Hoover's proclamations. They included the lethal column entitled: "The Oswald File Must Not Close" that was published just six days after JFK's death.

At the outset, Kilgallen's strong words were aimed at President Lyndon Johnson. She wrote:

> President Lyndon Johnson has been elevated so swiftly to his new high post that in one sense, he has been snatched up into an ivory tower. As Chief Executive, he is no longer in a position to hear the voices of ordinary

---

9 Kilgallen's eyewitness to history accounts completely dwarf those of so many authors and so-called assassination experts regarding credibility since she was there in Dallas, at the Ruby trial, etc. unlike any of them. Based on my research, any book that does not include her research and conclusions distorts the truth and should be dismissed as unreliable.

people talking candidly. If he could walk invisible along the streets of the nation and listen to ordinary people talking, he would realize that he must be sure that the mystery of Lee Harvey Oswald is solved and laid before the nation down to the smallest shred of evidence.

The famous reporter then added:

If Oswald is President Kennedy's assassin, he is the most important prisoner the police in this country had in 100 years and no blithe announcement in Dallas is going to satisfy the American public that the case is closed. The case is closed, is it? Well, I'd like to know how, in a big, smart town like Dallas, a man like Jack Ruby—owner of a strip tease honky tonk—can stroll in and out of police headquarters as if it was a health club at a time when a small army of law enforcers is keeping a "tight security guard" on Oswald. Security! What a word for it.

Finally, Kilgallen wrote, "Justice is a big rug. When you pull it out from under one man, a lot of others fall too." This bold and unnerving statement signaled to anyone complicit in the assassinations that she was a threat to exposing their involvement. Dorothy had to have known she could be placing herself in danger but remained undaunted with the lone-wolf investigation.

Kilgallen's harsh accusing words, as will be explained for the first time in detail, agitated LBJ as well as Hoover and others she had in her crosshairs. All were now watching closely the increasing attention given by the most powerful journalist of her era to the greatest murder case of the century.

In fact, in the column entitled "Still Live Topic" (also released as "The Tragedy We Cannot Forget"), Kilgallen continued the drumbeat to learn the truth about what happened to JFK and Oswald, writing on December 11, 1963: "What happened in Texas on Nov. 22 and two days later is extraordinary, so it is inevitable that people should continue to discuss the events, debate them, and argue about them. But even I am amazed at the sustaining interest in the assassination and its aftermath."

Extolling her propensity for mixing with the rich and famous, Kilgallen then wrote of a party she attended. Stage and film director Joshua Logan (*Picnic, Bus Stop*) hosted it. The guests included celebrated author Truman Capote, wealthy sportsman Alfred Vanderbilt Jr., American impresario, theatrical showman, and lyricist Billy Rose ("Me and My Shadow"), and the former president of Mexico. She wrote:

> As I moved from group to group, it seemed to me that there was no one who did not want to talk, for a moment or for quite a long time about President Kennedy, Jacqueline's astonishing fortitude after his death, the killing of Lee Harvey Oswald, and the mysterious figure who shot him, Jack Ruby. One might think that this collection of sophisticates and celebrities might be "tired" of the topic by now, but they were not obviously.

After I had scanned these columns, an important photo popped up based on research at the National Archives. My eyes brightened as I saw Melvin Belli holding a news conference with Dorothy right alongside. Following up, I discovered there was NBC footage available.

Kilgallen and Belli at Ruby trial news conference

To then aid readers with the visual nature of the Ruby trial, Kilgallen's coverage of it, and other matters about the famous journalist, I created a website, www.thedorothykilgallenstory.org, available today. It includes the Belli news conference.

At this point in time, it greatly impressed me to learn that this college dropout, who had worked her way to stardom as a columnist (Voice of Broadway—part gossip, part Hollywood show biz, part Broadway, and part true-crime reporter), landed the only

Dorothy at the typewriter

interview Jack Ruby permitted at trial. Ruby co-counsel Joe Tonahill, in an interview posted at www.thedorothykilgallenstory.org, stated in part, "She told me she had had a contact with a friend of Jack's from San Francisco. I believe it was an opera singer that he was very fond of. She wanted to pass a message along to him. I told Jack that and he said, 'I'd like to talk to [Kilgallen].'"

Dorothy being frisked at the Ruby trial

Asked why Ruby had decided to speak to Kilgallen, who had told revered CBS *Person to Person* television program host Edward R. Murrow how much she loved being in the "newspaper business" (www.thereporterwhoknewtoomuch.com), Tonahill said, "I don't think there was any doubt about it…Jack was highly impressed with Dorothy Kilgallen." He added, "Ruby figured she was a very classy person, she had good programs, *What's My Line?* and she was a highly intelligent person and I think of all the writers that were down there during the Ruby trial…about four hundred from all over the world…she probably was the one that, to him, was the most significant 'cause he was in the entertainment business."

Tonahill added:

> Jack had a bodyguard shield around him of four deputy sheriffs sitting behind him and everywhere he went, and I told them Kilgallen wanted to ask him some questions and speak with him at recess and that he'd agreed to it. And they said "okay." So when the judge declared the noon recess, Jack went over and spoke with her…in the courtroom right behind his chair where he was sitting…there was a rail there and he got up and she was on the other side of the rail and Jack was on this side and they had a little conversation. I think the press had already left the courtroom.
>
> [Jack] wasn't uttering nonsense because this interview with her was very significant in his classless life, you know I think he enjoyed it very much and cooperated with Kilgallen in every way that he could and told her the truth as he understood it. And it was just a very agreeable conversation between them and I just can't understand people doubting the sincerity of that interview because to me, and I watched them, a very sincere discussion was going back and forth.

Later, Tonahill, who knew Ruby had watched episodes of *What's My Line?* at his Carousel Club, wrote, on his letterhead, a letter to respected researcher David Henschel, dated April 23, 1998:

TONAHILL, HILE, LEISTER & JACOBELLIS
LAWYERS
TONAHILL BUILDING
P. O. BOX 670
409-384-2501
JASPER, TEXAS 75951

JOE H. TONAHILL
CURTIS W. LEISTER ★
MIKE JACOBELLIS
J. KEVIN DUTTON
J. J. BRAGG
★ A PROFESSIONAL CORPORATION

OF COUNSEL
RICHARD C. HILE ★
SUITE 330
1601 RIO GRANDE
AUSTIN, TEXAS 78701

April 23, 1998

The trial was traumatic, explosive, and loaded with pressure situations in a hostile venue. Yes, we learned that Ruby often watched *What's My Line* on his Carousel Club TV set. He insisted on absolute privacy and a quiet atmosphere when listening to his favorite Kilgallen episode.

I was present when Kilgallen interviewed Ruby during a noon recess in the courtroom. I arranged for the prison guards to delay taking Ruby back to his cell in order that she could get the interview.

I did hear Kilgallen deliver the message to Ruby from the San Francisco lady opera singer who was longtime personal friend of Ruby's. Earl Ruby lied—Ruby was a close friend of the singer's.

While Kilgallen's column, "Ruby Stars at Last," published in *Collateral Damage*, provided insight into his mindset at the time of his trial, another column may be more important. On February 23, 1964, the revered reporter had written a column called "Nervous Ruby Feels 'Breaking Point' Near." The first paragraph read, "Jack Ruby's eyes were as shiny brown-and-white bright as the glass eyes of a doll. He tried to smile but his smile was a failure. When we shook hands, his hand trembled in mine ever so slightly, like the heartbeat of a bird."

Continuing, the article, which showcased Kilgallen's gifted manner with words, stated, "'I'm nervous and worried,' he told me. 'I feel I'm on the verge of something I don't understand—the breaking point maybe.'" When she told Ruby, "I think you're holding up pretty well," he replied, "I'm fooling you, Dorothy. I'm really scared." Whatever Ruby told Kilgallen during their second interview caused her to write, "I went out into the almost empty lunch-time corridor wondering what I really believed about this man."

Joe Tonahill's observation—"Ruby told [Kilgallen] the truth as he understood it"—may be compared, as will be explained, not only with his Warren Commission testimony (revealed by Kilgallen before the report was to be released), but also a psychiatric exam and a polygraph test given to Oswald's killer. In each instance, I carefully dissected what Ruby said as I believed Dorothy would have done if she had been privy to the documents, impossible regarding the psychiatric exam and polygraph test since neither had been released to the public before she died.

Whatever Ruby told Kilgallen during their interviews, the substance of which led her to immediately visit New Orleans, the location of Carlos Marcello's underworld empire, none of the three (exam, polygraph test, WC testimony) gave any indication Ruby had acted any way other than alone when he assassinated Oswald. With regard to the psychiatric exam that was sent to me by a very reliable confidant confirming that, like Dorothy, I was privy to the best sources coming my way, the front page of the report dated December 27, 1963 (before his trial), read:

> December 27, 1963
>
> CASE OF JACK LEON RUBY, AGE 52
>
> STATEMENT OF PROBLEM
>
> A psychiatric evaluation of this defendant, who is charged with the slaying of Lee Oswald on November 24, 1963, is requested.

In order then, sections were divided into Medical History, Physical Exam, School History, Work History, Family History, Siblings, Personality as Described by Patient, Previous Offenses, and Reaction to the Death of President Kennedy and Present Offense.

Highlights include under "Personality as Described by Patient," Ruby was quoted as saying:

Patient said several times that he "loves" the police. He states
that on one occasion when a police officer was killed on duty he gave
$150, the largest contribution. He attended all policemen's funerals.
He said that two officers, Blankenship and Carlson, came to his club
one night and arrested him for selling beer after hours "but then they
found out I had good friends and they came out the next night sort of
apologetic. And just then there were two fellows who demanded drinks

Regarding his being present inside Dallas Police Department
headquarters following JFK's assassination where he attended Oswald's news
conference, Ruby said:

went in the hall. Everybody says, "Who, Jack." It was just a
tragic feeling. Everything was so bustling, so crude. My whole motive
was to find out how I could get into the radio station. I can't get
Joe DeLong. I even had an officer page him so I could get the right
number from him. I was in this swarm of people and suddenly Oswald
comes. The reporters asked me who was this one and who was that one.
I was in a complete change of mental reaction, already I am with the
deal. They are going to take him to the big assembly room. History
is being made. I am standing on the table above everybody and people
are asking me 'Who is that?' I even passed out some of my cards to
these newspaper men from all over the world. I just had my cards
printed with the Patty girl on them and I am proud of them. The

Concerning Ruby's comments to the interviewer regarding the specifics
of shooting Oswald including the observation that Oswald looked like Paul
Newman, etc., Ruby said:

interview was all over with Oswald. I said, 'The little guy looks
like Paul Newman'." The patient was asked whether he had his gun
with him at the time. He said that he had taken it out of his pocket
and left it in the car when he went into the synagogue, that it is
sacrilegious to go into the synagogue with a gun, but that he put it
in his pocket again. He had between $1,600 and $1,800 on him at the
time. He said if he had wanted to shoot Oswald he could have shot
him very easily when he was in the assembly room. He said that out-

doing little crazy things. I had parked the car with the dog in it and as I came out curiosity got
the best of me. I wanted to see what was going on. I was only about
a third of a block away. I noticed a policeman guiding an automobile
out of the City Hall so I walked down and there was nobody around me
and suddenly out of the elevator or whatever it was I see this vicious
person, this animal. If I had had to pay for a parking ticket where I
parked my car it would never have happened. I thought maybe Henry Wade
or Captain Fritz was talking to the newsmen after the transfer of Oswald
was over. I thought I might get a scoop for my friends at the radio
station, but I saw Oswald. He had a very smirky, cunning, vicious look
like an animal, like a Communist. I thought I might be looking at a
rat. I don't recall if I said, 'You killed my President', or if I
said anything. I don't recall if he said anything."

Patient was then asked why he didn't shoot more than once. He said,
"They grabbed my hand. After they brought me upstairs in the elevator
I felt relieved. I don't remember just how they wrestled me to the
floor. I think I said, 'You don't have to beat my brains out, I am
Jack Ruby.' It flashed through my mind, 'Why are all these guys jump-
ing on me?' I am very known person with the police and with everybody
else. I am not somebody who is a screwball."

When asked what impelled him to shoot, he replied, "I don't know. Here is a vicious animal -- and what the world has lost. I went crazy. I didn't think what could happen to me." He was asked whether the police said anything after he shot and he said, "I don't know, I think before I went to the ground a cop said, 'Jack, you rat'."

Based on the exam, the examiner concluded:

There seems to be no feeling of guilt whatever on the patient's part about the slaying of Oswald. He seems to feel that it was some agent outside of himself that carried out the act, and that Oswald was really not human. It was only when he was questioned about Oswald's wife and children that he was unable to use his defense of denial, that the man was not a real human being.

Those interested in Ruby's examination answers, part of history, may make what they will of his statements, but it seems clear that he had landed on, or been told to stick to, the story that he had accidentally been across the street from Dallas Police Department basement and then entered before he shot Oswald, quite contradictory to the Ruby trial transcripts, as will be explained, where it was learned he said during a verified telephone conversation, "I will be there," when Oswald was transferred. Of special interest for sure is that Ruby admitted "several times he 'loves' the police" which confirms what he said during the same conversation where he told whomever he was talking to that the police helped him get into the DPD basement when the transfer took place.

Regarding the polygraph test given on July 16, 1964, a portion of the opening page reads:

As early as December of 1963, Jack Ruby expressed his desire to be examined with a polygraph, truth serum, or any other scientific device which would test his veracity. The attorneys who defended Ruby in the State criminal proceedings in Texas agreed that he should take a polygraph examination to test any conspiratorial connection between Ruby and Oswald. To obtain such a test, Ruby's defense counsel filed motions in court and also requested that the FBI administer such an examination to Ruby. During the course of a psychiatric examination on May 11, 1964, Ruby is quoted as saying: "I want to tell the truth. I want a polygraph..." In addition, numerous letters were written to the President's Commission on behalf of Ruby requesting a polygraph examination.

With this in mind, certain questions and answers are of interest. They include:

Q. Did you know Oswald before November 22, 1963?
A. No.
Q. Did you assist Oswald in the assassination?
A. No.
Q. Between the assassination and the shooting, did anybody you know tell you they knew Oswald?
A. No.
Q. Aside from anything you said to George Senator on Sunday morning, did you ever tell anyone else that you intended to shoot Oswald?
A. No.
Q. Did you shoot Oswald in order to silence him?
A. No.
Q. Did you first decide to shoot Oswald on Friday night?
A. No.
Q. Did you first decide to shoot Oswald on Saturday morning?
A. No.
Q. Did you first decide to shoot Oswald on Saturday night?
A. No.
Q. Did you first decide to shoot Oswald on Sunday morning?
A. Yes.
Q. Were you on the sidewalk at the time Lieutenant Pierce's car stopped on the ramp exit?
A. Yes.
Q. Did you enter the jail by walking through an alleyway?
A. No.
Q. Did you walk past the guard at the time Lieutenant Pierce's car was parked on the ramp exit?
A. Yes.
Q. Did you talk with any Dallas police officers on Sunday, November 24, prior to the shooting of Oswald?
A. No.
Q. Is everything you told the Warren Commission the entire truth?
A. Yes.
Q. Did you shoot Oswald because of any influence of the underworld?
A. No.

Under the banner "Interpretation of the Test" were these words:

During the proceedings at Dallas, Texas, on July 18, 1964, Dr. William R. Beavers, a psychiatrist, testified that he would generally describe Jack Ruby as a "psychotic depressive." In view of the serious question raised as to Ruby's mental condition, no significance should be placed on the polygraph examination and it should be considered nonconclusive as the charts cannot be relied upon.

Based once again on the overheard Ruby conversations on Saturday before he shot Oswald on Sunday, these answers indicated Ruby was lying during this examination. When combined with the false testimony he gave to the Warren Commission as will be indicated, it appears that the only time he told the truth occurred when Dorothy Kilgallen, who Joe Tonahill said Ruby was "highly impressed with," interviewed him. Also recall that of their conversation, Tonahill stated:

[Jack] wasn't uttering nonsense because this interview with her was very significant in his classless life, you know and I think he enjoyed it very much and cooperated with Kilgallen in every way that he could and told her the truth as he understood it. And it was just a very agreeable conversation between them and I just can't understand people doubting the sincerity of that interview because to me, and I watched them, a very sincere discussion was going back and forth.

For certain, Kilgallen was upset when Ruby attempted suicide while in prison three times. And like the rest of the world, wondered what he meant when he uttered these words following his Warren Commission testimony:

The world will never know the true facts of what occurred. My motives. The people who had, that had so much to gain and had such a material motive to put me in this position I'm in would never let the true facts come above board to the world.

Without question, common sense dictates that Ruby's admissions only reinforced Kilgallen's belief that Oswald's killer was part of a plot to kill JFK and the cover-up.

* * *

Still hopeful that the US government might release the remainder of the JFK assassination documents as required by law, a breath of hope occurred on December 15, 2021, when the Biden administration announced that 1,500 documents would be released. Before doing so, the president, like those before him, had hidden the documents from the American public, a cover-up for certain. What were he and the other presidents hiding, what was the motive? Certainly Biden's explanation prior to the December date was lame. He had announced:

> Temporary continued postponement is necessary to protect against identifiable harm to the military defense, intelligence operations, law enforcement, or the conduct of foreign relations that is of such gravity that it outweighs the public interest in immediate disclosure.

What, I asked myself as I believed Dorothy would have wondered, could possibly be a credible reason for the documents, all of them, not being released so as to "protect against any identifiable harm" to the subjects mentioned. To anyone possessing common sense, Biden's excuses made no sense whatsoever if you take each excuse and analyze it. Perhaps most ridiculous was possible "identifiable harm to military defense" six decades after the assassination. Close in second place was possible harm to "law enforcement," whatever that meant.

Regardless, when the limited documents were released, I combed the pages for days on end, and during various media interviews, I provided strong opinions that were based on my research and my books, including *Collateral Damage*, and thus my unique perspective of what happened in Dallas in 1963. I did not agree with some so-called experts who called all of the documents "minimal and worthless," and "a waste of time." Despite there being at least a third of the 1,500 documents labeled as "missing" or "redacted," there were some jewels of information in the documents, including several connecting to my theories. For instance:

> A 3/25/1974 CIA document connecting Robert Kennedy, Sam Giancana, and Johnny Roselli regarding an attempt to "quash" a Grand Jury organized

crime indictment against Giancana" and thus "forestall public disclosure of Roselli's association with the US Government."

What was this all about? I wondered. Why was RFK involved in quashing the indictment?

The CIA agent who signed a document dated 4/17/1975 that deals with Lee Harvey Oswald's address book (the entries are all of Russians who work for Radio Moscow) is James Angleton, the same one who signed the August 1962 CIA document, as will be explained, that connects Marilyn, JFK, and Dorothy Kilgallen regarding matters involving Marilyn's death.

This document made me wonder more about Angleton, who he was, and what the agenda was of the CIA:

A 6/5/1968 CIA document dealing with Jim Garrison's investigation with one item reading, "Belli defense attorney for Jack Ruby; Jim Garrison was a weekend guest of Belli when Garrison visited SF in October 1967" and most interestingly, "Belli was reportedly involved in illicit drug trafficking with Morris Elowitz in 1958. Elowitz was a suspected contact of [mobster] Lucky Luciano."

This document indicated Belli's connection to the mob as noted in my books.

Regarding Sam Giancana, a 12/20/1977 CIA document reported that "Sam Giancana, Head of the Chicago Cosa Nostra, is still running things by remote control from a hide-out in Mexico."

The document seemed to confirm that even fourteen years after JFK was assassinated, Giancana, who helped catapult JFK into the White House, was still operating, albeit in Mexico.

A 4/4/67 CIA document detailing the report by a "sensitive Soviet Source" which reads in part, "The Soviets felt that President Kennedy's death was a great loss, not only for the US and SU, but for the whole world. According to the source, the Soviets felt that they could trust President Kennedy and deal with him on a cooperative basis."

This document appears to negate all the crazy theories about Soviets being involved in JFK's death.

A 9/25/1998 CIA document appearing to negate any connection of Oswald to the CIA's "Office of Operations."

This document appears to negate allegations made by Oswald/CIA theorists thirty-plus years after the assassination.

There were other points of interest, but disappointingly, no references to Dorothy Kilgallen or Jack Ruby, or any connections between RFK's illegal actions against Marcello that triggered JFK's assassination. What the unclassified documents as a whole do indicate is that those investigating the assassination headed down so many rabbit holes focused on Oswald that they missed the obvious, that, as Dorothy knew, focusing on Ruby was the key to resolving what happened to JFK.

CHAPTER 11

Lightning struck when Kilgallen was able to print the series of articles of enormous historical importance, which proved to be the most unparalleled exclusive in her illustrious journalistic career. These articles, published from the eighteenth of August to the twentieth, 1964, exposed the Jack Ruby testimony at the Warren Commission before its official release date.

The Kilgallen exclusive, one of hundreds secured as a powerful force bar none in the newspaper world, prompted fellow reporter Marianne Means from the Hearst Headline Services in Washington, DC, to write:

Dear Dorothy, it is not my custom to write praise of other [Hearst] writers no matter how good they may be (and as you are). But I must really compliment you on the Warren Commission Scoop…you have literally gotten this town in a tizzy, everybody turning to it second-hand for themselves. Congratulations. A very good job. Yours, Marianne Means

Regarding the Ruby testimony, recall that the famous reporter enjoyed her front-row seat at his trial while paying close attention to the overall testimony from those who provided firsthand accounts of everything surrounding the JFK assassination and Oswald's death and that she was the only reporter to interview Ruby. Exactly how and from whom Dorothy obtained the Ruby testimony has always remained a secret, that is, until now as will be explained. Before identifying the source, documents secured by this author through the National Archives provide Kilgallen's limited explanation as to how she accomplished this blockbuster achievement.

The proof is included in a letter/memo from J. Edgar Hoover to J. Lee Rankin, general counsel to the Warren Commission, regarding the events that took place so that Kilgallen received the transcript of Ruby's secret testimony before its release in the Warren Commission report. (*see right, top*)

Above his familiar signature, Hoover acknowledged that Rankin had requested an investigation as to how Kilgallen "came into possession" of the transcript of Ruby's testimony. The memo then states that accompanying pages "set forth the results of interviews with Joseph Kingsbury-Smith, publisher of the *New York Journal-American*, and Dorothy Kilgallen on August 21, 1964."

The first attached page read: (*right, below*)

Which FBI agent wrote the account remains unclear, but of interest is Kingsbury-Smith telling the interviewer that the publisher asked Kilgallen to "identify the

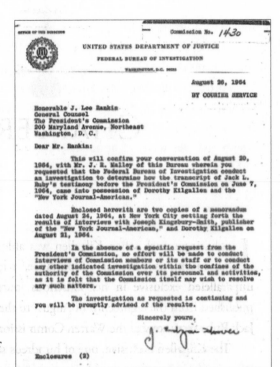

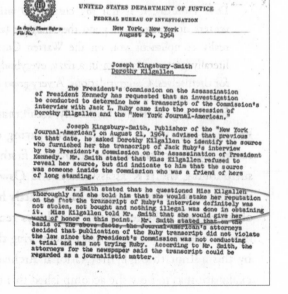

source who furnished her the transcript." The response was that she "refused to reveal her source, but did indicate to him [the publisher] that the source was someone inside the Commission who was a friend of hers of long standing."

Further, Kilgallen told Kingsbury-Smith that she would "stake her reputation on the fact the transcript of Ruby's interview definitely was not stolen, not bought and nothing illegal was done in obtaining it...that she would give her word of honor on this point." Concerning the transcript's publication, the publisher said he consulted with his attorneys and decided printing the transcript "did not violate the law," and that it "could be regarded as a journalistic matter."

The next two pages of the memo chronicled an interview by the agent or agents on August 21, 1964, at Kilgallen's "Town House at 45 East 68th Street, New York, New York."

Whoever wrote the memo recalled that Kilgallen "refused to reveal the source" but acknowledged it was "a responsible person who had a legal right to the transcript." She told the agent or agents "that she was the only person who knew the identity of the source and that she 'would die' rather than reveal his

> Joseph Kingsbury-Smith
> Dorothy Kilgallen
>
> Dorothy Kilgallen was interviewed on August 21, 1964, at her Town House located at 45 East 68th Street, New York, New York.
>
> Miss Kilgallen stated that she refused to reveal the source who gave her the transcript of the Jack Ruby interview by the President's Commission on the Assassination of President Kennedy.
>
> Miss Kilgallen stated that she would identify the source only as a "responsible person who had a legal right to the transcript." She stated that she was the only person who knew the identity of the source and that she "would die" rather than reveal his identity. Miss Kilgallen said that she based her refusal to identify her source on the right of a newspaper reporter to protect his sources of information.
>
> Miss Kilgallen specifically was asked whether or not the source was a member of the President's Commission itself or a staff member or employee. She refused to answer.
>
> Miss Kilgallen specifically was asked if the source was someone not on the Commission, such as Ruby's defense counsel or someone else who was present during the interview or who might legally have received a copy of the transcript. She refused to answer.
>
> Miss Kilgallen also said that she would refuse to give the date on which she received the Ruby transcript and would refuse to identify the city in which she obtained it.
>
> Miss Kilgallen did state that her source was a man and not a woman. She said her source is a friend of hers of long standing. She stated that the source gave her the transcript as a "friendly gesture."

identity." This was based, Kilgallen asserted, "on the right of a newspaper reporter to protect his sources of information."

Asked if the source was "a member of the President's Commission itself or a staff member or employee," or "someone not on the Commission such as Ruby's defense counsel," Kilgallen refused to answer. Kilgallen also would not divulge the date she received the Ruby transcript or "identify the city in which she obtained it."

Kilgallen, the memo stated, admitted to the agents that the source was "a man not a woman…a friend of hers of long standing" and the source "gave her the transcript as a 'friendly gesture.'"

The next page read: (see right)

Kilgallen stated "that she did not pay money for the transcript and did not give or promise her source anything else of value in exchange for the transcript." The agent said Kilgallen "refused to

> Joseph Kingsbury-Smith
> Dorothy Kilgallen
>
> Miss Kilgallen stated that she would swear that the transcript was not stolen and nothing illegal was done in obtaining it. She stated that she did not pay money for the transcript and did not give or promise her source anything else of value in exchange for the transcript.
>
> Miss Kilgallen refused to say if she first approached the source or if the source first approached her about the transcript.
>
> She stated this source gave her a typed transcript of the Ruby interview. She kept the transcript several days and had copies made including photostats. Miss Kilgallen then gave the transcript back to her source.
>
> Miss Kilgallen recalled from memory that the transcript she received was numbered from Page 1 to Page 103. She said that one page was missing. She believes the missing page was numbered 59, otherwise the transcript appeared to be complete. Page 103 of the transcript was a notarized statement from the stenographer who was present during the interview.
>
> Miss Kilgallen stated the "New York Journal-American" does not know the identity of her source and in fact, she told the newspaper less than she told the interviewing agents.
>
> Miss Kilgallen did not furnish any other information of value. She stated that she is the only person who knows the identity of her source and she will never reveal it.
>
> Miss Kilgallen volunteered to go to Washington, D.C. to testify on this matter before the President's Commission. She emphasized, however, that she also will refuse to identify her source to the Commission or anyone else. She stated that regardless of the consequences, she will never identify the source to anyone.

say if the source first approached her about the transcript." She told him the source had given her "a typed transcript" that she "kept for several days and had copies made including photostats [early projection photocopies]" before giving the transcript back to her source.

The agent, or likely agents, interrogating Kilgallen reported that she said the "transcript was numbered from Page 1 to Page 103." She said one page was missing and believed it to be page 59. Page 103, Kilgallen stated, included a "notarized statement from the stenographer who was present during [Ruby's] interview."

Of special importance is the final paragraph of the memo, which read:

> Miss Kilgallen volunteered to go to Washington, D.C. to testify on this matter before the President's Commission. She emphasized, however, that she also will refuse to identify her source to the Commission or anyone else. She stated that regardless of the consequences, she will never identify the source to anyone.

Though Kilgallen showed calm on the outside when she received the Ruby testimony, her heart was likely beating like that of a hundred-yard-dash Olympic sprinter. She knew she would have a chance to read his testimony before any other reporter did so. She could also publish it for the world to read while comparing his testimony at the Warren Commission with the Ruby trial testimony notes she had collected.

Based on Kilgallen's reputation for truth-telling, Kingsbury-Smith decided to rush the documents to print as soon as possible after consulting with his attorneys. The paper would have an exclusive, a scoop of unimaginable proportions, since millions of people were awaiting the Warren Commission report with anticipation on a daily basis.

In fact, one may only imagine what an incredible "exclusive" Kilgallen scored in light of the historical importance of Jack Ruby's Warren Commission testimony. Perhaps only the later disclosure of the Nixon White House tapes, exposure of the Pentagon Papers, and Edward Snowden's leak of classified information from the National Security Agency (NSA) in 2013 provide similar comparison.

Bottom line: Kilgallen had embarrassed the FBI director by exposing the Ruby testimony. And Hoover was not one to be embarrassed. She had made a fool of him, and in response he intensified surveillance of her by FBI agents.

When the story was published, Kilgallen added her own perspective based on, she said, "reading the transcripts three times in one sitting." She wrote: "Ruby was told to tell his story and he did, in thousands of words and hundreds of sentences, some of which rambled on to the point of being without sense. But, in the end, Ruby told much about himself." Kilgallen then added, "He opened the floodgates of his mind and unloosed a stream of consciousness that would have dazzled a James Joyce buff and enraptured a psychiatrist. Jack Ruby bared to the Chief Justice his emotions, his fears, his triumphs and his ego—a large ego for such a small man."

Kilgallen's hairdresser and confidant Charles Simpson had his own viewpoint of the danger she faced by crossing swords with what he called "the wrong people." He said during his taped interview, "She printed it [Ruby Warren Commission testimony] on the front page of the *Journal-American* before the president received it, and therein lies the tale. From then on, we were stalked. Marc [Sinclaire] and me, our phones were tapped [since] they were trying to figure out where she got her information, that she could get this information before the president got it."

True to Kilgallen's strength and integrity, she never disclosed the name of the source even though the consequences could have been possible prosecution. One may only imagine the pressure she endured when at least one, and in all likelihood two FBI agents descended on her home. Without

Charles Simpson

legal counsel to ensure her rights, she faced down the agents, forcing them to return to Hoover with the proverbial tail between their legs. Just imagine the director's strong vocal response to their not having been able to break Kilgallen and discover her source. These were tough agents who had interrogated heavyweight criminals and brought them to their knees, and yet they had to tell Hoover that Kilgallen had won the interrogation battle.

Kilgallen's acquisition and printing of the documents had begun with an apparent clandestine meeting with her friend, or more likely as will be explained, an "associate" of her friend, an "intermediary" chosen by the friend, at the commission. Based on her scathing *Journal-American* columns and articles, her source must have been aware of the reporter's disdain for Hoover and questions she had about the commission's intention to pursue the truth about JFK's death.

Kilgallen told no one of her secret source, but when she ran into Howard Rothberg, an interior designer and friend who was a founding member of

her P. J. Clarke's "Science Club," she showed him a thick grouping of papers hidden inside the *Life* magazine cover depicting Lee Harvey Oswald holding the Mannlicher-Carcano rifle the authorities swore he used to assassinate John F. Kennedy. When Rothberg asked, "What's this?" Kilgallen calmly replied, "It's just part of the Warren Commission report."

Nearly six years later, after publishing Kilgallen's story in what became the bestselling *The Reporter Who Knew Too Much*, I am able to identify the "source" who passed Ruby's testimony to Kilgallen in late 1964. As will be explained, it is based on shocking new evidence connected to "a man not a woman…a friend of hers of long standing" who gave her the transcript as a 'friendly gesture.'"

CHAPTER 12

Kilgallen's caustic columns about her disbelief in the "Oswald Alone" theory must certainly have drawn the attention of those who had the strongest motive to assassinate JFK and who covered it up. Regarding the former, she had to have known that New Orleans Mafia kingpin Carlos Marcello was the main suspect since he risked losing his freedom and his multi-million-dollar empire in 1963/64 if evidence surfaced that he was involved in the JFK assassination.

That Marcello not being pegged for orchestrating the assassination paid off was confirmed when in late 2021, while employing Dorothy Kilgallen's dogged investigative skills, I discovered a 1968/69 Marcello FBI file disclosing that his empire's net worth in the late sixties was more than $60 million ($480 million in today's currency).

The primary source for the information came from two informants who apparently became close to Marcello to the extent of the document providing data about his eating habits and rendezvous with various women other than his wife.

FEDERAL BUREAU OF INVESTIGATION

REPORTING OFFICE	OFFICE OF ORIGIN	DATE	INVESTIGATIVE PERIOD	
NEW ORLEANS	NEW ORLEANS	4/8/69	10/29/68-3/28/69	
TITLE OF CASE		REPORT MADE BY		TYPE
CARLOS MARCELLO, aka		SA JOHN C. MC CURNIN, II		- S
		CHARACTER OF CASE		m

INFORMANTS:

Identity of Source	Contacting Agent
NO T-3 is NO 1434-C-TE	SA THOMAS L. COLARELLI; SA JACK EVANS MEHL
NO T-9 is NO 1232-C-TE	SA REED W. JENSEN

In addition to these informants, others were listed, and thus the FBI file included never-before-exposed information that Marcello had been in contact with his lawyer Frank Ragano, also the attorney for James Hoffa and mafioso Santo Trafficante. In addition, the file exposed a 1969 Marcello meeting with F. Lee Bailey, and that Marcello was aware that New Orleans DA Jim Garrison met with Bailey and Ruby's attorney Melvin Belli the same year.

> On 2/5/69, source advised that FRANK RAGANO and F. LEE BAILEY were staying at the Bourbon Orleans Hotel yesterday and were to meet today with CARLOS MARCELLO and WILSON ABRAHAM for unknown reason at an unknown location.

> On 2/7/69, NO 1734-PC advised that F. LEE BAILEY and MELVIN BELLI met with District Attorney JIM GARRISON of Orleans Parish for unknown reason.

That Marcello met with Bailey, who, it may be recalled, I knew in the 1970s when we handled what was known as "The Headless Torso" case, is quite surprising but certainly connects the two men and Ragano, attorney for Marcello, Santo Trafficante, and James Hoffa. How Bailey entered that rat's nest is a mystery for sure, one that deserves further investigation.

Of greater interest is that Belli was in "Orleans parish" and for "unknown reasons" met "with District Attorney Jim Garrison." Belli appearing in the very city where Marcello ruled with the very DA who declined to investigate Marcello regarding the JFK assassination is alarming and causes one to believe the evidence I uncovered that Belli knew about the assassination before it happened is quite credible due to the potential Belli/Marcello connection.

The FBI file also proves Ragano, Trafficante's lawyer, met with Marcello, connecting those three men for certain.

> NO 1734-PC advised that Dr. FRANK RAGANO, TRAFFICANTE's attorney, was in telephonic contact with CARLOS MARCELLO that morning and was planning to meet with CARLOS MARCELLO in Bay City, Texas. NO 1734-PC knows that CARLOS MARCELLO had in his briefcase a transcript of the Laredo trial and also a map of the Waterford Oil Company property located adjacent to Churchill Farm Estate.

As far as Marcello's wealth goes, the document includes information like the following, proving the immense wealth the Mafia don had accumulated after both JFK and RFK were no longer among the living. Whether Marcello had a hand in RFK's demise is a matter for further research, but there is no question that Marcello benefited from JFK's death, since he became a multi-millionaire.

NO 1734-PC advised that CARLOS MARCELLO has essentially
four large tracts of land; 1) Churchill Farm Estate; 2) Cyprus
Gardens, which is a piece of property of approximately 150-170
acres in size, which is located between the Woodland West
Subdivision and the Timberlane Country Club on the west
bank of the Mississippi River in the Harvey-Gretna, Louisiana
area; 3) the piece of property on Veterans Memorial Highway
across from Dorignac's Super Market, approximately 50 acres
in size, valued at $1,250,000; and 4) a piece of property in
St. Charles Parish on Highway 90 West, which presently houses
a marina known as Al and Maria's on the road to Thibodaux,
Louisiana.

Finally, the document proves Marcello and James Hoffa were apparently connected as well.

without success. Source advised that CARLOS MARCELLO is a
good friend of a lobbyist in Washington by the name of IRVIN
DAVIDSON, and DAVIDSON in turn introduced MARCELLO to JIMMY
HOFFA. In this regard he knows of one specific occasion
when HOFFA and CARLOS MARCELLO met, and he does not recall
the date, but it was when BARRY GOLDWATER was running for
President and came to New Orleans for a speech. NO 1734-PC

Without question, Marcello's financial success was only possible since he did not have Robert F. Kennedy hounding him any further since RFK was no longer attorney general, having resigned in 1964. However, when the man who hated Marcello more than the devil announced his intention to run for president, a shiver must have crept up the Mafia don's spine. Why, because Marcello had to have known that RFK, using common sense, believed Marcello must have had a part in JFK's assassination based on his need to render Bobby powerless. With this in mind, no one had a greater motive than the New Orleans gangster to eliminate Bobby than Marcello since he would have believed that if elected to the White House, RFK would come after Marcello.

Suspecting that the Mafia don could have orchestrated RFK's death and that, by doing so, somehow involved Sirhan in the plot as a "patsy" of sorts, something Marcello had arguably accomplished with Lee Harvey Oswald regarding the JFK assassination, seems logical, but to date, no absolute proof exists to substantiate this theory. There is evidence based on several sources, including an eyewitness account from longtime paddock captain John Shear, that in 1965 Sirhan worked at the Santa Anita race track outside Los Angeles partly controlled by Melvin Belli's client Mickey Cohen, a fast friend of Marcello's.

This connection between Cohen and Marcello is confirmed through Cohen's autobiography, *In My Own Words*. He wrote, "[Marcello] is a beautiful person, a real gentleman who would break his nuts to do good for you or anyone he feels is right." No wonder, since within hours of Cohen's release from prison in early January 1972 after serving ten and a half years of a fifteen-year income tax evasion sentence, an FBI file noted, "[Cohen] in the company of an unknown individual, visited the office of Carlos Marcello, New Orleans LCN (La Cosa Nostra) boss and spent approximately an hour with Marcello. Marcello reportedly gave the subject $3,000 in cash [more than $18,000 in today's currency] which, according to the source, was not a loan."

Further research is underway on my behalf to solve what still remains the mysterious death of Robert F. Kennedy. It will involve extensive probing of the actions of Thane Eugene Cesar, whom Robert F. Kennedy Jr. has accused of actually being the one who killed his father. To that end, connecting Cesar and/or Sirhan to Carlos Marcello is the object, and a tip from a credible supporter of my books recently told me, "All of the major racetracks in in the LA area, including Santa Anita, were hooked into the Marcello wire service and bookie network."[10]

* * *

In *Collateral Damage*, I had included a reliable account by Gianni Russo, a former "associate" of Mafia don Frank Costello and coauthor of the book *Hollywood Godfather* with Patrick Picciarelli, to the effect that Russo was able to connect Marcello with Lee Harvey Oswald. This happened when Russo visited New Orleans and based on his account, I had hoped to find a credible one connecting Marcello with Jack Ruby.

In late 2021, such an account, another example of highly competent evidence about the assassination being forwarded along, came my way based on an interview with highly respected native Texan Kathleen Lieberman. What she told me was based on a firsthand account, that of her having seen Carlos Marcello and Jack Ruby together at the Adolphus Hotel in Dallas

---

10 To alert Robert F. Kennedy Jr. of my continuing research about his father's death and also provide him with an opportunity to discuss with me at a media appearance for this book his strong belief that RFK was not complicit in Marilyn Monroe's death, I emailed a letter to him on May 4, 2022. As of the deadline for submitting the manuscript, he had not replied.

near Dealey Plaza during the summer of 1963 just months before the JFK assassination. Lieberman had met Marcello when she was a young girl and visited her grandfather's Dallas home. She recalled:

> One morning my grandfather and I went to the Adolphus Hotel. We went to the coffee shop where Marcello, a woman, and two less-attached men were hanging around waiting for my grandfather's arrival. I knew him as Uncle Carly. I was passed around the table being hugged and ended up sitting in his lap for quite some time. Later other people came in to talk business with Carlos.
>
> Some people I knew as friends of my grandfather that visited his home or met at the Ole South Pancake House in Fort Worth came in. I got excited to see one of them, Mac Wallace, and I ran to greet him. He picked me up and carried me to a table. Carlos had a serious look on his face and Mac put me down and pointed to a different table and told me to sit there and not to say a word. My grandfather would go to that table and sit while Carlos conducted business.
>
> Another man that came in was Jack Ruby, but I didn't recognize who he was until later. What I do remember is telling my grandmother I was at the Adolphus and the man who owned the Carousel and another man that owned another club was there too. I didn't know it was the Carousel Club until later. When a kid hears Carousel they think of the carnival ride, but my grandmother called it a club. For a long time I thought it was a club for kids like the Mickey Mouse Club. The other man and Ruby talked a bit to the side closer to the table where I was while Marcello talked privately with Mac Wallace. That's the reason I heard them talking.
>
> My grandmother didn't like hearing anything I told her about my outing with my grandfather. She didn't like those men. Then she asked me if any women were there. I told her "No." I lied. There was that one woman. She was fancy.
>
> My grandmother was class. She had perfect hair, a perfect figure, beautiful eyes, and she looked every bit like an Iconic Movie Star. She didn't need much makeup because of her French olive complexion, light grey eyes framed by her thick rich mink hair with a natural wave cut in a typical short French hairstyle on a narrow tall neck. The lady present that day was a stripper, but as a kid to me she was fancy. She sat next to Carlos the whole day.
>
> Fast forward. I am now married with two children visiting my grandparents around 1977. I answered the phone as my grandparents were both

out. A woman asked for my grandfather. Then she asked who I was and I told her. She asked if I remembered her. I said no. Then she asked me if I remembered going to the Adolphus Hotel and she told me everything I wore that day. Then it jogged my memory, and I did remember her with Carlos Marcello that day. She wanted to meet with my grandfather because she wanted him to make a movie.

The woman told me she had a picture of the actual shooter in JFK's assassination. I thought she was a remnant of my grandfather's alcoholic days as he had many "hangers-on." She went on to say Oswald did not fire a shot and he was a patsy. The actual shooter was down in the sewer shooting out from the sewer slot at the street level. Her picture was of him walking out of the sewer. The shooters from the Book Depository were there to deflect where the shots actually came from with everyone looking up instead of downwards the shooter had time to flee undetected. The assassination was planned to be executed from below not from above.

When my grandfather arrived home I delivered the message. He called her and set up the meeting for that same evening. He asked if I wanted to go with him, and I declined as I had already promised to do something with my grandmother that evening. I had waited up for his return. When he did his face was white. I had never seen him scared and he looked like he had seen a ghost. He took me by the shoulders and told me never to tell anyone or it would get me killed. I asked if it was the real deal and he replied, "Yes, it is the real deal, now forget everything you heard." We never spoke of it again. She called several times after that, but he refused her calls. He wanted no part of it. This led me to believe that he knew who the shooter was, but I have no proof of that conclusion; only speculative.

Despite Lieberman's adolescence at the time, her story certainly rings true. In fact, the account seems rather chilling in nature, with the obvious question being, what was Ruby doing in the presence of Marcello during that summer of 1963?

* * *

Of historical interest at the same time Lieberman contacted me was a document forwarded by Rosie Walker, an historian living in Texas. It confirmed the Houston-based November 21, 1963, "Golden 27" Dinner, the last formal event JFK ever attended, since he was assassinated the next day.

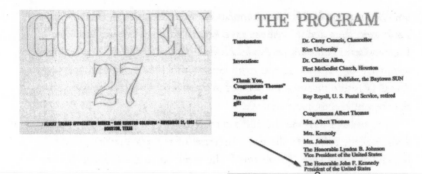

Adding to the validity of this event having happened (Kilgallen always, I knew, confirmed accounts by credible sources to ensure they were accurate), is the event being included in the little-known itinerary President Kennedy followed during the final two days of his life. Here is the schedule according to a National Archives document (spelling and punctuation not corrected, emphasis added):

November 21, 1963

President Kennedy had breakfast with his children. He said goodbye to Caroline when she left for school at 9:15. President Kennedy arrived at his office for the last time at 9:55. His last meeting was Thomas Estes US Ambassador to the Upper Volta, and Charles Darlington the US Ambassador to the Republic of Gabon. The President left the White House for the last time at 10:50 and helicoptered to Andrews Airforce Base where he and the First Lady departed for San Antonio Texas at 11:05 AM. John Jr had accompanied them the airport. In San Antonio the President partakes in the dedication of the Aerospace Medical Health Center, Brooks Air Force Base. He then went on to Houston. In Houston he makes brief remarks to the League of United Latin American Citizens at the Rice Hotel in Houston. **He then addresses a dinner in honor of Representative Albert Thomas.** The President and First Lady then traveled to Ft Worth were they stayed at the Texas Hotel.

November 22, 1963

The President was awakened at 7:30. After eating a light breakfast he headed out to the square in front of the hotel and addressed a few thousand people . When someone yelled out were was Jackie- he pointed to their

8th floor suite and said "Mrs. Kennedy is organizing herself, It takes her a little longer, but of course she looks better than we do when she does it". The President then took part in a Breakfast in the hotel. The First Couple together with the Vice President and Governor Connaly then proceeded to take the short flight to Dallas where Air Force 1 landed at 11:38. At 11:55 the President's motorcade left Love Field in Dallas. At 12:30 the first of two shots hit the President, it was followed by a second fatal shot that hit the President in the head. At 1:00 Dr William Clark pronounced President Kennedy dead at Parkland Memorial Hospital.

* * *

As my research refocused on Dorothy Kilgallen's death, I turned to published articles of hers denouncing the official investigation of the JFK and Oswald assassinations and the "Oswald Alone" Hoover proclamations. To several friends, including CBS's Marlon Swing, she said, "This has to be a conspiracy."

Meanwhile, Kilgallen had been in the midst of completing her new book for Random House about the assassinations. That book would never be published, although *Murder One* would be released two years after her death. It was based on a collection of her Voice of Broadway columns and thus did not include any of Kilgallen's evidence about the events in Dallas.

Kilgallen's main hairdresser Marc Sinclaire confirmed that Kilgallen was working on the assassinations book. Producer Joseph E. Levine also confirmed that Dorothy had shown him some text from it when they had a meeting on November 3, 1965, to discuss television adaptation of the book.

In addition, just prior to appearing on *What's My Line?* on the last night of Dorothy's life, co-panelist Bennett Cerf, the publisher at Random House, stated that she had shown him pages from her assassination book she'd brought to the program. He said she "was quite excited" about what she had written and intended to complete a manuscript within a month or so.

Kilgallen had received a book advance of $10,000. Ruby co-counsel Joe Tonahill, who initially believed Kilgallen had intended the Ruby trial evidence to be part of *Murder One*, reversed that opinion in 1978 when queried by one of this author's researchers about believing the assassination evidence she had compiled would be in a separate book. In a videotaped interview,

Marc Sinclaire stated, "I saw her open notes on the assassination and look at them. *Murder One* wasn't the book she had in mind [for those notes]."

In October, 1963, during a makeup session for *What's My Line*, the columnist told her makeup man, Carmen Gebbia, she was "all excited." When the friend asked, "Is it Kennedy?" Kilgallen replied, "Yes, and it's very cloak-and-daggerish."

Kilgallen informed Gebbia that she was about to venture to New Orleans to "meet someone who is going to give me information about the case." She told the makeup man, "If it's the last thing I do, I'm going to break this case." Regarding her opinions about the Warren Commission, Kilgallen told Mort Farber, an attorney and music talent agent, it's "laughable...I'm going to break the real story and have the biggest scoop of the century."

Interestingly enough, it appears that Mort Farber confided in his son David, who told the *Daily Mail*:

> My father was a noted New York attorney. Among his clients was an investigative newspaper columnist named Dorothy Kilgallen. She confided in [my father] about stories she was about to break. The night before she died, she called my father and told him she had "busted" the JFK assassination. She was going to New Orleans... to confirm a couple of things, but she felt it was going to be the biggest story in American history. That night, without further explanation, she died.

Little doubt exists that making these sorts of promises, in effect making fun of J. Edgar Hoover and the Warren Commission members' report, put the famous reporter in further danger than before. As will be explained, it appears that she knew more than anyone else at the time regarding disturbing facts about the inner workings of the commission and if that lethal information had been included in the book she was writing for Random House, there was yet another motive for Kilgallen having to be silenced.

* * *

Dorothy's dogged investigative instincts on fire, Kilgallen traveled to New Orleans, apparently due to whatever Jack Ruby had told her during their two confidential conversations. Of note is that Dorothy did not stay in Dallas or head for Washington, DC, to investigate the potential that LBJ had orchestrated JFK's death. She also did not investigate the nation's military establishment, or head to Miami to probe whether Cuban rebels upset over the Kennedy administration's handling the Bay of Pigs botched invasion might have killed JFK.

No, the finest journalist of her day and arguably in history, headed for New Orleans where Carlos Marcello ruled, the same Marcello whose two Dallas underlings, Joseph Civello and Joe Campisi handled Marcello's interest, the same Campisi who was the first Jack Ruby visitor in jail after he killed Oswald. He was also the same Campisi at whose restaurant Ruby ate dinner the night before he assassinated JFK's alleged assassin.

In February 2022, a Texas resident named Douglas Toney, a credible, primary source for sure, contacted me after watching the presentation of mine on YouTube regarding *Denial of Justice* in 2019 at the Allen Public Library near Dallas. Toney adds a significant link between Campisi and Jack Ruby never exposed before. Toney told me:

> My father John and his friend Joe Cody were Dallas police officers and friends of Jack Ruby.
>
> My mom and dad were friends with Jack Ruby, and I knew Joe Campisi as a friend of the family. We loved to go to Campisi's on Mockingbird Lane in Dallas, the original Egyptian Lounge. I first had a new food there called pizza!
>
> Dad knew Jack for many years. He used to joke that those other cops in the Carousel Club would look at those girls' titties, but he didn't want anything to do with that.
>
> Joe Cody was a good friend of Jack's. Good enough that Joe bought him that revolver, the 38-special revolver snub nose, the one in the photograph of Ruby shooting Oswald. Joe told me that Jack was worried about getting robbed at the Carousel. Jack wanted to install an alarm. Joe suggested he get an alarm that sounded six  times! He then went to Ray's Hardware, where many if not most of the Dallas Police purchased their guns and bought the gun for Jack.
>
> Dad said he didn't even know that Jack Ruby owned a handgun. Evidently he and Joe Cody had never talked about Joe buying the revolver for Jack before Oswald was shot. I was at Dad's house in Irving, Texas,

when he saw the news report that Jack had shot Oswald.

I was young. I do not know if it was a live broadcast or a report after the fact. Dad reacted to the footage of Jack shooting Lee with genuine surprise. There was nobody else in the room. He said something to the effect, "Jack, dadgum, what have you done!" Certainly, Dad had no idea this was coming. Joe Cody provided the weapon and he told me the story behind the gun. Joe providing the gun was totally unrelated to the murder of Lee Harvey Oswald.

Once again, I had landed on an historical piece of evidence just as had happened when Kathleen Lieberman contacted me. Each time this occurred, I smiled, since by continuing to use what I called "The Dorothy Method," credible primary-source evidence came my way as it had when Dorothy was investigating the JFK assassination. That Kathleen and Douglas trusted me with their credible accounts was a reminder once again of the days when, while preparing for trial to defend a client, credible witnesses trusted me with evidence that strongly led to the truth being exposed at that trial.

Of note was also Douglas Toney giving me this account of how his father became immersed in the arrest of Lee Harvey Oswald:

> Dad was one of the arresting officers of Oswald in the Texas Theater. He said he was there because he disobeyed an order. The Dallas Police Department had ordered all officers to converge in downtown Dallas. Dad then heard about an officer down in Oak Cliff, so he went to Oak Cliff instead. He then heard a report about a suspicious person in the Texas Theater. Dad said they saw Lee moving behind the screen.
>
> The officers then began telling customers that someone outside wanted to talk to them. They escorted them out in this way so as not to cause a panic and get them out of harm's way. He said it was mayhem when they grabbed Lee and Dad broke his thumb diving over a theater seat. He said nobody knew who had ahold of who in the pile. An officer in the pile hollered, "Let go of my arm, you SOB! You're breaking it!"
>
> Dad said another officer had Oswald in an arm lock. I know one of the officers made a name for himself telling the story like he single-handedly

made the arrest. That's not how it happened. Dad was afraid to report his broken thumb. He said the FBI was questioning everyone. He said that Russian involvement was talked about a lot. He went to his friend Jack Brundrett (veterinarian for the Dallas Zoo) to set the broken thumb.

* * *

Returning to the task at hand, discovering the truth about Dorothy's death, I learned that her hairdresser Marc Sinclaire, prominent in New York Society circles to the extent of having his own press agent, had described in a videotaped interview the bizarre set of circumstances regarding her visit to New Orleans. He said, "She didn't tell me why we were going. She just asked me if I could go with her, and I said 'yes.' She told me how I was to travel, where I was to go, what I was to do. I'd never been to New Orleans before, so I didn't know anything about it." (www.thedorothykilgallenstory.org)

Concerning the overall plans, Sinclaire added, "We didn't even travel on the same plane together. I went directly to my hotel, we talked [on the phone], and then I went over to her hotel and had dinner and then I went back to mine." Sinclaire then said, "And the next morning, I was supposed to do her hair and makeup, and she called me at my hotel and she said, 'I want you to go to the airport, I've left a ticket for you, and I want you to go back to New York, and never tell anyone you came to New Orleans with me,' and I said 'Okay' and I left." Summing up, Sinclaire added, "I knew enough not to ask any more. There were certain things where she drew a blank wall and she didn't want me to know any more about it."

When he and Kilgallen spoke back in New York City, Sinclair said, "I did know from Dorothy finally that there was a conspiracy [to kill JFK]. That it was a group of people, not one."

In a videotaped interview, Kilgallen's alternate hairdresser Charles Simpson said during this time that Kilgallen had told him, "I used to share things with you...but after I have found out now what I know, if the wrong people knew what I know, it would cost me my life." (www.thedorothy kilgallenstory.org)

Curiously, on November 4, 1965, four days before Kilgallen died, a *Journal-American* reprint of an Associated Press article appeared regarding an

126

important development in Jack Ruby's case. A portion read, "[Dallas] District Attorney Henry Wade said today his office is willing to recommend that Jack Ruby's death sentence be reduced to life imprisonment." Among Wade's comments were, "There is an advantage to keeping Ruby alive for interviews and historical purposes. There are still a lot of unanswered questions."

Wade did not elaborate, and no follow-up article appeared. Ruby's sentence was never commuted to life imprisonment as he died in prison before a new trial could be held based on the Texas Supreme Court reversing the guilty jury verdict due to Judge Brown's error regarding pre-trial publicity prohibiting Ruby from getting a fair trial. One must wonder what that new trial would have been like, including whether Ruby would have named names as to who may have ordered him to kill Oswald.

Meanwhile, on Saturday, November 6, two days before Kilgallen died, Marc Sinclaire spoke with her. He recalled, "We talked for about an hour. Her life had been threatened."

During the early evening hours of the next day, Kilgallen readied herself for the final *What's My Line?* program (https://www.youtube.com/watch?v=6gn6jS1UK78). When the program ended at 11:00 p.m., Kilgallen and CBS producer and close friend Bob Bach sped by limousine to a famous watering hole, P. J. Clarke's, for a nightcap. She ordered her drink of choice, vodka and tonic.

The table where Dorothy always sat was located near the rear exit. Due to my having interviewed Pat Moore, a revered waitress at Clarke's, called "the Vatican of Saloons" by the *New York Times* for nearly forty years, I had learned Dorothy's "regular table" was not number 36, as some had speculated, but an oval table labeled "B" behind table 37, where tables "A," "B," and "C" were positioned.

Moore told me, "Dorothy always sat under the huge, octangular clock fastened to the back wall at table B, she and all of her friends." Moore also told this author there was a large Bentwood chair facing away from the back wall and whoever sat there was considered to be sitting "at the head of the table." [Author's note: In 2016, while continuing my research of Dorothy's life and times and her death, I sat at that same table and felt a chill when I did so.]

Based on Bob Bach's account, as midnight neared toward the day of her death, Kilgallen told him she had a date. They parted when after he walked her to her limousine.

An hour later, Kilgallen walked into the lobby of the nearby Regency Hotel. As bubbly as ever, she walked down some steps into the basement bar and sat at a table near the back. Kurt Maier, the piano player, recalled her still being there as late as 2:00 a.m. Kilgallen was, he said, joined by a man but he could not identify who it was.

Fortunately, the eyewitness account of Katherine Stone, a contestant on Kilgallen's final *What's My Line?* program is preserved (https://www.youtube.com/watch?v=DUOcxyDIYuI). Excerpts from Stone's 1999 interview may be viewed at www.thereporterwhoknewtoomuch.com.

During the program, Stone, wearing large, black eyeglasses frames, attempts to stump the panel, but Kilgallen was too sharp for her. She guessed that Stone's occupation was, of all things, selling dynamite.

Stone was at the bar after she was asked to join the *What's My Line?* staff there but she did not know Kilgallen would be among them. Describing the décor, Stone recalled, "There was this big, beautiful, long baby grand piano, it was over there on the left, and then over to the right, way back in the corner, was sort of like a curved booth." Pointing to that area in a photograph, Stone said, "This is where [Dorothy] was, definitely in that corner, right there."

With brightness in her eyes, Stone added,

Katherine Stone, a *What's My Line?* contestant and one of the last people to see Kilgallen alive, points to the booth at the Regency Hotel Bar where Kilgallen was engaged in conversation with the "mystery man"

And the man was sitting right next to her, and I mean close because they were talkin' where they didn't want anybody to hear or what, you know. I could see they both had a drink. There wasn't any laughing, people jokin', this and that and the other. They were talkin', and the reason I know this is for the fact I kept an eye on her 'cause I wanted to talk to her afterwards to tell her, you know, that I enjoyed being there, happy she guessed my line, and so on and so forth. In other words, you wouldn't have felt like going up there. I knew they were talking business, serious business of some kind. I had that feeling.

Stone added, "I'd look over and want to see what was going on 'cause I wanted to talk to her. So that's the reason I was paying so much attention and I wasn't having many cocktails, you know." Asked during the interview if she could identify the man, Stone, unfamiliar with Kilgallen's private life, said she did not know but "had the impression he was younger than Dorothy."

Regarding Kilgallen's state of mind both during the program and at the bar, Stone said, "People wanted to know if I thought she killed herself from drugs and pills and I told them I didn't believe she overdosed. She was as sharp as could be on the program and looked normal at the cocktail lounge. I thought maybe this man might have done something to her, that he might have killed her." Stone agreed that maybe "the man gave her something, got her out of there."

Press agent Harvey Daniels, whose clients included the Regency Hotel, corroborated Stone's recollections of Kilgallen being with a man in the Regency Hotel bar at 1:00 a.m. He saw Dorothy and said she was "bright, cheery, and a little high."

CHAPTER 13

I f ever a death scene appeared staged, and I had witnessed several as a criminal defense attorney permitting an expertise with such matters, Dorothy Kilgallen's qualifies for certain. Why, because the highly respected media icon's body, as first mentioned in *The Reporter Who Knew Too Much*, was discovered in her East 68th Street Manhattan townhouse bedroom, one she never slept in with her hairpiece, false eyelashes, and makeup in place wearing bedclothes she never wore to bed.

Marc Sinclaire, initially quoted in *The Reporter Who Knew Too Much*, stands out as a most credible eyewitness. During his videotaped interviews, he recalled entering Kilgallen's home on the morning of November 8 at just before nine in the morning. She had an appointment at Kerry's school and asked Sinclaire to fix her hair. (www.thedorothykilgallenstory.org)

Marc Sinclaire

As was his routine, Sinclaire said he headed for a small dressing room on the townhouse's third floor where Dorothy normally had her hair done. The dressing room was next to her main clothes closet.

Sinclaire recalled, "When I entered…she was not in that room, but the air-conditioning was on, and it was cold outside. So, I turned on my curling irons and I walked into the [adjacent] bedroom, not thinking she would be there." [Author's note: In those days there was no central air-conditioning; each room had a wall or window unit.]

This was the master bedroom, adjacent to the Black Room, where the couple entertained guests, and Dorothy, Sinclaire said, had not slept in the master bedroom for some time. When the hairdresser asked why she didn't use that bedroom since it was so much more convenient, Kilgallen told him that was where she caught Richard with one of his paramours, apparently a male "business partner."

"Dorothy would have never slept there," Sinclaire stated. "She hated that bedroom, and we only used it because of the dressing room. Or we would have never used it at all."

With much emotion, Sinclaire explained that Kilgallen normally slept in her private office, the "Cloop," on the fifth floor. Richard slept in a bedroom on the fourth floor. Sinclaire then described what he discovered:

> She was sitting up in bed, and I walked over to the bed and touched her, and I knew she was dead right away. The bed was spotless. She was dressed very peculiarly. I've never seen her dressed like that before. She always [was] in pajamas and old socks and her makeup was off and her hairpiece was off and everything. She was completely dressed like she was going out, the hair was in place, the makeup was on, the false eyelashes were on.

Sinclaire added:

> The matching peignoir and robe, a book laid out on the bed, a drink on the table, the light was on, the air-conditioning was on, though you didn't need an air conditioner; you would have had the heat on. And she was always cold. And why she had the air-conditioning on I don't know.

For some years, there seemed no alternative reason as to why the air-conditioner was running when Dorothy's body was discovered other than Sinclaire stating "that perhaps someone had turned on the air-conditioner to keep the body at a certain temperature." However, as has often happened during my writing of the books touching on Dorothy's life and times and her death, new, reliable evidence from highly unusual sources appears on the scene. One such example occurred when I was contacted in February 2022 by Dr. Charles A. Mathis, MD, a fellow at the prestigious American College of Cardiology. He practices in, of all places, Elkhart, Indiana, eighty-plus miles from where I grew up in the small town of Auburn.

In line with my having discovered a plethora of credible evidence included in my books through those who may not be famous on a national level like Dr. Mathis, a respected cardiologist, here is what he told me after learning that the official NYC medical examiner's office's "verdict" regarding her death had been, as will be explained, "Acute Ethanol and barbiturate intoxication… Circumstances undetermined."

> After listening to your presentation at the Allen Library near Dallas in 2019 regarding the book, *Denial of Justice*, on the suspicious death of Dorothy Kilgallen, I wanted you to know that given the fact that Dorothy was found in an inappropriate cold environment as the air conditioner was turned on and being that the recorded outside temperature at the time was approximately fifty-five degrees, my professional medical opinion is that cold environment could have possibly been used to enhance respiratory depression with hypoventilation.

In laymen's terms, Dr. Mathis explained this meant that "Dorothy could not breathe as well" as normal stating that in "a cold environment, alcohol and barbiturates are all respiratory suppressants" and that "if someone is trying to kill someone, the cold temperature and the presence of alcohol and barbiturates meant they wanted the person to not breathe well."

Dr. Mathis's astute observations, in line with Marc Sinclaire recalling that "Dorothy was always cold," certainly point to the "prolonged sedation" becoming murder, an indication that Kilgallen did not overdose on barbiturates combined with alcohol intake.

* * *

During Marc Sinclaire's interview about the death scene, he further explained that a glass discovered in the bedroom was "on the right-hand side, way away, way over [from Dorothy], and the book on her lap (*Honey Badger* by Robert Ruark) was turned upside down." He added that the book wasn't in the right position where if you'd been reading it you'd lay it down right side up and yet it was upside down.

Sinclaire continued to describe the scene:

Rigor mortis had set in on one hand, the right hand, and it had drawn up the covers a little bit. And there was lipstick on the [left] sleeve of the bolero jacket …and the light was on and she was sitting up.

I went back in the dressing room, picked up the intercom, and rang for James [the butler]. I said, "James, I am unable to wake Miss Kilgallen. Could you please come up?" He *ran* up the stairs. I could hear him. He came up the front stairs and he ran like he was very excited and of course the door was locked. But I had come in from the back door. I don't think they expected me, no one knew I was coming. And this was before nine thirty in the morning, nine, five after nine.

So I opened the door to the bedroom and James came in, and at that time I noticed a sheet of paper laying on the floor that had been pushed under the door. And James came in and he was very flustered. He wasn't himself at all.

Sinclaire's statement regarding Kilgallen wearing a robe with her hair, makeup, and false eyelashes in place with the covers pulled up matched the descriptions in the NYC medical examiner's documents, providing credibility for his account. He added, "And I was very upset, so I turned to [James] and I said, 'I'm going home. You can reach me there if you want to,' and I left the building." Sinclaire then added a rather mysterious comment: "When I got downstairs and went out the front door, there was a police car sitting in front of the house…. There were two officers in it. Sitting right dead in front of the house. They didn't pay any attention to me when I came out. I find it very strange that they were sitting there dead in front of the house and Dorothy was dead upstairs. Yes, I find it very strange."

Shown a newspaper story reporting the maid having discovered the body, Sinclaire said, "They mixed that all up. But I don't think I was the first one to find Dorothy. I've never thought that happened." To that end, newspaper reports would signal the body being discovered at three different times by three different people.

Charles Simpson, Kilgallen's alternate hairdresser, confirmed Sinclaire's eyewitness account in a videotaped interview available on the Dorothy Kilgallen website mentioned before. He said that Sinclaire "called me on the phone and told me that he had found her dead. And he said, 'When I tell you the bed she was found in, and how I found her,' he said, 'you're going to know she was murdered.' And when he told me, I knew." Simpson added, "When Marc told me that day and then we got back together and he talked to me and told me where he found her, and how, it was abnormal, the whole thing was abnormal. It was just abnormal. The woman didn't sleep in that bed, much less the room, and if she still were sharing that room with Richard, that was Richard's bed. That's the one he set fire to. It wasn't her bed."

Simpson was referring to an earlier incident on December 15, 1953, when the drunken Richard had accidently set his bed on fire with a lighted cigarette after falling asleep. His screams alerted Kilgallen, and fortunately she awoke in time to save her alcoholic husband.

Confirming what Marc Sinclaire said regarding his not being the first person to discover his close friend's body happened when new evidence pointed to Kilgallen's butler, James Clement, as having done so before Sinclaire. Confirmed through an author interview with Clement's daughter Brenda DeJourdan, Clement swore he found Dorothy's body lying flat on the nearby bathroom floor.

Learning as I did some of the facts surrounding Dorothy's death was saddening for sure. This bright, robust woman who had everything to live for, both with her career and the love she shared with the three children, Dickie, Jill, and Kerry, had been cut down in the prime of her life. As her "voice," I was determined to "investigate, investigate, investigate" until I could expose what had caused that death and who was responsible.

* * *

The cover-up of Dorothy Kilgallen's death began with the discovery of an empty Seconal bottle found on a night table by the bed. A young NYPD detective named John Doyle and a junior medical examiner, Dr. James Luke, jumped to the conclusion that she had overdosed on the sleeping pills. "Just another celebrity who's a druggie," they apparently concluded.[11]

---

11 At the time, there existed absolutely no evidence that Kilgallen had a drug or alcohol problem as proven in previous books. Most importantly, if one watches her final *What's My Line?* program hours before she died, Dorothy is alert with no slurring of works and as usual, asks the best questions and is the one to guess unusual occupations before her fellow panelists may do so. As noted, that program may be viewed at https://www.youtube.com/watch?v=F6g5wE2deXU.

Deciding the next step regarding my research journey was a step into the world of Dorothy's autopsy, with my again believing that is what the revered reporter would have done if she had investigated the suspicious nature of the death of another person under similar circumstances. Locating her autopsy report (a combination of typed and handwritten pages) was quite difficult since I was not a member of her family, but in a stroke of good fortune, I discovered the document was hiding in plain sight at the National Archives (the complete document is included in *The Reporter Who Knew Too Much*).

The conclusion of the autopsy was spread to the media using these words:

Final Cause of Death:

Acute Ethanol and barbiturate intoxication...

Circumstances undetermined.

12/1/65 James R Luke M.D.

As will be explained, this "verdict" was as misleading, or in fact, dead wrong, similar to those "verdicts" issued when Marilyn Monroe had died and when the infamous Warren Commission report was released. In each case, a cover-up, or cover-ups, occurred, ones lasting to present day.

Excited at discovering the autopsy report, I read more carefully Dr. Luke's words on the second page, and when I did, it was noticeable that in his "Report of Death" he had adopted an accidental death theory based on information collected at Kilgallen's death scene. He thus concluded the autopsy report with the words, "Cause of Death: Pending Further Study" but did "Further Study" mean awaiting the toxicology results from the ME lab? Or, in the alternative, had something else changed his mind so that he could not definitively conclude that Kilgallen had died accidently from the alcohol and drug overdose, presumably from ingesting too many Seconal pills?

The "Final Cause of Death" on the autopsy report beneath the typed information includes the handwritten date "12/1/65." This suggests nearly three weeks passed between when Dr. Luke dictated the words, "Pending

Further Study" on November 8 and when he wrote in longhand, "Final Cause of Death: Acute Ethanol and barbiturate intoxication… Circumstances undetermined" on the first of December.

Suspicious of what Dr. Luke's two conflicting conclusions meant, and relying on my experience as a criminal defense attorney where I examined multiple autopsy reports while reading the NYC medical examiner report, I noticed that while Seconal was mentioned, a second barbiturate, Tuinal, a step up the ladder regarding the dangerous potency of sleeping pills, was indicated in a handwritten page dated 11/15/65, shown on the right.

A close-up view (*below right*) provides better clarity of this section:

This information made me suspicious as I felt Kilgallen would have been, based, it may be recalled, on her being "sent to the NYC morgue" early in her career where she viewed dead bodies and would have examined autopsy reports. I became even more so when I would learn that Dr. Charles Umberger, the NYC medical examiner's office director of toxicology in the Department of Pathology at the time of Kilgallen's death, conducted analysis of her bodily fluids *three years* after she died.

Regarding Umberger, retired Dutchess County sheriff's detective Dennis O'Keeffe told me he knew Dr. Umberger, known to the detectives as "Charley Joe." O'Keeffe added, "Joe really knew his stuff. He was very likeable, comedic. Wore expensive suits that were always wrinkled." Regarding Dr. Umberger's habits, O'Keeffe said the doctor "was known for saving beakers of bodily fluid specimens in hopes that technology advancements would aid future homicide investigations [forensic cryonics] as happened in Kilgallen's case." This disclosure apparently meant that Umberger believe Dorothy had not died accidentally.

According to John Broich, a medical examiner's office toxicologist and confirmed to me by his wife Eileen and son Chris, Dr. Umberger asked Broich to examine "a basic beaker with an extract from Dorothy's brain, and another beaker labeled 'drink.'" Also provided to the chemist were "two glasses which had contained alcoholic beverages" that had been discovered at Kilgallen's bedside table. Dr. Umberger told the chemist his examination had revealed one was a "drink" glass from which "the alcohol had evaporated, [which] was hers [Kilgallen's]" without indicating how he knew this to be true.

Broich said, through further testing, he and Umberger discovered evidence that three barbiturates, Seconal, Nembutal, and Tuinal, were present in Kilgallen's bloodstream. In addition, Broich reported that a rim specimen taken from one of the glasses attributed to Kilgallen contained traces of Nembutal. When Broich told Umberger of his discovery, Broich said Umberger "grinned" and told him, "Keep it under your hat. This was big.'"

Both men strongly believed that capsules of the drug had been opened, thus contradicting the notion that Dorothy had accidentally overdosed but in fact had been poisoned, murdered, with Broich's wife Eileen recalling her husband telling her, "Dorothy was bumped off." When I asked why neither of the two men reported their findings to the medical examiner, Eileen said her husband was scared to do so based on corruption within the ME's office.

One further clue that came my way dealt with additional information provided to me by Dr. Charles Mathis, the Midwest cardiologist who, as noted, I had interviewed in February 2022. Weighing in on another subject of interest regarding the forensics involved with Dorothy's death, he said,

> The presence of multiple kinds of barbiturates [in her system] would seem to be very unusual and prompt the question whether such a combination was used to maximize both the immediate and prolonged sedation.

Dr. Mathis's notation of the "presence of multiple barbiturates" being "unusual" certainly lends itself to the theory that the person who mixed the barbiturates was not Dorothy. As was mentioned in *The Reporter Who Knew*

Too Much and both *Denial of Justice* and *Collateral Damage*, whoever mixed those barbiturates likely did so first at the Regency Hotel bar and then at Dorothy's home with the weaker of the barbiturates utilized to perhaps make her "dizzy," and then the stronger ones used to end her life.

Dr. Mathis was also disturbed by a lipstick stain on Dorothy's bolero jacket when her body was discovered as recalled by Marc Sinclaire: "And there was lipstick on the [left] sleeve of the Bolero jacket. How did it get there?" Dr. Mathis wondered with his conclusion that foul play must have occurred since a woman would not normally have her lips on the garment.

Regarding the amount of alcohol Kilgallen drank, the medical examiner's report provided the only data. It listed the blood alcohol content as .15 but, as noted, this was the level the mid-afternoon of the eighth, meaning that level could have been much higher hours earlier when she presumably died. Whatever reason, the drum roll to Dorothy's death would have begun with drinking the vodka setting her up for the drug overdose shortly thereafter.

It seems a virtual certainty that Kilgallen drank vodka at the Regency Hotel bar based on past habits. However, the possibility that her drink was spiked with a deadly dose of barbiturates at the bar is more difficult to prove. Hairdresser Marc Sinclaire was curious about this aspect of Kilgallen's death, stating, "She was given it [the pills] somehow. I don't know if it had been injected, given in the back of the car, done in a drink. I don't know that, and I don't know if she left under her own power from the Regency Hotel."

If Kilgallen's drink was spiked, then she may have begun to experience a few signs of the effects of the drugs. These included confusion, unsteadiness, drowsiness, wobbly legs, and a possible partial loss of faculties.

Due to her being out of sorts mentally, the "mystery man" Katherine Stone saw could have escorted Kilgallen out of the hotel either through the front door, a side door, or a back entrance. Then he would have accompanied her to her townhouse just a few blocks away, probably by taxi. During this time, Dorothy's unsteadiness most likely increased. Since there was no police report providing any details about her actions at all that evening, and Katherine Stone was never interviewed by the police, no credible evidence exists from the time she was seen in the bar to when she died.

If Dorothy was drugged to a state of semi-consciousness, without any commotion, she and the mystery man could have quietly entered the townhouse. If he was someone she knew and trusted, logic dictates that the two would have headed to the Cloop on the fifth floor where she slept. But apparently that was not the case and for whatever reason, arguably because she continued to be drowsy from the barbiturates, they headed to the third floor.

Under this probable scenario, Kilgallen, either from the drinks or food she had eaten during the evening, had an upset stomach. While she went to the bathroom, the "mystery man" could have offered to fix them both a drink, accounting for the glasses noted later.

Following this theory, while Kilgallen was in the bathroom taking the Pepto-Bismol, the "mystery man" could have poured vodka into Kilgallen's glass. In all likelihood, this is when he could have broken the barbiturate capsules in two and sifted the deadly powder into her drink. This would account for the barbiturate (Nembutal) residue being on one of the glasses per the revelation discovered by Dr. Umberger.

As the minutes passed toward a half hour or so, Kilgallen, after sipping from her drink as she conversed with the "mystery man," could have begun to sink into a state of uneasiness. When I asked Dr. Charles Mathis to review this summary of what may have happened, he agreed that within forty minutes or less, dependent on how the combination of Seconal, Nembutal, and Tuinal affected her, Kilgallen would have, in all likelihood, experienced bradycardia.

This involved a slow heart rate accompanied by dizziness and fainting. Try as she may, it would appear the famous journalist and television star could not fight back against the poisonous drugs accelerating through her system, and she was dead.

His mission complete, the "mystery man" then could have quietly exited the townhouse, probably using the stairs. Whether he left a fingerprint or two or any other incriminating evidence behind is unknown, since there was no police follow-up.

At the time, Kilgallen's home staff consisted of James and Evelyn Clement and Ellen O'Hara, "a stooped, yet dynamically energetic elderly

Irish woman." Kerry Kollmar described her as "the kindest, warmest person in the household of my childhood."

When I interviewed James Clement's daughter Brenda DeJourdan in 2017, she first recalled the following:

> I remember my father telling Dorothy, "Be careful, let Jack Ruby alone." My father was fearful of her safety.
>
> Dorothy didn't believe JFK was killed the way they said it did. She thought it was a government cover-up and set out to investigate it.
>
> My father said to Dorothy, "For your safety, let it go, let it alone, the JFK assassination, only going to open up problems."

DeJourdan, with regard to the night Dorothy died, told me that her father had told her, "A gentleman was with Dorothy when she came into the townhouse." She added, "Somehow my father saw him; there was evidence of his being there. Dad said he didn't know the gentleman but when my father went to bed, he was still there." Continuing, Brenda said, "My father said he heard a noise, and it could have been the man leaving." Explaining, she said, "On the first floor, there was a door to the backyard, a screen door, and that night it was unlocked. My mother said, 'Maybe that is what you heard, the screen door closing.'"

Regardless, an undeniable fact remains—the three barbiturates *were* in her bloodstream. And the other solid fact that she did not die of an overdose is her daughter, Jill, telling two friends, one from childhood that I interviewed, "My mother was murdered." Jill denied this ever happened, but the two recollections are quite credible especially in tandem with James Clement's daughter Brenda telling this author that Jill told Clement, "They murdered my mother," without referencing who "they" were. An additional account comes from Marianne Harrison, Jill's closest childhood friend. She told me she learned from Jill that Dorothy "had been quieted."

Regarding the cause of death issued, when asked about Dr. Luke's statement during a February 25, 2020, phone interview with me, Dr. Michael Baden, who assisted Dr. Luke with Kilgallen's autopsy, stated that in his opinion, due to Dr. Luke's admission that he did not know what the cause of death really was, "What Luke said went beyond the bounds of what he should have told the media."

AUTOPSY PERFORMED BY DR. JAMES LUKE, JUNIOR MEDICAL EXAMINER
In the presence of Dr. Sturner and Baden.
November 8, 1965

In 2021, I confronted the famous Dr. Baden (O. J. Simpson, John Belushi, and Kobe Bryant cases, among others) during an interview for both of us on a prestigious New York City radio program. He was shocked when told his name was on Dorothy's autopsy and then backtracked with regard to any mistakes made with her case. Baden did admit that "we really didn't know how she died," meaning the ME team, a revelation that I found disgusting, very unprofessional, one that deprived Kilgallen of the justice she deserved.

Unfortunately, when Dr. Luke had announced to the media and thus to the public that "combining alcohol and sleeping pills was a common form of accidental death," the media and the general public took "accidental death" as the one and only explanation. But "accidental death" was not the accurate explanation, a distortion of the facts for certain.[12]

* * *

Now that I had discovered sufficient evidence in my mind to prove that Dorothy was silenced, I began a journey to uncover who had silenced her. Strong response to *The Reporter Who Knew Too Much* culminated in hearing from literally thousands of people around the world who contributed "tips" regarding new information about Dorothy's life and times and her death.

Predictably by being a woman of the truth and unafraid of those in power, Kilgallen had accumulated a long list of enemies. They certainly included J. Edgar Hoover, mobster Carlos Marcello, whom Dorothy had investigated in New Orleans, and even Frank Sinatra. She and the latter feuded, as will be explained, until the day she died.

Despite these men being front and center, I landed next on a romantic interest Kilgallen had right before she died based on the homicide detective's best friends—motive, means, opportunity, and benefit from the crime.

---

12 Certainly a similarity in the deaths of Marilyn Monroe, JFK, and Dorothy Kilgallen is the bogus nature of the autopsies. This occurring reminded me of a statement made to me by a homicide detective during one of my murder trials. He said, "If you want to coverup the truth, start with falsifying the autopsies."

Dorothy and husband Richard Kollmar were estranged as he had fallen from being a successful Broadway producer and restaurateur to becoming a philanderer and a drunk. She first enjoyed a torrid love affair with pop singer Johnnie Ray ("Little White Cloud That Cried") and then fell for a Midwestern journalist bent on climbing the ladder of success through a relationship with Dorothy named, I discovered, Ron Pataky.

Much more about each of these relationships is included in *The Reporter Who Knew Too Much* and *Collateral Damage*, but through a slow process of investigation that included tips from Pataky's relatives, I was able to peg him as being the most logical choice for the "mystery man"

Ron Pataky and Dorothy Kilgallen

Katherine Stone saw Dorothy with at the hotel the night she died. He had met her through a media junket in Europe regarding several 20th Century Fox films. He can be seen in video of that event along with Kilgallen at www.thedorothykilgallenstory.org.

There certainly is solid evidence connecting Pataky (twenty-nine), and thus *twenty-two years younger* than Kilgallen (fifty-one) when he met her in June 1964, three months after the Ruby trial, to Dorothy's death in my previous books including numerous lies Pataky, a pathological liar for sure, told about both the relationship and his whereabouts on the day Dorothy died. This said, the most incriminating, the most damaging for sure regarding his being complicit in her death gains noteworthy credence from poems he wrote within a year or two after the famous journalist died. The first poem is:

There's a way to quench a gossip's stench
That never fails
One cannot write if zippered 'tight'
Somebody who's dead could tell no tales.

Even a casual perusing of the words Pataky wrote and especially him referring to "a gossip's stench," and then "one cannot write if zippered 'tight'" followed by "somebody who's dead could tell no tales," shocks the conscience since common sense indicates the poem is about Kilgallen. The second poem, then, reinforces Pataky's guilt as her killer. It reads (*see right*):

Based on my research proving how Kilgallen died, it is not a stretch at all to realize that Pataky has provided information about her demise that only the killer could know. A close reading of this poem certainly indicates that he may have very well been "spilling his guts" to the "wrong people," described below, about Kilgallen's JFK assassination evidence. Regarding the "fetching" of two drinks with the intention to "make one of 'em poison," this appears to spell out how he may have silenced Kilgallen. Read in its entirety, it is not a stretch to believe that the poem may have been somewhat confessional in nature, Pataky's guilt splashing on the page as he posted the poem on his website.

I had also provided testimony that Marc Sinclaire and Charles Simpson believed he was complicit in her death. As fully explained in *The Reporter Who Knew Too Much*, I am today even more certain because Pataky had the motive, means, and opportunity: motive, because Kilgallen was going to discard him believing he had leaked JFK assassination evidence she shared with him to the "wrong people"; means, because of propensity for violence (arrests in the past including gun use); and opportunity, because Pataky, without question, was with her at a hotel bar the night before she died. He certainly benefited from the crime, since Kilgallen could not end the relationship as planned, an action that would have destroyed his career.

During several interviews I conducted with Pataky, he denied any love affair with Dorothy as well as having had anything to do with her death. More evidence to the contrary exists in the follow-up book, *Denial of Justice*.

To be certain, my long and winding journey to proving Pataky guilty took a strange twist when I learned about "Don" (he requested anonymity for fear of repercussions), a former Las Vegas Sands Hotel casino pit boss who actually knew of Pataky. Don, who had experienced firsthand the workings of the underworld, the CIA, and the FBI during this period of time, told this author that Pataky had landed "in some kind of trouble prior to Kilgallen's death."

Don, who knew Frank Sinatra on a personal as well as professional basis due to Sinatra's association with the Sands (confirmed through the source's Facebook page postings), had been sent by Mafia associates in New York City to Vegas to check on a blackjack dealer who was supposedly cheating. Ultimately, he confirmed the dishonesty of the dealer while joking, "That dealer never cheated again," indicating Mafia operatives eliminated him through a contract hit.

As our conversation continued, Don turned to his firsthand knowledge that Pataky was "saved" from the "trouble" by what Don called "rogue government agents." He added that these "rogue" agents were apparently working for the FBI or CIA in tandem with underworld figures who were closely monitoring Kilgallen's JFK assassination investigation and her intention to publish the Random House book.

According to Don, a member of the New York Mafia at the time who had no reason to lie, Pataky, in exchange for being "saved," agreed to become a mole, be "recruited," and then "managed" to the extent that he would provide his handlers with the secret information Kilgallen had "tripped on" about the assassination—information "that was lethal in nature."

My heart nearly stopped when Don then told this author that Kilgallen's "fate was sealed," that she "was dead!" as he put it, when Pataky betrayed her by "squealing" about the "damaging" evidence she possessed. The source's eerie account substantiates the belief that those who had been monitoring the dogged journalist's investigation of JFK's demise had decided to take action after these "wrong people," likely including J. Edgar Hoover and/or Carlos Marcello (the latter of whom Kilgallen had connected to Lee Harvey Oswald and Jack Ruby), evaluated Pataky's shocking disclosures.

Combined with additional evidence already collected about Pataky's complicity in Kilgallen's death, I've doubled my efforts to get her the justice she deserves by persuading law enforcement to re-investigate her death. I will never give up but, unfortunately, the Judas died at the age of eighty-six in May 2022. During several interviews including those where I begged him to tell the truth about what happened to Dorothy when she died, he nearly confessed his guilt in setting her up for the kill. I strongly believe that if law enforcement, including most recently Detective Phillip Panzarella of the New York Police Cold Case Squad, had interrogated him as I strongly urged, Pataky would have incriminated himself in Kilgallen's death.

According to top-notch researcher David Henschel, who along with respected researcher Kathryn Fauble has been most helpful during publication of several of my books, "If Pataky's loved one(s) had a celebration of life, it was not announced online." In addition, Henschel confirmed through solid evidence, "Nobody has submitted a message of sympathy or a reminiscence." This news is not surprising since during my conversations with Pataky and via his emails, he appeared be a lonely, miserable, bitter man consumed with guilt.

* * *

Regarding the 2018 book *Denial of Justice*, which followed *The Reporter Who Knew Too Much*, it was birthed when another one of the defining moments in my research journey appeared on the horizon from an unlikely source. This having happened made me realize once again that somehow, and for some unknown reason, I had become a magnet for securing the best evidence about the assassination.

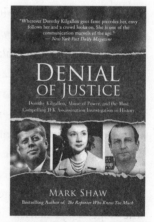

What came my way were the monumental two-thousand-page Jack Ruby trial transcripts, never published in a book before. Certainly my experience as a criminal defense attorney, one familiar with many trial transcripts while filing appeals, somehow had prepared me for this blessing.

How did this happen? One day, I was contacted by Greg Mullanax, a highly respected California attorney who said he had read *The Reporter Who Knew Too Much* cover to cover one evening and had "a gift" for me:

the trial transcripts. He forwarded them along electronically, and I am very grateful to Greg for doing so since the transcripts are, without question, the most credible evidence about the JFK assassination, packed as they are with eyewitness testimony under oath from those on hand when JFK's assassination took place. Excerpts are available at www. markshawbooks.com.

This author with the foot-and-a-half tall, 2,000+ page Jack Ruby trial transcripts

The trial transcripts opened the door to learning why Kilgallen had become so involved with investigating the assassination. It took me almost a month to read through all of the pages, but as I did, my eyes widened since there was definite proof of a plot to kill JFK (again, I dislike the word "conspiracy," a catch-all word that dampens what really happened on that day in Dallas).

Why no one before me had exposed these documents was a mystery, although many of those who advocated the "Oswald Alone" theory would have avoided this historically relevant evidence for sure. Why? Because without question these documents blasted any sense of accuracy regarding the "Oswald Alone" theory by confirming a plot to kill the president based on Ruby's conduct.

Most importantly, during a stop at a parking facility across from the Carousel Club the day before he shot Oswald, Ruby was overheard on the pay telephone by prosecution witness G. C. Hallmark, general manager of Nichols Brothers Parking. According to Hallmark, Ruby said the following to whomever he was speaking with at the time regarding

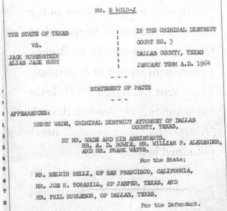

his "making like a reporter," apparently with the intention to gain entrance into the Dallas Police Department basement where Ruby would ultimately shoot Oswald:

Concerning the transfer of Oswald the next day, Hallmark recalled Ruby stating that "he would be there" when it happened.

Certainly these accounts differed from those Ruby provided during his polygraph examination and his testimony at the Warren Commission. Exposing these excerpts as well as Ruby admitting that the Dallas police assisted his entry into the DPD basement confirm that he certainly did not just "happen by" when Oswald was being transferred. Without doubt, Ruby was stalking his prey so that he could tie up a loose end by silencing Oswald for good.

In yet another example of the best sources of what happened to JFK coming my way, Rosie Walker, a prominent author in Beaumont, Texas, sent me in late 2021 Texas radio announcer Gordon Baxter's "Ruby Trial Notebook," never published before.

One such entry confirms Dorothy Kilgallen's appearance at the trial, and another confirms

Q   Directing your attention to the 23rd day -- Saturday, after the assassination of President Kennedy, at around 2:50 P.M., did you see the Defendant, Jack Ruby, on that occasion?
A   Yes sir, I did.
Q   What parking lot was that, what is it called?
A   The Nichols Brothers Parking, 1320 Commerce Street.
Q   Is it a fact, Mr. Hallmark, that Ruby has parked his car there for a number of years at that place, is that right?
A   Three years, yes.
Q   And his place of business is close by, is that right?
A   Yes sir, it is.
Q   Now, when he came into your garage, did he ask permission to use the phone?
A   Yes sir, he did.

Q   The 23rd, Saturday afternoon, around 2:50 P.M. What did he say with reference to being a reporter, if anything.
A   He said that he was making like a reporter.

A   The conversation was about the -- what I understood to be, the almost immediate transfer of Oswald from the City to the County Jail. Mr. Ruby informed whoever he was talking to, that people were strewing flowers at the scene of the assassination, and that possibly the transfer would be delayed.
THE COURT: The what?
A   Delayed.
Q   Now, did Ruby say anything with reference to whether or not -- concerning whether he would be there or not; what did he say on that?
A   He told whoever he was talking to, that he would be there.
Q   He would be there?
A   Yes.

the appearance of a witness who heard Ruby say "he would be there when [Oswald's] transfer was made," another firsthand account obliterating Ruby's story that he just happened to be at the DPD basement when the transfer took place. Baxter's entry reads (emphasis added):

Claude Hallmark- Gen. Man. Alright Auto Parts. -Sat 23rd 2:50 PM- Saw Ruby at parking lot. Asked to use phone- "Making like a reporter" he said. Asked for Wes Wise [radio reporter] talked to someone else- **Ruby told party transfer would be delayed**, because people were throwing out flowers at assn. scene. **Ruby said he'd be there when transfer made.**

Of special interest is confirmation that Ruby would "be there" when Oswald's transfer occurred, but Gordon Baxter's notation from trial testimony that "Ruby told party [he was speaking with]" that the "transfer would be delayed" is quite revealing as well. One must ask where Ruby gained this information with the obvious conclusion to be reached that it was passed on to him by Dallas police that he said he "loves" according to his psychiatric exam.

The notebook also chronicles Melvin Belli's statement to the court, "I just want to get this out about the case. I don't think there was a connection between the Dal. Police & Ruby and I want this thing cleared up & out of the case," verifying Belli avoiding this area of significant interest, another indication he had been chosen to represent Ruby and make certain he was convicted since Belli knew of Ruby's strong connections to the police as proven in Dorothy Kilgallen's columns. Baxter's account of the trial may be compared to that of Waymon Rose, the jury foreman. His notebook is available in *Denial of Justice*.

CHAPTER 14

Having already published the four books touching on the assassination, I was reluctant to launch into another one. However, literally hundreds of readers of these books asked the same question: Is there a connection between the deaths of Dorothy Kilgallen, Marilyn Monroe, and John F. Kennedy? With this question in mind, I decided to look into the matter, never realizing what unusual twists and turns this literary journey would take during the research.

As often happens when there has been an investigation of one matter of interest, in this case Dorothy's demise, another appears logical, but I had no idea whether Kilgallen had been interested in how Marilyn died, whether she had truly committed "probable suicide" as was the official "verdict" in 1962. What I did know from previous research was that, based on a primary source account provided to me by Brenda DeJourdan, Dorothy's butler's daughter, the movie star had been to parties along with Kilgallen's close friend, actress Joan Crawford, at Dorothy's Manhattan townhouse, but whether they were friends was unknown.

What I noticed at the outset of my investigation were conflicting newspaper headlines regarding how

Marilyn with Lauren Bacall and Humphrey Bogart

Marilyn died. The one in Kilgallen's own newspaper as portrayed by Dorothy's journalistic sidekick, Bob Considine, read (*right*):

That account contrasted with the *LA Times* reporting (*below*):

Suicide or "Pill Overdose," that was the question and caused me to decide to see if there was a definite connection between the two media superstars. The starting point for considering this critical point of interest was checking records at the National Archives, a competent researcher's best friend regarding accuracy. When I did

so, I discovered a photograph depicting Marilyn and Dorothy on the set of a 1960 movie called *Let's Make Love* that had costarred the most famous movie

star in the world and French actor Yves Montand. During a "media day" of some sort at 20th Century Fox, three smiling faces appear, Montand, Marilyn, and Dorothy, although she appears to be a bit distracted as she gazes to her left.

My interest heightened, I considered whether Dorothy would have written about Marilyn shortly before she died. As had happened so many times before, my research struck gold when I discovered this Voice of Broadway column dated August 2, 1962, just two days before Marilyn's untimely death.

It read:

Marilyn Monroe's health must be improving. She's been attending select Hollywood parties and has become the talk of the town again. In California, they're circulating a photograph of her that certainly isn't as bare as the famous calendar, but is very interesting. And she's cooking in the sex-appeal department, too; she's proven vastly alluring to a handsome gentleman who is a bigger name than Joe DiMaggio was in his heyday. So, don't write Marilyn off as finished.

As before with Kilgallen's case, an "ah-ha" moment had happened, but before I could fully digest its possible impact, there was the discovery of another column Kilgallen had written in November 1960, less than two years before Marilyn died.

Unlike the bouncy column Dorothy wrote in 1962, this one about Marilyn had a sad note to it, with the first two paragraphs reading:

Picture an orphan girl who has never had a dime. Someone leads her into a toy store and tells her, "you can have anything you want." She chooses one toy after another. But while they are being wrapped, she finds it hard to believe that the toys are really hers.

That's Marilyn Monroe. It's a short version but the most famous of all blondes today is facing her third divorce because she was, in truth, an orphan girl suddenly let loose in the biggest toy store of all: the world. She could have anything she wanted because she was fabulously beautiful and appealing and inevitably some toys were men.

Kilgallen then chronicled Marilyn's unsuccessful love affairs, first early on in life with high school friend James Daugherty, then New York Yankees baseball star Joe DiMaggio, and then famed playwright Arthur Miller (*Death of a Salesman*). This leads to the final sentence in the column, one that certainly captured this lovesick celebrity's unfortunate state of affairs at the time: "Marilyn is alone again, the orphan in the toy shop. Perhaps the item she wants this time has already been sold."

Fortunately, when Dorothy wrote the column "MM Has Hollywood Talking Again" two years later, Marilyn was in a much better frame of mind. And when I found that column, it marked a defining moment that served as a turning point regarding my eventual investigation of her life and times and her tragic death on August 4, 1962. Doing so reminded me of the days when a single piece of evidence changed the course of one of my murder cases from being hopeless into one where reasonable doubt could save an innocent client from life in prison.

Why? Because what the gifted columnist had written was completely at odds with the actress presumably having the mindset to commit suicide. Instead of indicating a troubled woman with thoughts of killing herself, Kilgallen had portrayed a woman who was on the upswing, one who was "the talk of the town again," one who was "cooking in the sex-appeal department," one who had offers to appear on Broadway, a lifelong dream of hers. This was the happy Marilyn, the one with the smile that lit up the movie screen, and to my shock, I had never seen Dorothy's column published in any book to date, since authors had apparently never fully probed the Marilyn/Dorothy connection regarding Marilyn's life and times and her death.

Marilyn's cheery mindset was confirmed after I read an excerpt from Marilyn's housekeeper Eunice Murray's book, *Marilyn: The Last Months*. She wrote, "Marilyn was shy, open, generous and kind and despite her lack of education, an extremely bright girl with an intuitive intelligence that was most unusual." Murray added that as "spring of [1962] approached, Marilyn's life was on the upswing," echoing the column Dorothy Kilgallen had written.

When strong evidence like that is discovered, it makes sense, per the "Dorothy Method" of proper investigative procedures, to seek confirming evidence from credible sources, and I had done so with the 2021 publication of *Collateral Damage: The Mysterious Deaths of Marilyn Monroe and Dorothy Kilgallen, and the Ties that Bind Them to Robert Kennedy and the JFK Assassination.* For the first time, the book connected the life and times and deaths of the three twentieth-century luminaries who had died just forty months apart, a true contribution to history that I believe will stand the test of time. As noted before, by having investigated the JFK assassination first, then Dorothy's death, and then Marilyn's out of order since Marilyn died first, then JFK, then Dorothy, the organizational skills I learned while preparing for opening statements or closing arguments at trial paid dividends some fifty years later since by utiliz-

ing these skills, I was able to piece the puzzle together like no one before me.

In late 2021 and early 2022, however, I learned even more about Marilyn's positive state of mind, that it was unlikely she would have taken her life based on two reasons, what at first glance don't seem strong reasons but must be taken into account. Finding these jewels, more appropriately what might be called clues, reminded me again of Dorothy's meticulous investigative instincts, ones I was trying to emulate. For instance, the phrase "little things mean a lot," held true since to Kilgallen "little things" ended up being "big things" during her investigations. For example, she learned that Jack Ruby, while telling anyone who would listen that he was distraught to the extent of being sick to his stomach when JFK died, had tried to sell "twist boards" to *Dallas Morning News* personnel just a few hours after this terrible sorrow. That didn't make sense to Dorothy, and from that point on, she focused on Ruby and left Oswald to those who chased his story far and wide with little good fortune when it came to exposing the truth.

What were the clues I discovered? Marilyn loved animals (during her early years she begged first husband Jim Dougherty to permit a sheep being soaked with rain in the cold to enter their home), loved her dog Maf (short for Mafia), given to her by Frank Sinatra, and would not have abandoned her canine friend. Second, Marilyn had achieved a lifelong dream, owning a home, and it certainly meant the world to her, so much that she intended to spend the rest of her life there. With this in mind, according to Murray's

book, the two of them had visited "a
furniture store on Wilshire Boulevard on
the day Marilyn died where they purchased
a bedside table for Marilyn's bedroom."
Murray added, "At least one thing is
obvious: on Friday [August 3, day before
she died] Marilyn had no somber plans to
end her life. There was too much to look
forward to."

To my mind, Kilgallen would have
taken the "clues" discovered in Murray's
book and followed up on them, and I thus
did likewise, since I was now quite curious

Marilyn, with her new friend, Maf,
headed to NYC

as to whether the truth about Marilyn's death had been exposed. To that
end, I began to repeat the research journey utilized when investigating
what turned out to be Kilgallen's murder. Again, my experience in the
courtroom helped and thus I immediately sought the autopsy performed
when Marilyn died.

Suffice it to say that the LA County deputy medical examiner, Dr. Thomas
Noguchi, a very controversial public official who would later be criticized for
his handling of actress Natalie Wood's death and others involving celebrities,
completely botched the autopsy, which concluded that Marilyn committed
what he called "probable suicide." This "verdict," I would discover to my
amazement, had conflicted with the certificate of death specifying the cause
of death to be an overdose of drugs.

Marilyn's coroner examination, performed as Coroner Case #81128 at
10:30 a.m. on August 5, 1962, is packed with as much mystery as would
be the case when Kilgallen died three years later. Amazingly enough,
as would be with Dorothy's death, Marilyn was examined by a deputy/
junior/assistant medical examiner, one with less experience and expertise
than the chief medical examiner. One must question why this happened,
leading to speculation that those in charge of examining the two deaths
wanted only the appearance of an autopsy rather than a genuine and
thorough autopsy.

In Marilyn's case, three words in the "Official Copy" of the autopsy report, dated August 5, 1962, bear mention. Notice them just under the first paragraph: "ACUTE BARBITURATE POISONING; INGESTION OF OVERDOSE."

While there is no way to confirm exactly why the words "POISONING" and then "INGESTION OF OVERDOSE" were used, the former perhaps indicating foul play and the latter accidental death due to overdose, what is apparent *is the absence of any indication that Marilyn committed suicide*. One reaction to the wording is that whoever performed the autopsy either suspected foul play or, in the alternative, accidental death due to an overdose but never suicide.

The medical examiner employee selected to complete this document, and thus Marilyn's safekeeper as to the truth about what happened to her in the forensic sense, was Dr. Noguchi. Many accounts of a forensic nature have been offered through the years but in 2009, Noguchi, eighty-two at the time, presented his version of what happened in a widely circulated and most disturbing interview with a *Los Angeles Examiner* reporter.

Noguchi's conduct attracts suspicion from the outset in his having told the journalist he had no idea who Marilyn Monroe was: "I just assumed it was someone else who had the same name." Difficult to believe for sure since that "name" was famous throughout the world, but nevertheless, Noguchi stated that he had examined a woman who was five feet, four inches tall, weighing just over ten stone (140 pounds). He added that the police report included the fact that "various bottles of pills, including an empty bottle of Nembutal," were scattered close to the body.

Noguchi said he began the autopsy by inspecting Marilyn's body for needle marks "in case she had been injected for drugs" and for "marks indicating physical violence." The coroner stated that he found no needle marks (did he check under Marilyn's armpits, her toes?) but did discover "a dark reddish-blue bruise" on her left hip, one "judging by its color, fresh rather than old." No explanation was ever given as to the possible cause of the bruise but, as will be explained, I was able to do based on accounts of how Marilyn died never considered before.

Surprisingly, Noguchi said his internal examination produced "no visual evidence of any pills" in Marilyn's stomach. Since he was aware of the empty Nembutal bottle, he checked for "a yellowish dye with which Nembutal capsules were coated [in her stomach], but found none."

A step up from Seconal on the ladder of dangerous barbiturates, Nembutal, one of the three drugs discovered in Dorothy Kilgallen's system, has been called "Yellow Birds" or "Yellow Jackets" when marketed on the street as yellow capsules. The drug consists of white, odorless, crystalline granules or a white powder with a slightly bitter taste. It is very soluble in water or alcohol. The latter accelerates its effect above the normal forty-minute range, similar to Seconal.

Normal digestion of either Nembutal or chloral hydrate, which acts as a depressant on the central nervous system with sedative effects similar to those of barbiturates, normally requires water intake, and if Marilyn had consumed close to fifty pills, as was speculated, perhaps several glasses of water, it seems likely, would have been necessary to absorb that intake. When reading Dr. Noguchi's report, Kilgallen, whose own autopsy revealed traces of Nembutal, would have questioned why no drinking glass or glasses appeared in Marilyn's crime scene photographs.

* * *

Thomas Noguchi reported that he discovered "a milky substance" in Marilyn's stomach but again, he provided no explanation in his coroner's report. In addition to blood samples forwarded for toxicological testing, he sent Marilyn's internal organs as well. Noguchi said that "several hours after he had completed the autopsy" the results came back indicating 8.0 percent level of chloral hydrate in the blood, while the liver tests revealed 13.0 percent of pentobarbital (Nembutal). Each dosage alone would have been fatal.

This testing may be assumed to be competent, but then Noguchi dropped a blockbuster during his interview, admitting, "I made a mistake at this point," since, "the toxicology tests had only been performed on the blood and the liver, not on the internal organs." He added, "I should have insisted that all of the organs be examined." By the time he realized the mistake, he said, those organs had been destroyed. When I read this admission, I wanted to travel to LA and strangle Noguchi, still alive today. What incompetence!

Noguchi was certainly correct when he admitted that if he had done his job right and examined all of the organs, as was standard procedure, "I am sure that this could have cleared up a lot of the subsequent controversy, but I didn't follow through as I should have."

Noguchi then made a second mistake, one he later admitted, when he had given his boss, Dr. Theodore Curphey, what turned out to be a "jump the gun" autopsy report. Based on that report, which included no mention of any suicide having occurred, Curphey nonetheless announced to the public that Marilyn had died of a "probable suicide" (https://www.youtube.com/watch?v=b-3a6pWt43I) via the certificate of death, which, for the first time, included the words "probable suicide" as the cause of Marilyn's demise. Whether Curphey did this on purpose will be considered.

157

The result was that this less-than-truthful conclusion spread quickly to the world with headlines such as "Marilyn Monroe Kills Self," since the media failed to print the "probable" side of the findings and instead just intimated that she had committed suicide. This was a sensationalist conclusion just as erroneous as when Kilgallen's cause of death as "Overdose of Drugs" three years later was manipulated by the coroner into a self-administered overdose and reported to the public through the media. In each case, the women's reputations had been ruined, tragic for sure.

Upset that Marilyn had certainly not gotten a fair shake in the forensics department (deliberate or not? I wondered), a second Kilgallen column then provided the nexus to realize that foul play regarding her death was front and center in my search for the truth. That column, one with the misleading headline, "Martha Proves She's a Trouper," about actress Martha Raye, included several questions about Marilyn's death. Kilgallen wrote:

> The mail pouring in on the subject of Marilyn Monroe is amazing in volume and content. Many of her fans—and some people who knew her in life —want an investigation above and beyond what the Beverly Hills police have conducted. They simply aren't satisfied with the brief autopsy report that was issued in California (not that the California authorities care what Marilyn's fans think) and they pose some intelligent questions.

Chief among the questions were suspicious ones about the actions of Marilyn's housekeeper, why Marilyn's bedroom door was locked, and so forth, but it was these words that captured my attention for certain:

> I can't answer any of these questions, but I have a feeling the real story hasn't been told, not by a long shot.

Since, if Kilgallen, my inspiration, my muse, believed that the "real story hasn't been told," I was certainly of a like mind and now quite suspicious that Marilyn had been murdered. With my investigative juices on full tilt, I had, in essence, become the "voice" for Marilyn as I had for JFK and Dorothy, thus becoming an advocate for her with the determination to fight for justice as I had in the other two cases. With this in mind, I turned attention toward pointing the finger of guilt at the one man who checked all of the boxes regarding motive, means, opportunity, and benefit from the crime regarding the movie star's death. That search began by borrowing a few of Kilgallen's words in the column about Marilyn: "She's proven vastly alluring to a handsome gentleman who is a bigger name than Joe DiMaggio was in his heyday."

If, in fact, I asked myself, if Marilyn did not commit suicide, then who was the chief suspect, "the bigger name" Kilgallen alluded to in the column? First up was President John F. Kennedy since there was evidence she had become enamored with JFK when he was a senator but, of most interest to me was that the two bigger-than-life personalities had had a

Marilyn serenades JFK with "Happy Birthday, Mr. President"

love affair after Marilyn sang "Happy Birthday" to JFK during a May 1962 Democratic fundraiser at NYC's Madison Square Garden just a few months before she died.

Among those who were quite impressed with Marilyn's performance was Dorothy Kilgallen. In her Voice of Broadway column, she included a hint of things to come, writing, "It seemed like Marilyn was making love to the President in front of 40 million Americans." In *Life Magazine*, Kilgallen was quoted as adding, "The approval of the crowd was like an embrace."

CHAPTER 15

Following the investigative "path" I believed Dorothy Kilgallen might very well have followed, I quickly learned then that the love affair between the charismatic president and the charismatic movie queen was short-lived, apparently cut off by Papa Joe Kennedy due to the prospect of bad publicity for JFK when he ran for reelection in 1964.

Unable to give up my search for the truth about what happened to Marilyn, I asked the question "Who is another 'big name' who may have been involved romantically with the movie legend at the time?" Immediately I turned my attention to Robert F. Kennedy, shown with JFK and Marilyn at the birthday celebration after-event party in this photograph as the possible culprit in Marilyn's murder.

In light of my having recovered a state of mind that included the army of investigative instincts I once possessed while practicing criminal defense law, and by considering what Dorothy Kilgallen would have done based on this evidence, I was suddenly drawn to the National Archives to see if any government documents existed that could assist my probe. Several days of research later, I retrieved a copy of a document that I first thought was FBI but, after further research, realized it had been created by CIA agent James

Angleton as of August 3, 1962, the day before Marilyn died. [Author's note: Angleton, a higher-up CIA agent, would later become a controversial figure in the mysterious death of Mary Pinchot Meyer, one of JFK's mistresses, in 1964. The excellent book *A Very Private Woman* by Nina Burleigh tells the story.]

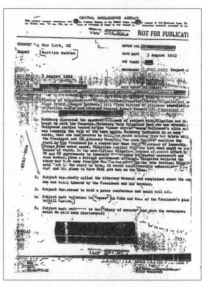

When I noticed the document's designation of the "Subject" as being "Marilyn Monroe," my blood pressure must have surged in anticipation of reading the memo. And when I then realized that both Kilgallen and JFK were prominently mentioned as well as Marilyn, a connection between the three of them for certain, I shouted "Wow!" loud enough for the neighbors to hear.

The document reads:

Wiretap of telephone…between reporter Dorothy Kilgallen and a close friend Howard Rothberg [A] wiretap of telephone conversations of Marilyn Monroe and Attorney General Robert Kennedy [B]. Appraisal of Contents [redacted]

1. Rothberg discussed the apparent…of subject with Kilgallen and the break up with the Kennedys. Rothberg told Kilgallen that she [Marilyn] was attending Hollywood parties hosted by the "inner circle" among Hollywood's elite and was becoming the talk of the town again. Rothberg indicated in so many words, that she had secrets to tell, no doubt arising from her trysts with the President and the Attorney General. One such "secret" mentions the visit by the President at a secret air base for purposes of inspecting things from outer space.

   • Kilgallen replied that she knew what might be the source of visit. In the mid-fifties, Kilgallen learned of secret effort by the US and UK governments to identify…crashed spacecraft and dead bodies from a British government official. Kilgallen believed the story may have come from the…in the late forties. Kilgallen said that if the story is true, it would…

161

> terrible embarrassment to Jack [Kennedy] and his plans
> to have NASA put men on the moon."
>
> 2. Subject [Marilyn] repeatedly called the Attorney General
>   and complained about the way she was being ignored by
>   the President and his brother.
>
> 3. Subject threatened to hold a press conference and would
>   tell all.
>
> 4. Subject made reference to "bases" in Cuba and knew of
>   the President's plan to kill Castro.
>
> 5. Subject made ref[erence] to her "diary of secrets" and
>   what the newspapers would do with such disclosures.

A slow, careful reading of the front page of the document causes one's heart to skip a beat for several reasons. First, it seems clear that both the telephones of Dorothy Kilgallen and Marilyn Monroe had been wiretapped. When this occurred is not specified but no question exists that, for whatever reason, each was under surveillance. Second, it is logical to believe that Kilgallen's column "MM Has Hollywood Talking Again" is based on Howard Rothberg's sources since the language in the column and in the document are nearly verbatim.

Third, Rothberg indicated to Kilgallen that Marilyn "had secrets to tell, no doubt arising from her trysts with the President and the Attorney General." And fourth, that "one such 'secret'" involves a JFK visit to "a secret air base for purposes of inspecting things from outer space." Both Rothberg and Kilgallen, it appears, knew that the president would have been "embarrassed" if that visit and its purpose were exposed in the media.

A close reading of the items numbers 2 through 5 dictates the lethal nature, the threats by Marilyn to completely destroy the Kennedy brothers' reputations and their professional lives especially through her "diary of secrets," but it is item #4 that is the time bomb. Why, because Marilyn's mention of "bases in Cuba" and that she had been privy to the president's "plan to kill [Fidel] Castro" would have been explosive, worldwide news if exposed.

In fact, not only would have the Kennedy Camelot image been obliterated but potential charges of treason may have been leveled against either one or both of the Kennedys since either through pillow talk or ego-out-of-control boasting, Marilyn had been made aware of matters of national security.

This said, the startling nature of the CIA document continues when one reads page two.

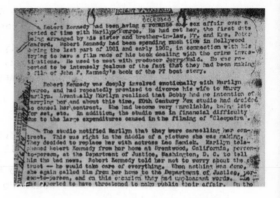

Robert Kennedy had been having a romance and sex affair over a period of time with Marilyn Monroe. He had met her, the first date being arranged by his sister and brother-in-law, Mr. and Mrs. Peter Lawford. Robert Kennedy had been spending much time in Hollywood during the last part of 1961 and early 1962, in connection with his trying to have a film made of his book dealing with crime investigations. He used to meet with producer Jerry Wald. He [Robert Kennedy] was reported to be intensely jealous of the fact that they had been making a film of John F. Kennedy's book of the PT boat story.

Robert Kennedy was deeply involved emotionally with Marilyn Monroe, and had repeatedly promised to divorce his wife to marry Marilyn. Eventually Marilyn realized that Bobby had no intention of marrying her and about this time, 20th Century Fox studio had decided to cancel her contract. She had become very unreliable, being late for set, etc. In addition, the studio was in financial difficulty due to the large expenditures caused in the filming of "Cleopatra."

The studio notified Marilyn that they were cancelling her contract. This was right in the middle of a picture she was making. They decided to replace her with actress Lee Remick. Marilyn telephoned Robert Kennedy from her home in Brentwood, California, person-to-person, at the Department of Justice, Washington, D. C. to tell him the bad news. Robert Kennedy told her not to worry about the contract— he would take care of everything. When nothing was done, she again called him from her home to the Department of Justice, person-to-person, and on this occasion they had unpleasant words. **Marilyn was reported to have threatened to make public their affair.** On the… [Emphasis added.]

Bolstering the CIA document's claim of Marilyn's affair with Bobby was a startling piece of evidence discovered in 2016 among JFK files released by the US government. It was an early 1960s letter (undated) from RFK's sister, Jean Kennedy Smith, who died in 2020 at age ninety-two, to Marilyn found in Monroe's belongings at her home. Written on her stationary (notice Palm Beach address), it read, in part, "Understand you and Bobby are the new item! We all think you should come with him when he comes back East!"

Through the years presentation of the letter has been criticized, even to the point that it was forged, but apparently Kennedy Smith acknowledged writing it, although she said the line, "Understand that you and Bobby are the new item!" was made in jest. In addition, the full content of the letter before that statement reads, "Mother asked me to write and thank you for your sweet note to Daddy—He really enjoyed it and you were very cute to send it." Following the text regarding "the new item!" is the closing, "Again, thanks for the note. Love, Jean Smith."

Based on primary sources, Marilyn joined RFK during a party at the home of Peter and Pat Lawford, the Kennedy brothers' sister, on February 1, 1962, some six months before her death. On the third of that month, Marilyn wrote a letter to her ex-father-in-law Isidore Miller and her stepson Bobby Miller describing the encounter.

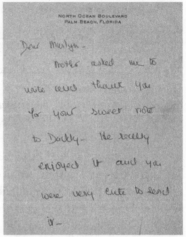

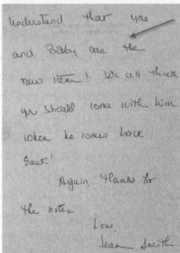

Jean Kennedy Smith's letter to Marilyn

Brother and sister, JFK and Jean Kennedy Smith

In part, it read:

Oh, Bobby, guess what: I had dinner last night with the Attorney-General of the United States, Robert Kennedy, and I asked him what his department was going to do about Civil Rights and some other issues. He is very intelligent, and besides all that, he's got a terrific sense of humor. I think you would like him. Anyway, I had to go to this dinner last night as he was the guest of honor and when they asked him who he wanted to meet, he wanted to meet me.

One may only guess what strong emotions Marilyn must have had, how giddy she must have been when she learned that RFK, apparently the guest of honor at the dinner, had been asked "who he wanted to meet," and he said, "he wanted to meet me." Her heartstrings must have been pulled by the man she described as being "very intelligent" and one who had "a terrific sense of humor." No wonder Jean Kennedy Smith wrote that she and Bobby were the "new item" in her letter to Marilyn.

The CIA report, especially the section where the RFK/Marilyn love affair is noted, was substantiated in a very controversial book: *The Strange Death of Marilyn Monroe* by Frank A. Capell, published in 1964, just two years after her tragic death.

Frank Capell's book

Since I referred to what Capell wrote in my book *Collateral Damage*, criticism of my doing so has been considered since these critics are correct that Capell had a dubious background and apparently was an overzealous anti-Communist. This said, close inspection of what he wrote is important. It includes: "This is the story of an American girl who was used by materialist avaricious people, by false friends with bad advice, by sex-depraved V. I. P.'s. She came under the influence of many whom she allowed, in child-like trust, to chart the course of her life and who led her to a premature grave. That she became immoral cannot be denied but she was also kind and generous."

Regarding specifics as to the "sex-depraved" VIPs, Capell wrote, "Marilyn Monroe's involvement with a V. I. P. during the period just preceding her death was well known to her friends and reporters in the Hollywood area. This important person was and is ambitious, ruthless and will stop at nothing which is to become President of the United States."

Since JFK was already president, it is no stretch to believe that Capell was referring to Robert Kennedy, and with this in mind, and putting aside what objections critics had, and have today, of the author's credibility, one major factor still exists, as I have pointed out in numerous interviews and presentations. It supports the fact that the powers-that-be in the Kennedy family, apparently Bobby and arguably Papa Joe, believed that Capell's account *was* accurate regarding the continuous love affair between Marilyn and the attorney general during the summer of 1962. [Author note: This is when RFK was attempting to get a film produced at 20th Century Fox based on his book, *The Enemy Within*, his vicious diatribe assaulting the very being of those in the underworld whom he detested such as Carlos Marcello and Sam Giancana.]

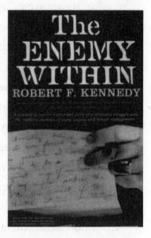

The proof that the Kennedys must have believed Capell's book had credibility follows a threat beginning in an FBI memo circulated in July 1964. Notice it is sent to Robert Kennedy from "Director, FBI," at the time, J. Edgar Hoover.

The Attorney General   July 8, 1964

Director, FBI   1 - Mr. Belmont
            1 - Mr. Mohr PERSONAL
43   1 - Mr. Evans
            1 - Mr. DeLoach
FRANK A. CAPELL   1 - Mr. Sullivan
INFORMATION CONCERNING 1 - Mr. Baumgardner
(INTERNAL SECURITY)   1 - Mr. Simpson

One paragraph (Memo to "The Attorney General") reads, "According to Mr. Capell, his book will make reference to your alleged friendship with the late Marilyn Monroe. Mr. Capell stated he will indicate in his book that you and Miss Monroe were intimate and that you were in Miss Monroe's apartment at the time of her death." Based on wording such as "Mr. Capell stated," he must had met with FBI agents about the book, providing the above heads-up information about it directly to these agents and thus to Hoover who was then aware, if he had not been already, of the love affair.

That statement is followed by yet another FBI memo, which contained the following opinion, apparently from an agent identified as "Mr. F. J. Baumgardner." He stated that *Some allegations of Capell are from public sources and are apparently true*, [emphasis added] some are completely false and others are extremely questionable and not subject to corroboration." What allegations were "apparently true" are not specified, but apparently Baumgardner found some credence to what Capell had written.

What reaction did the "heads-up" trigger from the Kennedys? While this author has not been able to discover whether the FBI followed up on the allegations against the attorney general, or whether he took any action (doubtful either happened; no media exposure discovered), there must have been some concern about Capell's revelations, true or false. Under the same banner as above—"SAC, New York"—the memo read, "You are instructed to follow this matter very closely" while requiring the New York office to apparently purchase books "in order that the Attorney General may be kept advised."

Common sense dictates that the mention of "purchase books" means that a statement by Joe DeCarlo, an enforcer for Melvin Belli's client and close friend of Mickey Cohen as relayed to this author and noted in *Collateral Damage*, is quite credible. DeCarlo had told close friends of his whom I interviewed, "There were not too many copies of the Capell book around; the Kennedys had tried to keep it off the market to the extent of even buying as many copies as possible." Logic follows that this was done to keep the public from reading them.

Criticisms of Capell are understood and warranted, but common sense seems to indicate that the Kennedys, but especially Bobby, were quite concerned about Capell's book, more concerned than seems necessary for a book that they knew was being denounced at every turn as mostly pure garbage in some of the memos. Regardless, Capell's allegation, if exposed to readers of his book and the media, that the VIP involved with Marilyn was an "important person," one "ambitious," and "ruthless" who "will stop at nothing...to become president of the United States," an obvious reference to RFK, the attorney general's name would have been dragged through the mud thus ending any aspirations Bobby had to become president.

To be certain, the apparent need by the Kennedys, in particular RFK, to get the Capell book off the market by purchasing as many copies as possible triggers the belief that Bobby knew one thing for sure: *what Capell had written was absolutely true, and thus covering up the truth, a Kennedy family specialty, was in order.*[13]

With all this evidence in mind, one may ask how serious the Kennedy brothers John and Bobby would have taken any publicity regarding their womanizing, their cheating on their wives if Marilyn had lived and held a news conference to "tell all" regarding her romantic relationships with each of them. One may assume that, at the very least, both men's political careers, as noted, would have ended but like those in the Mafia, when confronted with attempts to paint them in a bad light, the Kennedys were dangerous when cornered with any sort of attempt to disparage that Camelot-connected name of theirs to any extent at all.

Regarding JFK and how he reacted to any public attempt to expose his philandering, an incident author Seymour Hersh revealed in his 1997 bestselling book, *The Dark Side of Camelot*, is worth mentioning. The "incident" is a strange one involving what Hersh called "a middle-aged housewife named Florence M. Kater, who decided in 1959 that her mission in life

---

13 To read a damning article about Robert Kennedy, although he is not named, and his almost certain complicity in Marilyn Monroe's death, one should check the August 1963 edition of *Photoplay* magazine and the article written by journalist Martha Donaldson (recent research leads to the potential that Donaldson was the pen name used by Martha Gellhorn, best known for her marriage to Ernest Hemingway), entitled "Her Killer's Still At Large." Excerpts are included in *Collateral Damage*, including one that reads, "You can read about him almost any day in the newspapers and magazines and you will think, 'This is a good person. This is a truly honorable man'...But what you will never read, never see, never know is that this man is a killer. He is the man who killed Marilyn Monroe," an obvious reference to RFK.

would be to force the Washington press corps to deal with [JFK's] womanizing." The basis for her knowledge of the president's philandering was, Hersh reported, her renting an "upstairs apartment in her Georgetown home to Pamela Turnure, an attractive aide in Kennedy's office."

According to Hersh, Kennedy and Turnure were "conducting an indiscreet affair that involved many late-night and early-morning comings and goings to Kater's consternation." When, Hersh wrote, "Turnure moved to another apartment a few blocks away [in late 1958], Kater "ambushed Kennedy leaving the new apartment at three a. m. and took a photograph of the unhappy senator attempting to shield his face with a handkerchief."

Kennedy's reaction, according to Hersh? "The encounter rattled Kennedy and he struck back," the author wrote. "A few weeks later, Kater alleged, she and her husband were accosted on the street in front of her home by the angry Kennedy, who, waving his forefinger, warned her 'to stop bothering me' and then said, 'and if either of you spread any lies about me, you'll find yourself without a job.'"

Of course, this was JFK not RFK, but since their temperaments were closely bound, one may imagine RFK handling the matter using the same sort of threats. No matter, reported Hersh, Kater "mailed a copy of the photograph and an articulate letter describing her encounter with Kennedy to fifty prominent citizens in Washington D. C. and New York City, including editors, syndicated columnists, and politicians." J. Edgar Hoover also received a copy.

Fortunately for JFK, Hersh stated, "No responsible journalist touched the story," likely, it would seem, frightened of offending the Kennedy family. And what happened to Turnure? Hersh wrote that "after his election, Kennedy showed his disdain for Kater by appointing Pamela Turnure press secretary for his wife Jackie." Such conduct was certainly an affront to the first lady, who may or may not have known that one of Jack's sexual conquests was working in her office.

Summing up, Hersh wrote, "The obsessed housewife was a campaign-damaging bomb that did not explode. There were others, equally dangerous."

Like Kater, Marilyn was a time bomb waiting to explode, a threat to the Kennedy brothers, and she ended up dead. While there is no absolute proof that JFK knew of Bobby's involvement in ending Marilyn's life, the president had to have been quite suspicious that RFK was involved. Regardless, Joe's favorite sons emerged unscathed. Marilyn's threat was over, covered up through her death.

CHAPTER 16

Regarding the wiretapping of RFK and Marilyn's telephone conversations as noted in the CIA document, viable proof was discovered in late 2021 that her phones had been tapped through credible accounts by former *Hill Street Blues* TV star Veronica Hamel.

The actress confirmed that in 1972, she and her then husband became the new owners of Marilyn's Brentwood home. They hired a contractor to replace the roof and remodel the house, and the contractor discovered a sophisticated eavesdropping and telephone tapping system that covered every room in the home. The components were not commercially available in 1962, but were—in the words of a retired Justice Department official— "standard FBI issue." Hamel and her husband spent $100,000 to remove the bugging devices from the house.

Rightfully so, readers of *Collateral Damage* asked a most pertinent question: What events led to Marilyn's threat "to hold a press conference and… tell all"? Based on certain reputable accounts as noted in *Collateral Damage*, her anger toward the Kennedy brothers reached the tipping point during the last weekend of Marilyn's life when she attended a party at the Cal Neva Lodge on the northern border of California and Nevada. As best my research now indicates, JFK and RFK were not there, as originally believed, but certainly Frank Sinatra and Peter Lawford were present and reliable accounts indicate that Marilyn expressed her anger to the extent that she felt like she was being treated like "a piece of meat" by the Kennedy brothers.

Regardless, Dorothy Kilgallen, I believed, would have focused on the clues in the CIA document, if she had known about them, as I did where it was stated that Marilyn "repeatedly called the Attorney General and complained about the way she was being ignored by the President and his brother." One must thus imagine poor Marilyn, upset that she was apparently being forsaken by the Kennedy brothers during a time, as Kilgallen pointed out in a previous column, Marilyn was seeking love in her life.

It is thus no exaggeration to believe that tears must have streamed down Marilyn's cheeks as she sat by the phone. Especially hurtful for Marilyn would have been Bobby turning his back on her after she had been involved in what the CIA document called a "romance and sexual affair," which must have meant that she not only shared her body with him but her love as well. Further, the document stated: "Robert Kennedy was deeply involved emotionally with Marilyn Monroe, and had repeatedly promised to divorce his wife to marry Marilyn." Even though it was stated that "eventually Marilyn realized that Bobby had no intention of marrying her," the hurt in her heart continued on unabated as the days passed toward August 4, 1962.

* * *

Of certain interest to me based on previous research after having discovered the damning CIA document was the information included below the words "Appraisal of Contents." These were various notations signaling that Marilyn "had secrets to tell," and that one such "secret" was JFK's "visit...at a secret air base for purposes of inspecting things from outer space." Kilgallen is then quoted, based on her phone apparently having been wiretapped, regarding her knowledge of "the source of the visit" and that "it would be a terrible embarrassment to Jack [Kennedy] and his plans to have NASA put men on the moon." Ever observant of the consequences of one's actions, Kilgallen's comment about the impact of JFK's interest in UFOs being made public was right on point.

Since I do not believe in coincidences, it was apparently meant to be that I was contacted in late 2021 by a quite reputable source, Karen Jean Tanner. She shared with me a never-before-published photo of Kilgallen (on the right) at the Roswell, NM, UFO site in 1954 and a postcard Dorothy sent to her aunt, Betty Tanner, a NYC socialite and close friend of Kilgallen's that included mention of "spy reports" and stating "it has been interesting," confirming the experience at Roswell.

This photo, though fuzzy in nature, resembles others taken of Kilgallen's profile and solidifies the evidence pointing to her obsession with UFOs as noted in the CIA document as well as her columns about UFOs.

The postcard Tanner referred to is marked as being sent August 19, 1954.

One such column Kilgallen wrote about UFOs is shown below:

Those "Little Men" On Flying Saucers? Real, Says Kilgallen

Remember the creepy stories about flying saucers and little men from outer space? Dorothy Kilgallen has run into a new one in London. Here is her dispatch to the New York Journal-American on what a British official thinks about those "little fellows."

BY DOROTHY KILGALLEN
(DISTRIBUTED BY INTERNATIONAL NEWS SERVICE)

LONDON, May 22—British scientists and airmen, after examining the wreckage of a mysterious "flying ship," are convinced that these strange aerial objects are not optical illusions or Soviet inventions, but actually are flying saucers which originate on another planet.

The source of my information is a British official of cabinet rank who prefers to remain unidentified.

"We believe, on the basis of our inquiries thus far, that the saucers were staffed by small men —probably under four feet tall," my informant told me today.

"It's frightening but there is no denying the flying saucers come from another planet."

This official quoted scientists as saying a flying ship of this type could not have been constructed on earth.

DOROTHY

The text read:

By Dorothy Kilgallen
Distributed by International News Service

London, May 22 - British scientists and airmen, after examining the wreckage of a mysterious "flying ship," are convinced that these strange aerial objects are not optical illusions or Soviet inventions, but actually are flying saucers which originate on another planet.

The source of my information is a British official of cabinet rank who prefers to remain unidentified.

"We believe, on the basis of our inquiries thus far, that the 'saucers' were staffed by small men - probably under four feet tall," my informant told me today.

"It's frightening but there is no denying the flying saucers come from another planet."

This official quoted scientists as saying a flying ship of this type could not have been constructed on earth.

The British government, I learned, is withholding an official report on the "flying saucer" examination at this time, possibly because it does not wish to frighten the public.

When my husband, Richard Kollmer and I arrived here for a brief vacation, I had no premonition that I would be catapulting myself into the controversy over whether flying saucers are real or imaginary.

In the United States, all kinds of explanations have been advanced.

But no responsible official of the U.S. Air Force has yet intimated the mysterious flying ships had actually vaulted from outer space.

* * *

Discovery of the Angleton CIA document provided what many may call "smoking guns" on several levels, including the fact that there was little doubt both Kilgallen's and Marilyn Monroe's telephones had been wiretapped. Next up as I built a case against RFK's complicity in Marilyn's death as a prosecutor would do, was discovering solid evidence that the attorney general was actually in Los Angeles on the day Marilyn died as corroborated by this 20th Century Fox security log:

Before 11 a.m. on Aug. 4, 1962, a helicopter landed at the Twentieth Century Fox studio's helipad near Stage 14. Studio publicist Frank Neill, working that Saturday morning, said he saw Kennedy jump out of the helicopter and rush to a dark grey limousine waiting nearby. Neill said he got a glimpse of movie star Peter Lawford, brother-in-law to the Kennedys, sitting inside.

Later on that day, near midnight, Beverly Hills police officer Lynn Franklin, the most decorated officer as the time, stopped a limousine on Wilshire Boulevard in West LA. Driving was Lawford, with RFK in the back seat and Marilyn's psychiatrist, Ralph Greenson, beside Lawford.

Why Greenson was in the car has never been fully explained despite further research, but his being there is suspicious for sure.

Substantiating both the 20th Century Fox ledger and Franklin's account, as noted in his book, *The Beverly Hills Murder File*, is another account, this one most credible. Daryl Gates, later to become Los Angeles police chief, swore Robert Kennedy was in the city at the time Marilyn died. In his autobiography, *Chief: My Life in the LAPD*, Gates wrote, "I was working out of Chief Parker's office when Monroe died, and like the rest of the world, we were shocked...It is my own opinion that her death was accidental," while then adding, "The truth is, we knew Robert Kennedy was in town [Los Angeles] on August 4." By way of proof, Gates said, "We always knew when he was here. He was the Attorney General, so we were interested in him, the same way we were interested when other important figures came to Los Angeles [but] while we knew Robert Kennedy was in town that day, we paid no attention to where he went or what he did; whether he saw Monroe or not."

Each of these accounts, the 20th Century Fox log, Lynn Franklin's actually seeing RFK in LA on the evening when Marilyn died and Chief Gates's recollections, completely destroy the attorney general's alibi that he was in the San Francisco area on August 4. Common sense thus dictates that Lawford and RFK visited the movie star on the afternoon or early evening of her death begging Marilyn to retract her promise to go the media and "tell all" as noted in the CIA document. She refused, basically signing her death warrant.

When dealing with the means by which Marilyn died, my analysis focused on little-known facts about her death scene that were, in reality, major clues to what happened.

As mentioned in *Collateral Damage*, the clues that came to my mind included what medical examiner Noguchi described as "a dark reddish-blue bruise" on her left hip, one "judging by its color, fresh rather than old," and her housekeeper Eunice Murray "doing the wash" in the middle of the night when police arrived. In addition, as noted, normal digestion of either Nembutal or chloral hydrate, the drugs discovered in Marilyn's bloodstream, requires water intake, and if Marilyn consumed close to fifty pills, as was speculated, arguably several glasses of water would have been necessary. Kilgallen, when she read Dr. Noguchi's report, would have questioned why in the crime scene photographs, there appear to be no glasses present, and for sure, no glasses present partially filled with water easily reachable by her friend Marilyn.

As I believed Dorothy would have surmised, the fresh bruise was a major element of deciding that before she died, Marilyn's body had somehow been carried, perhaps from the front door by intruders who had surprised Marilyn late at night. Other explanations exist but it seems reasonable to believe that while moving her body through the hall, the hip could very well have been injured when it hit a table, a door knob, or another object.

Regarding Murray doing the wash (there is conflicting information as to whether Marilyn's home included a washing machine), logical reasoning permitted the conclusion that the intruders, probably two, recruited to end Marilyn's life, removed any outer clothing she was wearing, such as a robe. They then carefully positioned her body on the floor face down before dipping a bulb syringe of some sort into the mixed solution, lubricated the tip with perhaps Vaseline or another substance, and inserted the tip into Marilyn's rectum, with some spillage possible. Quickly, the lethal dose would have infiltrated her blood system and begun the march to her death.

Then, after placing Marilyn's nude body face down on the bed and positioning the phone receiver in her hand for effect, the two soldiers cleaned up as best they could and quietly left the home. If this happened, then they made at least two mistakes: first, there was no glass on the nightstand to indicate Marilyn had taken the pills with water, and second, they did not consider that some liquid would ooze out of Marilyn's rectum onto the sheets. Proof that the latter happened, it would seem, is a logical, common-sense inference although other explanations may be considered as well, regarding the reason why housekeeper Murray was doing wash when the authorities arrived in the middle of the night. When I completed my research I believed that Kilgallen would agree with the conclusion reached.

In mid-2021, support for the essence of my conclusions came from two credible sources, one still alive and one who had passed from this earth.

The first one is based on an excerpt from the book *Marilyn, Joe & Me* by June DiMaggio, Joe's niece and a dear friend of Marilyn's for eleven years, much of it when she was married to the baseball legend, and coauthor Mary Jane Popp, which I discovered on July 28, 2021.

The chilling account of what happened to Marilyn on that evening of August 4, 1962, reads as follows:

Joe and Marilyn during happy times

On the night Marilyn Monroe was murdered, the police were trying to locate Joe to tell him that she'd been found dead. Unable to find him right away, they knocked on my door between 11 pm and midnight and told me what happened. When I heard the news, I went into shock. I couldn't believe what they were telling me, and I didn't know where Joe was for sure so I called my Mother since I believed Joe might be in San Francisco

My mother already knew. Marilyn had been talking with her on the phone, mother told me, when intruders entered Marilyn's house. In her terror, Marilyn dropped the phone, but the killers never hung it up. Mother told me that she had heard it all – the voices in the room, the struggle, the silence. All accounts that I know about of state that when Marilyn was found, her phone was still off the hook.

Mother told me that she *knew* who killed Marilyn, but that knowledge absolutely terrified her, and to protect us, she said she would never reveal the details of what she knew.

I begged mother to tell me over, and over, and over again. She was not only traumatized but stubborn, the Swiss German in her rising to the surface. When Joe asked her to tell him, she just said, "No, I want my family to live."

Nothing that I said was able to bend Mother's iron will once she had made up her mind that if we knew, we could be in danger. Whoever killed Marilyn must have been very, very powerful to frighten my mother into everlasting silence. My smart, spunky mother was terrified to the very end and took the truth to her grave.

Even after the FBI traced that last call that Marilyn made to Mother, not even the country's G-men could make inroads with her. As she told me directly and in no uncertain terms, she wouldn't tell anything to the FBI or to another living soul.

Whenever we begged her, she would press her lips together and draw her fingers across them, to pantomime that she was zipping them tight. When I kept at her, she admitted her terror that if she told, "they" would kill her family.

The primary source for June's story is her mother, Rosalia, who relayed the events of August 4 to June after Marilyn died. If one closely examines what Rosalia said, many questions arise, such as who "the intruders, the killers" were that June's mother mentioned, and what were the details regarding "the voices in the room, the struggle, the silence." In addition, when Rosalia told June "that she knew who killed Marilyn," and that the "knowledge absolutely terrified her," who was Rosalia talking about, the ones that she had to "protect" the family from at all costs?

That Rosalia was "traumatized" by what happened and answered Joe's inquiry by refusing to reveal the details of that evening since "I want my family to live," who was Rosalia referring to at that time? Providing her own feelings, June wrote, "Whoever killed Marilyn must have been very, very powerful to frighten my mother into everlasting silence. My smart, spunky mother was terrified to the very end and took the truth to her grave."

Joe and his father and mother

Of special importance is that June then added, "Even after the FBI traced that last call that Marilyn made to Mother, not even the country's G-men could make inroads with her.... Whenever we begged her, she would press her lips together and draw her fingers across them, to pantomime that she was zipping them tight. When I kept at her, she admitted her terror that if she told, 'they' would kill her family."

Most importantly, through the excellent reporting of Mary Jane Popp, one must inquire, as Dorothy Kilgallen would have done, into who the "they" were, the ones Rosalia was referring to in her account. Doing so reminds one of Bobby Kennedy's use of "they" when describing who assassinated his brother and Melvin Belli's use of the same word when mentioning "they killed Dorothy, now they will go after Jack Ruby."

Learning of June's story, certainly her belief that Marilyn did not commit suicide, caused me to re-examine the evidence I had exposed in *Collateral Damage* regarding the legendary actress's death. Of special interest was June stating, "Whoever killed Marilyn must have been very, very powerful." June also indicated that Marilyn intended to re-marry Joe DiMaggio and either attempt to conceive a child or adopt one, with the wedding planned to take place, sadly, on the same day as Marilyn's funeral. The marriage intention appears to be confirmed in Eunice Murray's book where she writes that Marilyn told her, "I think [Joe] would like to move in," after he sent her a package containing a pair of his pajamas.

The second credible account, another example of the most reliable sources contacting me, arrived through an email from a Boston-area woman named Donna O'Laughlin.

During an interview with Donna in July 2021, this is what she told me:

In about 1975, I lived in a small town in western Massachusetts. My grandfather had been quite wealthy through the scrap metal business and then he and my father used some of the money to open a ski area called Brodie Mountain. Frank Sinatra played there and my family became friends with the Kennedys. [Note: Brodie has been confirmed as being a ski resort in New Ashford, Massachusetts, in the Taconic Mountains in the far northwestern part of the state.]

I recall that Ted Kennedy had contacted my uncle John, and Joan was around, in fact, Ted invited Donald Kelly, my dad, to go to Cuba, and House Speaker Tip O'Neill went with them.

At the time, I was working at a hospital as a nurse, and when I got home there was some hassle and my mother said to two guys, "Don't bring a gun into the house," but they said, "It's unmarked and can't be traced."

Late that evening, the two guys who had the gun talked to my dad and then the men got drunk and went to bed and I was, at about 19 years old at the time, left with the men in the front room. They had a Coke cooler full of beer, and were what I would call unsavory characters.

The two men's names were Steven McClusky of Boston who looked like Oliver Hardy, and Frankie Martin, who owned a restaurant in our small town. There was talk by the two men having "hit" my grandmother's husband in New Jersey who no one liked or trusted. They said, "We went to get her in New Jersey and no one has to worry about your grandmother anymore."

"That guy's name was Tony Mazol," one of the men said, "and we bludgeoned him to death with a baseball bat and then pinned it on his retard son."

The two drunken men then said they did the "dirty work for the Kennedys," meaning, to me, they were hit men. Then out of the blue, one of them said, "You know, Marilyn Monroe didn't commit suicide." When I asked about that, one of the men replied, "Yeah, she didn't kill herself. The Kennedys authorized her being killed. And here's how they did it. She had had an affair with JFK and Bobby, and Jackie was mad and went to Joe Kennedy and said she wanted a divorce."

Then one of the men said, "Marilyn was calling the White House so she's gotta go to appease Jackie. Marilyn's dangerous, Jackie will leave, and so Bobby opened the bedroom window in Marilyn's home (the men didn't say they were involved) so Bobby was there that night, the night she died."

There was also talk of Marilyn's having a diary, that she might "open her mouth" and so Bobby unlocked the window and the men went in (didn't say who the men were, only that they worked for the Kennedys) and lifted her up, rear end up. They took her own medication, diluted it, and put it into a syringe and injected that into the mucus membrane inside the bowel. To me, as a nurse, that meant that it went directly into the colon area since that membrane absorbs instantly, and thus no needle marks are evident.

The proof of how they did it as the men described, comes from the gray discoloration on Marilyn's face you can see in photos of her where they forced her down. When she died, the circulation stops and frees the liquids into the face. It's called "mottling."

Of course, I was petrified the next day and thought they would come after me but they didn't do so I went to my dad and told him what happened and he said, "Never tell anybody what happened." I never told my fiancé, or my husband, and the only ones I told before you are my two children.

Regarding Peter Lawford, the men told me, "He was involved, was with Bobby and the poor son of a bitch was never the same again."

Backing up her story, Donna O'Laughlin forwarded this photograph to me:

When one assesses the veracity of a source, character comes into play, and during my interaction with Donna, I was most impressed with her character. She even sent me a newspaper clipping detailing how her father traveled to Cuba while telling me the hilarious story that he surprised Fidel Castro with a box of cheap American cigars

At the Brodie Mountain Lodge. Left to right, back row—Ted Kennedy, Joan Kennedy, and Donna's father Don with his arm on Donna's mother's shoulder. Donna's uncle Jim and aunt Dorothy are positioned in the front row to the right side.

Donna had purchased for her dad that paled in comparison to the rich flavor of the Cuban cigars her father smoked during a dinner with the Cuban leader. Apparently, Castro feigned being upset with her dad to the extent of scaring him into believing he might be in danger before laughing about the incident.

City businessman talks trade with Castro

While Donna's account doesn't coincide with RFK's motive of silencing Marilyn based on her threat to hold a news conference exposing her love affairs with both Kennedys and the matters of national security as exposed in the CIA document created by James Angleton, no question exists that if Joe Kennedy ordered Marilyn's death, Bobby would have carried it out through operatives who did "dirty work for the Kennedys." Appeasing Jackie as a reason for Joe's order makes sense due to Marilyn having had "a tryst with JFK and Bobby" causing Jackie to be "mad and went to Joe Kennedy and said she wanted a divorce."

To this author, Donna's account seems quite credible especially in view of her, based on experience as a nurse, using the medical term "mottling" to describe Marilyn's facial condition when she died. The astute observation enhances the belief that Marilyn's death, as Dorothy Kilgallen may very well have surmised, happened because of what may be called a "double whammy": both Jackie's threat to leave JFK if Marilyn wasn't "punished" for the love affair with JFK and Bobby's need to silence the movie star due to the lethal nature of what Marilyn threatened to tell the media as noted in the CIA document. Either way, Marilyn was dead.

One point of interest hit me one day regarding the CIA document dated August 3, 1962. Sadly, the agents there, including Angleton, knew from the substance of the document that Marilyn was in danger. Unless they were brain dead (or most likely, didn't care), her threats against the Kennedys to go public with not only the love affairs but more importantly, the matters of national security, put a target on the film legend's back.

Common sense dictates that if RFK called his close friend, LA Police Chief William Parker and suggested/ordered him to do everything possible to make certain that Marilyn's death was designated as a suicide, that was a done deal based on Bobby's power base. To that end, Parker, it would appear, deftly decided, instead of launching any viable investigation into her death (there never was one conducted), to appoint a friendly psychiatric panel of experts to delve into Marilyn's mental state with the "verdict" mentioned that she was a loose cannon psychologically and prone to suicide. End of story, with Parker having already influenced medical examiner Curphey for the required result. Curphey then distanced himself from the autopsy report by appointing Dr. Noguchi to handle it, and the web of deception crawled into the "Probable Suicide" media announcement discussed before.

Dr. Cyril Wecht, called by famed attorney F. Lee Bailey, "the best medical expert witness in the country…you are going to get the truth… The bigger and tougher the case to solve, the more you need Cyril Wecht," compared what happened in Marilyn's case to that occurring when Kilgallen died. Dr. Wecht stated that "if Dr. Milton Helpern, the New York medical examiner, received the same sort of order that Dr. Curphey received, then the addition of 'Circumstances Undetermined' to the cause of Kilgallen's death was Helpern's hiding behind that wording." In each case, Wecht was surprised, but not that surprised, that neither Curphey nor Helpern handled the high-profile cases and instead handed them off to deputy/junior/assistant medical examiners Dr. Noguchi and Dr. James Luke, "since that way Curphey and Helpern still got the publicity but could pass off any criticisms to the younger junior MEs." [Author's note: When noted forensic scientist Dr. Cyril Wecht was asked about the autopsy "verdict" in Marilyn's case, he told the *Los Angeles Times*, "I have conducted more than 16,000 autopsies and seen many others, and I have never seen the word 'Probable' with the word 'Suicide' used in a report."]

When the question is asked as to why Bobby Kennedy would take a chance and actually appear in LA on the day Marilyn perished, I noted that one had to take into account how scared the attorney general had to be that she would follow through with the threats made per the CIA document and "tell all" to the media. One must thus consider RFK's frazzled mind at the time, since unlike all of those who had attempted to cut him down to size as now arguably the second most powerful man in America who expected one day to be president, he was about to be exposed by a woman he considered to be just a dumb blond actress. Attempting to shut her mouth, he must have believed, was worth the risk of being in LA on the fateful day when he had Marilyn silenced to save his own skin. And he was there; no doubt about that based on the accounts of objective witnesses with no reason to lie.

Adding to the intrigue of what happened to Marilyn is an interview I conducted with Michael Berryman, noted actor in films such as *One Flew Over the Cuckoo's Nest* and his creepy performance as Pluto in the uncompromising Wes Craven horror film *The Hills Have Eyes*. It is an account of his father, famous neurosurgeon Sloan Berryman's involvement in the death of Marilyn Monroe:

> We lived in Santa Monica and my father, Sloan, was a noted neurosurgeon who was called in to examine the body of Marilyn Monroe. I am unaware of why my dad was selected or what he discovered when examining her body, but I believe it must have had to do with brain analysis of some sort.
>
> I believe my dad examined Marilyn's body even before the coroner did. Unsure why but on three occasions, men in black coats arrived at our home in big black cars and then came to the door. I opened it and they showed me their credentials as Secret Service agents. I do not know why the Secret Service appeared.
>
> My father would have taken notes regarding examination of Marilyn's body, but those notes were probably destroyed through the years. I do remember him telling me, "Marilyn was murdered with an overdose of barbiturates administered by enema."

Sloan Berryman's account, that an enema was given to Marilyn, adds credence to the theory that the reason Eunice Murray was doing the wash when police arrived in the middle of the night is the soiled sheets. Some critics have disagreed but common sense needs to be the byword here.

One disturbing point of interest is worth mentioning. Despite extensive research, no comment of any kind, no condolences, nothing, have been discovered from the Kennedy family, not Joe, not John, not Bobby, not Rose, not Jackie, not Ethel, not Jean Kennedy Smith, not even Peter and Pat Lawford who hosted Marilyn at their Santa Monica beachfront home, about Marilyn Monroe's death. To them, it was like this remarkable woman, the one who lit up the world singing "Happy Birthday" to JFK, and who was friendly with Jean Kennedy Smith, never existed. Shame on them.

CHAPTER 17

From the June 2021 publication of *Collateral Damage* through my submitting the manuscript for this book, new evidence/information appeared on the horizon from various unusual sources, including reader tips from far and near, government documents I knew nothing about, eyewitness accounts like Donna O'Laughlin's, and so forth. In each case, this new material adds to the story that needs to be told about Marilyn Monroe's life and times and her death.

Since understanding the Kennedy family mindset was an avenue I had wanted to pursue for some time, I discovered an ignored book, purposely or not, entitled *The Kennedy Neurosis* by respected author Nancy Gager Clinch, later to be known as Nancy Land Gager. Published in 1973, just ten years beyond the date of the JFK assassination and thus quite credible timewise, in keeping with my dedication to utilizing information 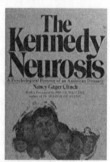 written close to when events of great importance occurred, Clinch takes on the Kennedy family with the subtitle reading, "A Psychological Portrait of an American Dynasty."

Though some critics at the time (one admitted he was a male chauvinist) attacked Clinch's analysis as being far too personal since she was a stout feminist and lacked post-graduate academic credentials in the field of psychology, a 1972 Kirkus Review at the time stated, "Never has the Kennedy mythos been so boldly or conjecturally dissected," leading the reviewer to praise the book "since it dims some of the healthy shine on that Camelot escutcheon [coat of arms]."

Clinch's credentials away from the academic world are first rate. At the time, she was codirector of the Center for Women Policy Studies in Washington, DC, and a member of the American Historical Association. A graduate of Wellesley College, she completed her studies at Oxford University.

This author's contribution to history provides a unique, reasonable perspective of the Kennedy family, permitting more introspection into their actions prior to and after both JFK and RFK were assassinated. Clinch wrote: "I do not see the Kennedy failures in performance as caused mainly by bad luck or the vagaries of politics and human nature. Rather, the factual failures were largely the result of psycho-historical circumstances that existed for the Kennedy sons even before they were born and that strongly affected the shaping of their individual characters."

Clinch then added that based on research of the inner workings of the Kennedy family, she saw in each son "unconscious emotional conflicts developed that were bound to disrupt their attitudes and actions as national leaders." She opined that was no excuse for personal responsibilities including those dealing with ethical matters of interest, behavior, it would seem, regarding what she called "the freedom both to choose responsibly and then to decide to do so." Calling political leadership psychologically moral, Clinch pointed out that the issue of concern regarding leaders like the Kennedys was whether the choices they made were due to "immature emotions."

As proof of the Kennedys' failure based on these emotions, she wrote that "In less than 10 years, this family produced a president of the United States, three United States senators, a U. S. Attorney General, and two additional presidential contenders." But, Clinch added, "the shining coin of success had its dark side," pointing out that of four Kennedy sons, three had died, one through war (Joseph Kennedy Jr.), two the result of assassination (JFK and RFK), and the fourth one (Ted), five years later, was disgraced when he was complicit in the death of a "young woman...under ambiguous circumstances." Further, Clinch wrote, "One daughter was killed in a plane crash and another daughter was confined since young adulthood in a home for the mentally retarded."

Regarding the so-called "Kennedy curse," Clinch, relying on hundreds of interviews with those close to the family, suggested that "many people, viewing the astonishing achievements on the one hand and the recurring disasters on the other, have seen the Kennedys as victims of a mysterious curse." To the contrary, the author believed the personal disasters were due to what she called, "the fate of all mortals who aspire too high—they are punished. This is the ancient Greek concept of *hubris*—or excessive pride and arrogance, which offends the gods," with the emphasis on the family's, especially the sons' "excessive pride and arrogance."

Continuing, her research had concluded that the Kennedy sons had been subjected to three "childhood patterns," what Clinch called "negative dynamics"—"patriarchy, competition and sexism." Regarding the destructive dynamic of "patriarchy," she singled out Papa Joe and his overwhelming dominance causing him to "not only set neurotically perfectionist goals in his off-springs' childhood, but to do so continuing through the sons' adult years." By doing so, Clinch's conclusion was that each of the sons was a mirror image of their father, and this observation is key since it is well known that Joe's lack of moral and ethical conduct stood out as a true failure as a father figure. One has only to view how he treated wife Rose by throwing his mistress, actress Gloria Swanson, in her face, being unscrupulous during the Depression as a money grabber when the rest of the US and the world was suffering, and even appeasing Adolf Hitler.

Finally, in this portion of the book, Clinch offered a most fascinating viewpoint of the essence of the Camelot aura surrounding the family. She wrote, "Camelot has often been used as a symbol for the Kennedys, but Franz Kafka's Castle would be more appropriate. The Kennedy Camelot was more an illusion of power than a reality, a dreamworld doomed to betrayal within. Like Kafka's hero, the Kennedys, in pursuing the illusory Camelot of omnipotence, succeeding only in erecting a Castle that imprisoned their true selves."

One may make what they wish of Clinch's observations, but it appears obvious that Joseph Kennedy projected neurosis—"mental, emotional, or physical reactions that are drastic and irrational"—into his sons' behavior up and down the line, especially by their having few ethics or morals, by the patriarch living his life and imposing his will through them. Each son, especially Jack and Bobby, suffered a fate that may be imposed on those with few ethics or morals—early death—with both dying through gunshot at the hands of assassins.

* * *

A second most important passage from author Clinch's profound 1973 book deals with substance for why the Kennedy sons, particularly Jack and Bobby, basically became, in essence, sexual predators during their adult lives. She wrote that the Kennedys believed they were privileged to always win due to their superiority. Clinch believed that the "Kennedy neurosis and neurotic contradictions of American society as a whole converged in what could be termed the Kennedys 'masculine mystique'—or, in contemporary language, the male chauvinism exhibited by all of the Kennedys."

As proof, Clinch pointed to the Kennedy father and sons as strongly attuned to the belief that men are "by nature" superior to women. She pointed to the Kennedy men being the only ones in the family selected to run for political office and that:

> All the Kennedy men were sexually promiscuous and tended to regard their wives as little more than attractive possessions and providers of "bed and board," giving emotional support when needed, bearing the full responsibility of raising offspring and engaging in the political activity considered appropriate to a supportive wife.

Clinch then pointed to Joe's extramarital conduct with Gloria Swanson, JFK's dalliances with many women, and the sexual activities of the other brothers. Perhaps as noteworthy, or one may say disturbing, are Clinch's strong words about the effect the Kennedys' father and sons' philandering had on the women in their lives, their wives. She wrote:

> The reactions of the Kennedy wives to their husbands' promiscuity have, of course, been largely concealed from public view. But memoirs of former Kennedy servants and other employees, and a few increasingly frank biographers, offer enough evidence to indicate the response of these dependent women—outer aloofness and a feigned ignorance, along with a good deal of repressed inner rage.

Recall these caustic words were written within ten years of JFK's assassination and within five of Robert's. They indicate what few people consider when detailing the Kennedy sons' cheating on their wives with mostly well-known paramours where they used the women for sex and then cast them aside as both JFK and especially RFK did with Marilyn. Some even laugh and say, "Wow, those two Kennedys were some studs" or something like that, not even considering the hurt the wives must have endured, especially when the sexual affairs were public knowledge. Shame on these two male chauvinists, shame on them for treating women, even their wives, with such disrespect with JFK having at one time spoken, it would seem for Bobby as well: "If I don't have sex *every day*, I get a headache."

Confirming Clinch's assessment are cold, hard facts: JFK had affairs with, among others, Judith Exner, whom he shared at the same time she was the mistress to Mafia boss Sam Giancana, society headliner Mary Pinchot Meyer, suspected spy Inga Arvad (proof existed she attended Herman Göering's wedding and was introduced to his best man, Adolf Hitler), actress Anita Ekberg, German call girl Ellen Rometsch, actress Gene Tierney, actress Marlene Dietrich, White House intern Mimi Alford, White House interns Priscilla Wear and Jill Cohen, also known as "Fiddle and Faddle," and of course, Marilyn Monroe. Bobby's conquests included Miami-based National Airlines flight attendant Amy Brandon, the owner of a prestigious Manhattan jewelry store, Barbara Marx, wife of actor Harpo Marx, such Hollywood stars as actresses Jayne Mansfield, Mia Farrow, and Lee Remick and singer Claudine Longet.

Of the brothers, former undersecretary of commerce Franklin Roosevelt Jr. told the *Washington Post*, "Everybody knew about the affairs. The two of them carried on like a pair of lovesick teenagers." No wonder, it would seem, since, according to acclaimed author and playwright as well as Ambassador to Italy Clare Boothe Luce, John Kennedy said to her, "Dad told all the [Kennedy] boys to get laid as often as possible."

Based on Clinch's observations and connecting the dots regarding JFK and RFK's extramarital affairs, is it any wonder that first Jack and then Bobby were, in fact, sexual predators seeking, like their father before them, trophy mistresses, and into their den of immorality came Marilyn Monroe, seeking love as Dorothy Kilgallen had written about in the aforementioned column entitled, "Marilyn, the Golden Girl, Loses Third Marriage, Pursuing Love." In effect, the powerful brothers took advantage of Marilyn based on their belief that, as Clinch wrote, "Men are, by nature, superior to women." Predictably, in line with their being supreme male chauvinists, the two men not only broke Marilyn's heart but, in RFK's case, orchestrated her death.

Clinch's words about the Kennedy men being womanizers of the first degree, believing women were inferior, triggers the question as to whether either JFK or RFK appreciated at all Marilyn's intellect or just wanted, as their father Joe, the trophy mistress. As proven in *Collateral Damage*, Marilyn was no "dumb blond," evidenced, at least in one instance, by not only being a voracious reader (she read, among other classics, *Ulysses* by James Joyce), but her being a worthy writer and a competent poet.

Perhaps the most important of Marilyn's writings other than the autobiographical *My Story*, a must-read, is preserved in the book *fragments*, a second must-read for anyone interested in the "true" Marilyn that is edited by Stanley Buchthal and Bernard Comment. Included are written answers she gave to an interviewer who, unfortunately, remains unknown. The famous movie star did not generally like interviews and, on most occasions, asked for the questions ahead of time. In this instance, the answers without the questions still provide insight into Marilyn's psyche at the time on many subjects of interest. The answers read in part:

> There was a pupil teacher relationship at the beginning of the marriage and I learned a great deal from it—a good marriage is a very delicate balance of many forces but there was much more to the marriage than that [apparently a question about her marriage to Arthur Miller]

> The love of my work and a few reliable human beings the hope of my future growth and development

> I am at ease with people I trust or admire or like the rest I'm not at ease with

> I love poetry and poets

> I have great feeling for all the persecuted ones in the world

> The lack of consistent love and caring. A mistrust and fear of the world was the result [apparently about her childhood]

And one of her poems highlighted in *fragments* read:

feel what I feel
within myself – that is trying to
become aware of it
also what I feel in others
not being ashamed of my
feeling, thoughts – or ideas
realize the thing that they are –

This was Marilyn the human being in action, not Marilyn the movie star. In the spirit of how I had "humanized" spiritual guru Thomas Merton in my book *Beneath the Mask of Holiness* while I was at seminary regarding his "human side" when he found love with a student nurse in part "qualifying" me for doing the same about Marilyn, I had humanized her in *Collateral Damage* so readers would know what the world lost when she died. Since the publication of that book, readers of my previous books have forwarded bits of memorabilia about her. They include:

Marilyn and Elvis Presley

A rare photo of Marilyn and Elvis Presley at an early age. Who could have known that years later, each of them would die too soon?

A rare photo of Marilyn with singer Ella Fitzgerald whose career the famous actress had boosted during the 1950s when Ella was not allowed to play at Mocambo, Hollywood's most popular nightclub, because she was African-American. Marilyn, who was a big fan of Fitzgerald's, called the owner and said that if he booked Ella, Marilyn would be there every night, which guaranteed huge press coverage. He booked Fitzgerald, and Marilyn was there, front table, every night. Ella praised Marilyn, stating, "After that, I never had to play a small jazz club again. She was an unusual woman, a little ahead of her time. And she didn't know it."

Of interest to me was viewing a rare photo depicting an introspective Marilyn apparently reading away at her Beverly Carlton Santa Monica apartment. Even then, the glamorous side of her shines through.

A special letter from acclaimed author John Steinbeck (*The Grapes of Wrath*) requesting Marilyn's autograph:

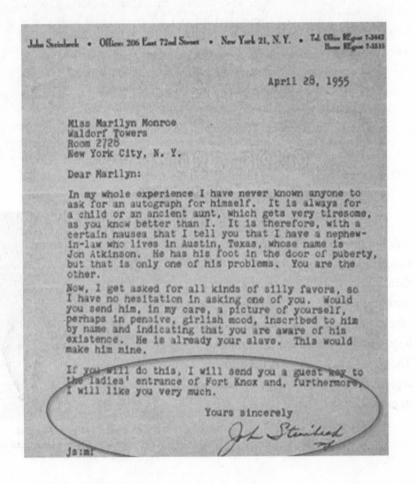

A fresh account of Marilyn Monroe by actor George Chakiris, the Academy Award and Golden Globe winner, appeared in his 2021 book, *My West Side Story*. He appeared with her in 1953's *Gentlemen Prefer Blondes* and 1954's *There's No Business Like Show Business*.

Regarding his recollections, Chakiris wrote:

She was very quiet. She seriously concentrated on her work and trained tirelessly to give her best performances. Whenever we would stop filming a scene, many cast members would just go back to their dressing rooms. But she would just go right back to her starting position, ready to begin again. That's how concentrated she was in her work. And I really admired her for that. Not everyone did that.

I do remember one time while filming "There's No Business Like Show Business," a little boy approached her and she greeted him with a huge smile on her face. And she took the time to talk to him. I watched her and she was practically glowing. It was such a sweet, genuine connection she had with this child. She wasn't like "leave me alone, I'm busy." She was generous to take time from her day just for a child.

I never understood how people could say such terrible things about her over the years. I can only speak from my experience, as just a dancer in the background, but my impression was that she was very sweet, kind, incredibly polite and eager to work hard as the rest of us. I always appreciated that about her. I have a feeling that if we had the chance to become friends, she would have been just the same. But truthfully, we were just there to work.

One version of how the photo to the right originated is that at a party at the Beverly Hills Hotel in which Monroe, then twenty-four, allegedly showed up in a revealing red dress, a columnist declared it "cheap and vulgar," adding she would have been better served wearing "a potato sack." The 20th Century Fox PR department then capitalized on the moment by putting her in one.

A rare photo—Marilyn Monroe, age twenty-four, wearing a potato sack, 1951

* * *

To my surprise, although "surprises" in my life became the norm long ago, in February 2022 I happened across new information that added context to Marilyn's appearance at Madison Square Garden to sing "Happy Birthday" to JFK while learning how the powerful Kennedy family, especially Joe, could cover up most anything while also exposing an angry side of Robert Kennedy I had never been aware of before. According to Seymour Hersh in his book *The Dark Side of Camelot*, just as the matter of whether Marilyn could sing the song was in progress, a full-blown scandal surrounding JFK was in full bloom.

The potential scandal had been brewing for some time and surrounded the suspicion that JFK had married a Palm Beach, Florida, socialite named Durie Malcolm, called by many in the media, "JFK's secret first bride." Hersh quoted Charles Spalding, "a retired New York stockbroker who had been a Kennedy intimate since World War II," as being the first to acknowledge for Hersh that he and other insiders had known for years that the rumor was true: Kennedy and Malcolm were married, albeit very briefly in 1947 prior to his marrying Jackie in 1953.

Hersh reported that when Joe Kennedy learned the marriage could be true, he had a "hemorrhage," especially since Malcolm had been twice divorced. Ordered by Joe that the matter be "taken care of," Spalding told Hersh he "removed the [marriage] papers" from the Palm Beach County Courthouse.

Hersh then quoted a reliable source who requested anonymity but who believed the marriage had happened, causing JFK to be a bigamist if he never divorced Malcolm, and thus tried to talk the author out of including it the book. The source told him, "You sit down and think about it. Jack was never married legally to Jackie, and all that's left of Jack are his two children and his grandchildren." Telling about the marriage would make Caroline and John Jr. "not legal. That's a very disruptive thing to do. The children had a hard enough time as it is—they lost their father."

JFK denied the marriage ever took place, telling Clark Clifford, a Washington, DC, attorney and political insider, "All I know is that some years ago,

I knew very briefly a young woman named Durie Malcolm. I think I had two dates with her. One may have been a dinner date in which we went dancing. The other, to my recollection was a football game." Malcolm, for her part, apparently signed an affidavit stating "I was not married to John F. Kennedy" while later, in 1996, telling the London's *Sunday Times*, "I'll tell you why, if you want to know the truth. I didn't care for those Irish micks, and old Joe was a terrible man."

Durie Malcolm

Spalding's wife Betty, Hersh stated, supported her husband's recollections based on Eunice Kennedy, Jack's younger sister, stating that "there was a drunken party and they [Jack and Durie] went off to a justice of the peace and got married" and "claiming that Malcolm 'wouldn't sleep' with Jack 'unless he married her.'" Later, Malcolm admitted, Hersh wrote, that the marriage "was true" and Hersh was told that "Joe went ballistic and got everything eradicated—all the records wiped out."

JFK and Jackie early on in their marriage

Deciding in April 2022 to investigate further into the "bigamist" claims, I discovered documents of certain interest at the National Archives with the apparent date of 11/14/61. Marked "Personal and Confidential," it was addressed to "Director, FBI," (Hoover) and CC'd to "Asst. Dir. C. D. De Loach."

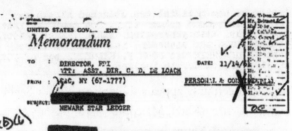

If one carefully reads the documents, the first paragraph begins with "[redacted] made available the attached excerpts from what appears to be a genealogy of the Blauvelt family, published in 1957, United States Library of Congress Catalog Card No. 56-10936." Of great interest is the next paragraph, one that reads:

> Copies of the material are attached hereto and it will be noted that in the left-hand column of p. 884 there is listed as a member of the family, 11th generation, DURIE (KERR) MALCOLM. [redacted] pointed out the statement is contained therein that the third husband of DURIE was JOHN F. KENNEDY, son of JOSEPH P. KENNEDY, one time Ambassador to England.

This information certainly appears to confirm author Seymour Hersh's account, one that Durie (Kerr) Malcom's third husband "was John F. Kennedy, son of Joseph P. Kennedy, one time ambassador to England." In the accompanying document, this having happened is noted again along with the addition of "There were no children of [Durie's] second or third marriages."

Notice that there is no information provided that the Durie/JFK marriage resulted in divorce, and if true, as Hersh had alleged, JFK was indeed a bigamist when he married Jackie, nullifying that marriage. Regarding who forwarded the documents to the FBI, the third paragraph of the memo identifies the person as a "he" with it then pointing out that "he said he was not going to publish this information but he thought it was significant and that it should be called to the Bureau's attention." The source did not divulge where he obtained "the material" but that "he knew of another person, unidentified, who had the information available and he did not know whether or not the other person would attempt to publicize it."

Finally, he "said he did not feel it would do the country any good to publicize the alleged first marriage."

Who was this source, and what was his motive to forward along what may be called a "juicy" story, one that would have shocked the American public, about the president of the United States? It appears to have been sent along in November 1961, nearly a year after JFK took office and based on my research, no media attention resulted.

Since the information was sent directly to Director Hoover, one must wonder what he decided to do with it, whether he directed agents to investigate perhaps even to the extent of checking the records in Palm Beach. What does seem certain is that the fact that it appeared JFK may have been a bigamist would be included in Hoover's "dirty secrets" file, which he used when necessary to let public officials, up to and including presidents, know that if they did not behave as he wished them to, the "dirty secrets" could lead to their downfall from grace.

This said, the bottom line is that once again, Joe Kennedy did his duty: covering up the fact that his son John was a bigamist.

* * *

JFK being a bigamist or not, as a backdrop to Marilyn singing "Happy Birthday" to JFK, rumors of the Kennedy-Malcolm marriage resurfaced over the years, even to the early sixties in several of the media, including the prestigious *Parade* magazine. Efforts to debunk those rumors by the Kennedys continued and Hersh wrote,

> The mini-crisis did not prevent the Kennedy brothers from going all out to get Marilyn Monroe to appear at a May 1962 Madison Square Garden rally in honor of the president's forty-fifth birthday. Monroe was then shooting Something's Got to Give for 20th Century Fox; the film was over budget and far behind schedule.

As confirmation of Robert Kennedy's involvement not only as a lover of Marilyn at that time but also inserting himself into her business affairs, Hersh detailed, through an interview with Milton Gould, a Fox attorney, that Marilyn was ordered not to attend the fundraising event in New York City. The attorney then received a phone call from Robert Kennedy asking Gould to "waive his objections." Gould resisted and of the call told Hersh, "Kennedy got very abusive. I said 'we're just not going to do it,' and he called me a Jew bastard and hung up the phone on me. He never apologized."[14]

---

14 Like father, like son, since in *The Poison Patriarch* I included a reputable account by Kennedy friend Morton Downey Jr. He told author Ronald Kessler, "Joe Kennedy's feeling toward Jews was that the only way he could be a success was that every day when he got up, he would focus on one deal involving a Jew, and he would win that deal. That was his whole driving spirit." Downey Jr. added, "Joe and his father would refer to Jews by a code word—'Canadian geese,' apparently because of a perception that Jews have long noses."

Regarding the marriage of JFK to Malcolm, the Kennedy machine rolled out Ben Bradlee, who published a September 14, 1962, article in *Newsweek* (Marilyn would be dead by then) dismissing all of the rumors. Hersh wrote, "As the Kennedys hoped…once the falsehood had been exposed to public light; it was reduced to a curious footnote to the Kennedy legend."

As I concluded my research into the matter, I noticed a familiar name at the end of Hersh's account of the suspected marriage. It was John Sherman Cooper, the respected senator from Kentucky who was a member of the Warren Commission and, as will be explained, pivotal in understanding the inner workings of that commission.

What author Hersh had done was to connect, of all people, Cooper's second wife, Lorraine, to the very man, Thomas Shevlin, a Palm Beach socialite, whom, according to Hersh, Joe Kennedy persuaded to marry Durie Malcolm once the noise died down about JFK's alleged marriage to her.

The kicker was that Lorraine Cooper's first husband had been Shevlin, and with this in mind, Hersh chronicled a dinner at the Coopers' years after the assassination hosted by Lorraine and John. Quoting Maxine Cheshire, a society reporter for the *Washington Post*, who was there, Hersh wrote, "We were eating soft-shell crabs in her dining room in Georgetown. And Lorraine told how Jack [Kennedy] would laugh at dinner parties and say, 'Lorraine and I are related by marriage.' And then the two of them would die laughing, and nobody else knew what they were talking about."

Efforts to reach Seymour Hersh, age eighty-four, have proved futile, and thus why he included the episode at the Coopers' home without a date in time is unknown and thus certainly provides no explanation as to why JFK would say that "Lorraine and I are related by marriage," since such appears impossible. This said, was the president confirming what everyone, including those inside the family of Malcolm, suspected—that he had been married to Durie, that the marriage had never been annulled (to annul it meant admitting the marriage once existed), that his children were bastards since he was a bigamist, thus nullifying his marriage to Jackie?

Of course, stepping in to cover up the sorry episode was Papa Joe, the family fixer. If he could fix an election as he did in 1960, covering up JFK's stupid conduct was easy pickings.

If any more credence to embracing author Nancy Gager Clinch's insight into the Kennedy family—a disoriented, dysfunctional clan for certain—is required, an episode described in bestselling author Barbara Leaming's superb book, *Kick Kennedy: The Charmed Life and Tragic Death of the Favorite Kennedy Daughter*, confirms the seediness of Joe Kennedy to a new level. Describing Kick, short for Kathleen, as "the incandescent life force of the fabled Kennedy family, her father's acknowledged 'favorite of all the children,' and her brother Jack's 'psychological twin,'" Leaming then chronicled Kick's life as had author Lynne McTaggart, who observed in her book *Kathleen Kennedy: Her Life and Times*, that "of all nine Kennedy children, she was the only one who didn't march down the prescribed road."

Nicknamed after her great-aunt, whom Kick said "was a lot of fun. She was a kick," Kick's life turned from beauty to sorrow after she met William Cavendish, set to become the future Duke of Devonshire in England where Joe Kennedy was serving as ambassador to the US. Deeply in

A young JFK with Kathleen Kennedy

love with Cavendish, Kick rebelled against returning to the United States following Germany invading Poland in 1939.

Despite the Kennedy family's objections, Kick returned to England as a Red Cross volunteer and she and "Billy," as he was called, resumed the love affair. Warned by her mother, Rose, that marrying outside the church (Billy wasn't Catholic) was a mortal sin, Kick nevertheless married her true love in May 1944 only to have him die a few months later due to a German sniper's steady aim.

Kick herself then died when she and her new love, Peter Fitzwilliam, a married man, were killed in a plane crash in France. Instead of celebrating her life, the Kennedys put the hush- hush out due to their being afraid of the scandal that could emanate from Kick's relationship with Fitzwilliam, more evidence of the diabolical aspects of the family, since at this point in time JFK had aspirations for higher office.

The incident that author Leaming portrays in her book reads as follows: "Rose lived with a husband who was not only compulsively unfaithful, but who went so far as to parade certain of his women in front of her; and she lived with sons Joe Junior and Jack, who thought nothing of mocking and disparaging a parent they found cold and at times absurd."

Leaming then added:

> Kick adamantly refused to join her elder brothers in this harsh treatment of Rose. On one occasion, not long before the family had been transplanted to England, she had made a great scene when old Joe Kennedy brought one of his many girlfriends to the family table at Cape Cod. Risking the rage of the father she adored, Kick had indignantly objected to the mistress's presence.

Summing up, Leaming wrote: "Rose, for her part, had long endeavored to armor herself against the potential for embarrassment. Even when Joe paraded his girlfriends in front of her, she simply 'acted as if they didn't exist.'" Leaming did point out that during the time Rose was pregnant with Kick, she attempted to leave Joe, but Rose's father wouldn't let her do so.

CHAPTER 18

While the music of Francis Albert Sinatra continues to mesmerize millions on a daily basis, consider this: that his life intersected with those of Marilyn Monroe, John F. Kennedy, and Dorothy Kilgallen, and each of them were killed at an early age.

To better understand the rat's nest Marilyn Monroe fell into when she fell under the spell of first John and then Robert Kennedy via Sinatra, inspecting his life and times in a concentrated fashion instead of piecemealing it provides stronger insight into the complex man he was from early on to the day he died on May 14, 1998. Other than his contribution to music through his recordings, Sinatra had few, if any, ethical or moral values, treated many women like garbage, was a thug who threatened anyone who disagreed with him including members of the media, and owed the start of his career and its lengthy run to Mafia killers with whom he associated throughout his life during eighty-two years on the face of the earth despite his denials at every turn.

The toupee-less Frank Sinatra

With this in mind, one must wonder how Sinatra was able to have at least one foot in four different "worlds"—entertainment, politics, relationships with various women, and associating with gangsters—and yet survived without someone killing him along the way. Such an observation causes it to seem like Frank's life was more fiction than fact, but if there was one main ingredient that stands out it is that he was a survivor. Even today, as it is with the Kennedys, especially JFK and Bobby, people do not want to believe the worst about Frank but instead enjoy his crooning without even a nod to the evil he caused in the world.

To be certain, Sinatra was, as George Noory, the esteemed host of *Coast to Coast* radio, wisely pointed out during an interview with this author, an "enigma." To that end Sinatra was a singer, an actor, a part-time political groupie of sorts, a common thug, a womanizer of the first degree and, at one point, a bagman for the Mafia. As expert a liar as anyone who ever lived, he continually denied any affection for gangsters, but photographs like this one where he exhibited the famous Sinatra smile amidst several of his Mafia "friends" are proof positive of his underworld connections.

Gianni Russo, previously mentioned as the author of *Hollywood Godfather* with Patrick Picciarelli, told me, "I was there that night at the Westbury Music Fair [in the mid-1950s] in Westbury, Long Island, when that photo was taken. The Gambino crime family controlled the ticket sales and there was a big scandal and a few people went to jail because of them scalping the Sinatra concert tickets and many other performers' tickets."

Frank Sinatra (back row, white shirt) and his mobster friends

Russo added, "The gentlemen in the photo include Carlo Gambino, Paul Castellano, Greg DePalma, and Tommy Bilotti. Castellano and Bilotti were shot in front of Sparks Steak House in New York City by John Gotti's crew. That's when Gotti took control of the Gambino crime family and announced that he was now the boss."

An LAPD report confirmed Sinatra's "relationship" with mobster Mickey Cohen (recall him being a close friend and client of Melvin Belli). It detailed discovering Sinatra's address in Cohen's personal address and telephone book. The memo also described how on December 23, 1946, "Mickey Cohen asked Jimmy Tarantino to get Frank Sinatra to come over to Cohen's house...And Cohen later attended one of Sinatra's broadcasts where he sat on stage." And finally, "that on one occasion Cohen accused an unknown individual of having threatened Sinatra."

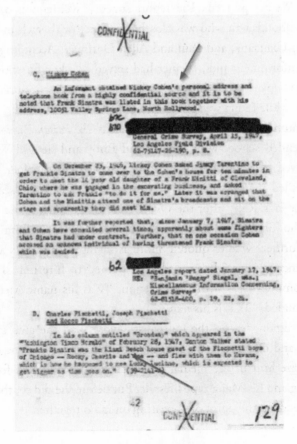

In the final paragraph, confirmation of Kilgallen's alleging that Sinatra and the Fischetti brothers were "friends," as previously noted, is confirmed through the memo mention of a column, written by Denton Walker in the February 28, 1957 edition of the *Washington Times Herald*. Walker wrote: "Frank Sinatra was the Miami Beach house guest of the Fischetti boys of Chicago—and flew with them to Havana, which is how he happened to see [mobster] Lucky Luciano, which is expected to get bigger as time goes on." What Walker meant by "get bigger" is unknown.

Sinatra's interaction with underworld characters even stretched to questions as to how Melvin Belli became Jack Ruby's attorney. Surfacing in the HSCA report was Los Angeles record producer Michael Shore, president of Reprise Records, a company owned by Frank Sinatra. Shore, dubbed by Sinatra "nothing short of a genius," was not only a friend of Earl Ruby's, but Irwin Weiner as well. The report stated: "Weiner was a prominent underworld bondsman who was closely associated with such men as James Hoffa, Sam Giancana, and Paul and Allen Dorfman. According to Federal State law enforcement files, Weiner had served as a key functionary in the relationship between the Chicago Mafia and various corrupt union officials, particularly while Hoffa was president of the Teamsters Union."

Continuing, the report, one I included in *The Poison Patriarch*, stated: "Shore attended school with Weiner and Ruby and he and Weiner have been involved in a number of business transactions." Weiner, the report added, recalled that Michael Shore discussed with him the search for an attorney for Jack Ruby after the Oswald shooting. Weiner said Shore told him "that he [Shore] had arranged with Earl to try to get him some legal help in." Further, Weiner quoted Shore as saying, "There was an attorney in San Francisco that I knew and Earl wanted to hire him. I forget his name." Prompted later with the question, "Was his name Melvin Belli?" Shore responded, "That is his name."

To be certain, few in the journalistic world had the guts to stand up to Sinatra, and of those, only one, Dorothy Kilgallen, had the courage to really criticize him in the media, to hold Frank accountable for both his womanizing and his Mafia-type lifestyle. But before she did so, the two were actually friends to the point of appearing on radio together.

Kilgallen was also a fan of Sinatra's music, often featuring him in her Voice of Broadway column. Like many other celebrities, she flocked to popular Broadway nightclubs including the Copacabana where mobster Frank Costello, allegedly the Copa's true owner through a front man, held court. Frank Sinatra often appeared there as well as J. Edgar Hoover, the pug-faced, power-hungry FBI director who enjoyed being treated as a celebrity despite having nothing to do with the entertainment arena. Of note was that Dean Martin and Jerry Lewis first launched their act at the Copa, and the Barry Manilow song "Copacabana" was named after the trendy nightclub.

Sinatra and Kilgallen in happier days

During this time, no better evidence of Frank and Dorothy's friendship exists than her permitting the singer of such hit songs as "My Way," "That's Life," and "It Was a Very Good Year" to write her Voice of Broadway column when she vacationed. The announcement stated, "Dorothy Kilgallen is on vacation. Her guest columnist today is the eminent crooner, Frank Sinatra."

Sinatra then began the column with the headline, "The Business of Warbling" before adding, "The question I run across most frequently is 'What is the most important experience in becoming a singer?'" He continued, "Well,

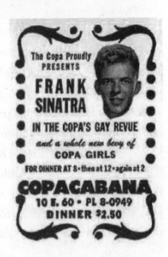

206

thanks to Dorothy and the column she's given me, I'll attempt to answer that and in doing so, I'll perhaps give some young boy or girl just starting out some advice that will help—advice based on my own experience."

Another indication of Kilgallen's admiration for Sinatra is based on a *Photoplay* article in June 1944 entitled, "The Stars I'd Like to Be Married To." Number one was Sinatra with her comment, "He heads the list just because, well, you guess why: Frank's used to getting screamed at by young fans, so he's less likely to fall prey to the next pretty wolf in sheep's clothing who tries to steal him away, and besides, he'll sing to you."

During this time, Dorothy Kilgallen decided to make a prediction of the upcoming presidential 1960 election in her Voice of Broadway column. She wrote that JFK would win since he "was adorable on television…his promises and connections would get him the labor vote and the machine Democrats… Sammy Davis' support would guarantee him the Negro vote…the majority of Jews would go to the polls for him, and no true Sinatra fan would dare vote for anyone else."

Frank Sinatra and JFK, circa 1960

After a New Year's Eve appearance at the Copa, Kilgallen wrote, "The list of celebrities who can't get in to see Sinatra is almost more glittering than the roster of those who make it in. Latest victims of the velvet rope include Zsa Zsa Gabor, international playboy Porfirio Rubirosa, and Marlon Brando." And just before the 1960 election, Kilgallen's Voice of Broadway column included a jab at Sinatra, a sign of things to come:

> Only a few months ago, Sen. Jack Kennedy had the crying towel out because "those columnists" were linking him with Frank Sinatra and the Senator protested the association was unfair because he "had only met him a few times in California…" So last week the Democratic candidate from the presidency was the guest of honor at a private little dinner given by Frank. No reason why he shouldn't of course but why try to kid the press.

Unfortunately, in early 1956, the friendship between the two superstar celebrities had begun to falter and a feud of unapparelled proportions was birthed when Kilgallen wrote several scathing articles about Sinatra, the Kennedy family friend and Mafia-connected singer, for a *Journal-American* series titled "The Real Frank Sinatra

Sinatra and the Fischetti brothers

Story." Included in the article was the mention of Sinatra being friends with such killers such as the dangerous Fischetti brothers, Rocco and Charles, cousins of the legendary Al Capone.

Regarding Sinatra's lifestyle, Kilgallen wrote:

> Success hasn't changed Frank Sinatra. When he was unappreciated and obscure, he was hot-tempered, egotistical, extravagant, and moody. Now that he is rich and famous, with the world on a string and sapphires in his cufflinks, he is still hot-tempered, egotistical, extravagant, and moody.

Striking back, Sinatra featured Kilgallen in his nightclub act. He told audiences she "looks like a chipmunk."

Sinatra must have been jealous of Kilgallen's extended popularity. Johnnie Ray's biographer, Jonny Whiteside, observed, "Rules must be followed. That was how they played it in Gotham. But Dorothy Kilgallen was in a position to change the rules anytime it suited her—and everyone from the Mayor on down to [mobster] Frank Costello who occasionally joined her table at P. J. Clarke's, knew it."

In her articles, which co-panelist Bennett Cerf praised as "wonderful" on the February 26, 1956 airing of *What's My Line?*, Kilgallen detailed Sinatra's various romances with, among others, Gloria Vanderbilt, Kim Novak, Lana Turner, and Ava Gardner. She wrote:

> A few of the women, like Ava and Lana, were public idols themselves and priceless examples of feminine beauty. Many more, of course, have been fluffy little struggling dolls of show business, pretty and small-waisted and similar under the standard layer of peach-colored Pan-Cake makeup. [They

are] starlets who never got past first base in Hollywood, assorted models and vocalists, and chorus girls now lost in the ghosts of floor shows past. Others belonged to the classification most gently described as tawdry.

In turn, Sinatra derided Kilgallen's "chinless" appearance, dubbing her "the chinless wonder." She responded by writing more about his Mafia connections.

* * *

If Frank Sinatra's ensuing over-the-top behavior toward Kilgallen indicated his low-life status in spades, his meddling in the 1960 presidential election projected him into a new frontier, that of changing the course of history through his connecting two of his worlds: politics and the underworld. At the time, Sinatra was buddy-buddy with the Kennedy family but especially close to JFK, who admired Frank's womanizing and his freewheeling lifestyle, even his connections to the Mafia. Frank was the playboy the future president wanted to be and thus the two appeared many times in public both before the election and afterwards.

Regarding Sinatra having been "recruited" to become involved in the elections, Papa Joe Kennedy was a realist, as noted, and knew Richard Nixon would occupy the White House instead of Joe's son unless JFK won the electoral votes in Illinois and West Virginia. Having been a fixer most of his adult life, Joe knew that certain mafiosi he was familiar with could change the outcome, and the patriarch reached out to Sinatra, who Joe knew had his fingers in the underworld.

The result (more details in *The Poison Patriarch*) was that the crooner, heeding Joe's orders, acted as a go-between by connecting the Kennedy campaign with Chicago crime boss Sam Giancana, a close "associate" to New Orleans Mafia don Carlos Marcello. Through Giancana's influence in both states but especially in Chicago where Giancana's close friend, Mayor Richard J. Daley, ruled, voters were bribed to back JFK and in some cases, voters cast those votes more than once. In the end, John F. Kennedy, thanks in great part to Francis Albert Sinatra's intervention, defeated Richard Nixon and became president based on the smallest margin in the twentieth century.

As part of the deal with Giancana and his Mafia "associates," Sinatra had to have been privy to "the deal with the devil" that Joe Kennedy made to the effect that if JFK won, the new administration would not pursue those underworld figures for years to come. Then, as noted, Joe broke his word, had JFK appoint Bobby attorney general, and one of RFK's first actions was to illegally deport Marcello and prosecute Giancana for tax fraud.

Based on this double cross, the drum roll had begun resulting in JFK's assassination in 1963 with the tragedy arguably never occurring had Sinatra not persuaded Giancana and his Mafia "friends" to believe Joe could be trusted. Indirectly then, Sinatra, by meddling in the election, was responsible for JFK's death, but he was never held accountable at the time, and his actions are never condemned by those who worship his music today.

Proof of Mafia intervention through Sinatra's actions during the 1960 presidential election comes from, as first noted in *Collateral Damage*, a little-known book by Charles Higham entitled *Rose*, a biography of Rose Kennedy where he touched on the West Virginia "swindle" that was bypassed by authors and historians favoring the Kennedy clan. Based on primary-source witnesses, some of the more than four hundred interviewed, Higham said that Rose was discouraged from campaigning in West Virginia because the state was anti-Catholic, "a desperately poor area, with mass poverty and unemployment, in which the Greenbrier Hotel resembled the Palace of Versailles at the time of the French Revolution."

Thus, the Kennedy Catholicism and wealth would be a detriment to gaining much-needed votes there.

This was not, however, the real reason Rose never set foot in West Virginia, Higham stated. It was because "Bobby invited a Las Vegas mobster to the state, where he was authorized to use criminal tactics in insuring votes," a plan originated by Giancana and approved by RFK. Regarding Rose's knowledge of this happening, Higham wrote, "She must be protected from knowing this at all costs."

* * *

Unfortunately for Marilyn Monroe, Frank Sinatra's seediness, his lack of moral and ethical values, became part of her life. "The Marilyn and Frank" story could take hundreds of pages to explain but the relationship would lead directly, as proven in this book and *Collateral Damage*, to Sinatra's becoming, at the very least, an enabler regarding Marilyn's murder in 1962.

Proof of Marilyn's connection to Sinatra and to Peter Lawford, JFK and RFK's brother-in-law in 1961, comes from this photo taken at Lawford's Santa Monica, CA, beach house. Pat Kennedy Lawford stands to the left with husband Peter sitting while Sinatra stands next to Marilyn and across from where actress Shirley MacLaine is sitting. The beach house was where Marilyn fell into the nest of the Kennedy brothers in the early 1960s by meeting them there.

Deciding a change of scenery might brighten her day, Marilyn had left the East Coast for Brentwood, California, where she made one of the worst mistakes of her life: dating Frank Sinatra for several months. Believing the move would help calm her worried mind, Marilyn purchased a home while agreeing to appear in the film *Something's Got to Give* costarring Dean Martin.

In December of 1953, presented with the opportunity to costar opposite Sinatra in the production of *Pink Tights*, she walked out of the production objecting to the script's role for her, to her lack of any director approval, and to the salary. Retaliating, 20th Century Fox, her studio at the time, suspended her.

In what would be their last appearance together, this one on the weekend before Marilyn died, she and Frank, along with Kennedy brother-in-law Peter Lawford, sat in the sun at the infamous Cal-Neva Resort teetering on the edge of California and Nevada near Reno.

Nevada Gaming Commission reports I examined seeking the most reliable sources have noted that the resort was owned by Frank Sinatra as the front man for "his friend of thirty years," mobster Sam Giancana. In fact, Marilyn had been detailed about her appearances at the resort, telling her friend Gianni Russo she occupied "cabin number 4, Sinatra cabin number 5," and that the Kennedy clan occupied "cabin number 3." Russo also said that "the Kennedy brothers, most notably John and Bobby, would go there often and be treated to a platoon of hookers, courtesy of Sinatra."

The infamous Cal-Neva Resort sign

American jazz and pop singer and pianist Buddy Greco's firsthand account as told to *Variety* was quite insightful. He reported, "When Marilyn arrived that Saturday, you'd never believe she had a care in the world. I was sitting with Frank, Peter Lawford, and a bunch of other people outside Frank's bungalow, when a limousine pulls up and this gorgeous woman in dark glasses steps out." Regarding Marilyn's attire, Greco said, "She's dressed all in green—everything green: coat, skirt, and scarf. Before I realized who it was, I thought: 'My God, what a beautiful woman. No taste in clothes, but what a beautiful woman!'"

Marilyn with Frank Sinatra at the Cal-Neva Lodge

Marilyn with Peter Lawford at Cal-Neva on the last weekend before she died

CHAPTER 19

At the January 1961 inauguration of JFK into the presidency, Dorothy Kilgallen attended the "Rat Pack" gala headlined by Frank Sinatra and his celebrity pals. She and Frank did not acknowledge each other's presence for obvious reasons.

Sinatra, who had ingratiated himself with all of the Kennedys, including, as noted, JFK's brother-in-law, Peter Lawford, had been most instrumental in setting up the entertainment for the inaugural. Among those performing were Harry Belafonte, Nat King Cole, and Sinatra himself.

In the February 2011 issue of *Vanity Fair*, an article by Todd S. Purdum titled "From This Day Forth" chronicled what the magazine called "a moveable, star-studded bash." Among the photographs presented was one depicting Sinatra sitting beside the new president at his inauguration.

Barely a year later, JFK was scheduled to visit Sinatra's compound in Palm Springs. Sinatra even went to the length of having constructed, Purdum noted, a heliport to handle the landing of Marine One. But when J. Edgar Hoover told Bobby Kennedy that JFK and Sam Giancana were sharing the same girlfriend, Judith Campbell Exner, and that Sinatra had been receiving telephone calls from her, JFK abruptly cancelled the visit, leaving Sinatra embarrassed over the slight.

Purdum said Sinatra never spoke to Peter Lawford, whom Sinatra blamed for the slight, again, an indication of Sinatra's wrath, adding the famous singer to the list—the long list, including Santo Trafficante, Sam Giancana, Carlos Marcello, and Mickey Cohen—who had long since lost any love for the new president and his brother Bobby who hounded each of them despite Joe Kennedy's promise not to do so.

Of the snub, Tina Sinatra told author Cari Beauchamp, "Dad was stunned when the administration began to prosecute the very people it had enlisted for help just the year before. He had gone to Sam Giancana out of friendship for Jack Kennedy and expected nothing back. What he did not expect was to be set up like a fool." Beauchamp added, "The rebuff of Sinatra sent reverberations deep into the mob, who had to wonder what was next."

Meanwhile, Marilyn, along with her prized dog Maf, given to her, as noted, by Sinatra, had moved into her new home in Brentwood, California, near Santa Monica. It had been purchased for $77,500 ($665,000 in modern currency). Marilyn paid for it partly in cash while assuming a mortgage for half the value. When she signed the documents, her face lit up like it was Christmas morning.

* * *

Meanwhile, one evening, Sinatra had walked by Kilgallen at the Stork Club. Noticing that she was wearing sunglasses, he dropped a dollar bill in her coffee cup. Then he said to a friend, "I always figured she was blind."

In another seething column answering a reader complaint about JFK being friendly with Sinatra, she called the singer "a successful tough guy who refers to women as 'broads' and gets off airplanes with a drink in his hand… in the true Sinatra fashion, no rules and plenty of booze and girls anywhere you look."

At an appearance at the Copacabana in New York City, Sinatra (called by Elvis Presley "a cretinous goon") hit Kilgallen with a nasty diatribe of his own. As a part of his act, he told the audience, "Dotty Kilgallen couldn't be here tonight. She's out shopping for a new chin." He then added to laughter and applause, "C'mon, let's all chip in and buy Dorothy a new chin," before lifting his glass toward the fans. "This is a toast to my enemies," Sinatra shouted before spitting the whisky to the floor. He then added, "That one was for Dorothy Kilgallen."

When friends told Sinatra that he was berating Kilgallen too often, he roared, "I'm not being rough enough." During a performance at the Sands Hotel, he held up a car key while asking the cheering audience, "Doesn't this look like Dorothy Kilgallen's profile?" Another quip was Sinatra telling his audience, "If you run into Kilgallen, do it drivin' a car."

Later, Sinatra, while performing at the Villa Venice outside Chicago with Dean Martin and Sammy Davis Jr., said, "I've met many, many male finks but I never met a female fink until I met Dorothy Kilgallen. How's that for an opener? I wouldn't mind if she was a good-looking fink. The town where she came from had a beauty contest when she was seventeen years old and nobody won."

After learning of Kilgallen's death from his PR man, Jim Mahoney, Sinatra showed little concern. He calmly said, "Dorothy Kilgallen's dead. Well, guess I got to change my whole act."

In November 1961, Kilgallen was asked by a *Time* magazine reporter about the rift with Sinatra and why he had gone to such extremes to bad-mouth her with the intent to soil the famed reporter's reputation with personal attacks on how she looked, deficiencies such as being the "chinless wonder." Kilgallen's answer was simple: "Sinatra's personal attacks are for one reason and one reason only: because I resisted his sexual advances." No specific information was provided, but apparently Sinatra never defended himself against the accusations.

While Sinatra definitely hated Kilgallen and had motive to see her eliminated, proving his culpability is difficult without new evidence surfacing. Certainly, his mob connections extending into NYC made it possible for him to order a "hit" on his archenemy, bringing to mind a quote from his mother Dolly. She had said of him, "Yes, my son is like me. You cross him, he never forgets."

Closer to the JFK assassination, FBI reports obtained through the Freedom of Information Act confirm that Sinatra gave Melvin Belli's client, Mickey Cohen, $20,000 ($150,000 in today's currency) just after the gangster's release from prison. Days later, Cohen received a cash gift from

Sinatra and his underworld "friends" at the Fontainebleau Hotel in 1968

Carlos Marcello, and the mobster was the first person that Cohen visited upon release from the penitentiary.

At one point, Sinatra visited Cohen's LA home requesting that the gangster attempt to mend the singer's ongoing feud with actress Ava Gardner. On another occasion when Sinatra's career was waning, Cohen organized a testimonial for him at the swank Beverly Hills Hotel. "I love Frank," Cohen said, "I have a very great respect for him, and even when he was at his worst, I was his best friend."

As noted in *Denial of Justice*, Sinatra's connections to Frank Costello and Mickey Cohen stretched from coast to coast. In California, Sinatra became close friends with Cohen after he assumed control of the LA Mafia. This happened following Bugsy Siegel's murder. Sinatra worshiped Siegel, the West Coast Mafia chief for Murder, Inc. Sinatra admitted he "wanted to emulate Siegel" with the "two men sharing certain similarities." These included being "notorious womanizers who took flamboyant lovers…traveled with entourages, possessed ferocious tempers, and had grandiose visions of empire-building."

According to the singer's FBI file I obtained through the Freedom of Information Act, Frank Sinatra "pimped" for John Kennedy. The notation read, "It was a known fact that the Sands Hotel [in Las Vegas] was owned by hoodlums and that while the Senator [Kennedy], Sinatra, Peter Lawford were there, show girls from all over town were running in and out of the Senator's suite."

Little question exists that Marilyn had an affair with the crooner as evidenced by her appearance at his performance at the Sands Hotel in June of the year before she died. An indication of the close nature of the relationship exists in the form of a memo distributed to the media at the time that I discovered in the National Archives. It read:

> Marilyn Monroe will be Mr. Sinatra's guest. It is Mr. Frank Sinatra's intention that Miss Monroe be accorded the utmost privacy during her brief stay at the Sands. She will be registered in Mr. Sinatra's suite. Under no circumstances is she or Mr. Sinatra to be disturbed by telephone calls or visitors before two p.m.

Regarding Sinatra's Las Vegas "life," the Vegas casino boss previously quoted about Ron Pataky, who likely set up Dorothy Kilgallen for the kill, told this author in April 2020, "Frank certainly did care about Marilyn. He had a side to him that wanted to look out for the injured, and she was one of them. I heard he even paid the bills for a psychiatrist she was seeing."

Nearly one year before Marilyn was found dead, a photograph of the two aboard Sinatra's yacht was taken. It showed Marilyn, wearing a white blouse and white pants, her eyes hidden behind sunglasses, next to Frank. The expression on her face is a pensive one as she listens to the suntanned singer.

Marilyn and Frank on his yacht

This calm, attentive look on Sinatra's face contrasts with the rough-and-tumble Sinatra's temper, one that had wreaked havoc on many a member of the media when they intruded on his lifestyle. In one instance he had beaten up a Hollywood reporter, but each time, when criminal charges appeared on the horizon, his influential friends in higher places made the charges go away.

One disturbing account of Sinatra, a Mafia wannabe like Ruby attorney Melvin Belli, is included in singer Paul Anka's book, *My Way*. He wrote: "There was the night in 1967 when Frank ran up a $500,000 gambling debt at the Sands, where he was headlining, then disappeared for the weekend. He certainly didn't come back apologetic."

Continuing, Anka said, "Sinatra seized one of the golf carts used for luggage, plunked his wife, Mia Farrow, in the passenger seat, and drove it into the glass entryway, shattering it." Anka says Sinatra wasn't angry at the moment, just very, very drunk. So drunk he kept trying to set fire to curtains in the lobby but couldn't manage to start a blaze. But soon afterward, Anka writes, "Sinatra was furious enough to call for a hit on the manager of the Sands, Carl Cohen. Howard Hughes had taken over, and the game had changed. Sinatra was being refused his gratis markers, and he was used to getting $50,000 worth of free chips."

As Anka described it, Sinatra jumped on a blackjack table, bringing all the action in the casino to a halt as he raged and cursed. Anka and Sinatra then moved to the coffee shop, where Cohen showed up to make peace. Anka wrote, "The first thing Sinatra did was hurl a chair at Cohen's security guard. Still, Cohen tried to calm him, explaining that Hughes was in charge and certain things couldn't be done. Sinatra responded by ripping away the tablecloth, spilling scalding hot coffee into Cohen's lap."

Anka also revealed the sordid details of the Rat Pack (Frank Sinatra, Dean Martin, Sammy Davis Jr., Joey Bishop, and Peter Lawford) in his memoir. At one point, Anka recalled that after Sinatra embarrassed Carl Cohen, he punched Sinatra in the face—and the singer's dental caps flew out of his mouth. Anka helped hustle Sinatra out before the police arrived. Within an hour Frank boarded a Learjet flight to LA, where he got his teeth repaired and plotted revenge. "[Sinatra] puts the word out to the boys he wants Carl dead," Anka wrote. "But the boys said no. You have to understand, the mob still ran the place, and Carl was one of the boys from Cleveland."

On many occasions, when Sinatra was accused of a crime, victims and witnesses suddenly disappeared or dropped charges when paid to do so. Besides being a big star, one must wonder whether his Kennedy family connection protected him from arrest or even imprisonment.

Amazingly enough, one primary source who witnessed the Sinatra method of dealing with those who offended him was Peter Lawford. When a violent argument between the two men happened after Lawford dined with Sinatra's love interest, Ava Gardner, Lawford said of the crooner, "I was panicked. I mean I was really scared. Frank's a violent guy and he's good friends with too many guys who'd rather kill you than say hello."

In October 1961, Kilgallen had written a searing, lengthy column where she acknowledged Sinatra's talents as well as his fame while still pointing out his many flaws. She wrote, "I have received many letters like this one," and included what she'd received:

> Dear Miss Kilgallen:
>
> I would find my day lost if I missed your column therefore I would like your opinion why the President and his charming wife would entertain a person such as Frank Sinatra at their home, while the President's brother, Robert Kennedy, is supposed to be going to investigate Sinatra's friends the Fischettis [gangsters]…Mary Ann Nolan

In the column, Kilgallen replied:

> Miss Nolan, you and all the others who wrote to me are an admirable but naïve minority. The majority of people in this country admire—openly or secretly—a successful tough guy who refers to women as "broads" and gets off airplanes with a drink of whisky in his hand. I suppose a parlor psychiatrist would deduce there are a great many conforming Milquetoasts in this land who would give anything to be cut loose from the wife and kids and the mortgage and community mores and live in the Sinatra fashion, no rules and plenty of booze and a girl anywhere you look.
>
> In any case, next to President Kennedy Frank Sinatra is the biggest man in America today. He is rich, powerful and adored by millions of fans. He is more famous than any writer, philosopher, clergyman or poet. If you don't believe me walk down your own street and ask the first 50 people you meet who is the author of the last Pulitzer Prize novel. Ask them who is Bertrand Russell. Ask them what Robert Frost does for a living. You'll be surprised at the blank looks. But ask them who Frank Sinatra is and you'll get 50 right answers. So why shouldn't President Kennedy entertain him, if he wants to. The election is over.

* * *

What can be said of Frank Sinatra? What is the proper legacy for him? As noted, one must realize that he touched the lives of three of most important people of the twentieth century, President John F. Kennedy, Marilyn Monroe, and Dorothy Kilgallen, and each one of them ended up dead before their time.

In fact, the trail of Sinatra's presence contributing to dire moments in history starts with Joe Kennedy, then to mobsters Giancana, Marcello, and friends, then to JFK becoming president, then to Joe's double-cross, then to RFK, then to JFK and RFK to Marilyn, then to Marilyn's murder, then to JFK's assassination, and then to Dorothy Kilgallen's murder. Truth be told, Sinatra was poison to many of those who touched his life.

CHAPTER 20

Research by this author, and others of note, has exposed Frank Sinatra's irreverent behavior but it pales in comparison to that of several public servants who abused the trust placed in them by the American people based on new evidence discovered and included in this book, or for that matter, any book, for the first time. As happens when an investigation is opened about one topic of interest, as noted before, new revelations may appear, but no one could have predicted, least of all me, that as my research continued, the motherlode of all JFK assassination breakthroughs would occur. And, as noted in the introduction, become the crown jewel of my contributions to history.

Regarding this new evidence, those involved are President Lyndon Baines Johnson, FBI director John Edgar Hoover, arguably Joseph/Robert Kennedy, and the entire Warren Commission save one senator, who, as will be explained, believed the final report, as he labeled it at the time, was "corrupted." Through him, as if he were speaking from the grave, a whole new perspective about the assassination comes forth, one that should shock every person who reads of the destructive nature of what happened just before and then after the commission was established on November 29, 1963, seven days after JFK was shot and killed in Dealey Plaza.

To put the shocking new evidence in context, it makes sense to first review many of the actions of the FBI director from the moment he learned that JFK had been assassinated.

His conduct includes:

Ignoring Dallas police chief Jesse Curry's directive to his police officers after he heard the first shots to immediately check the Dealey Plaza overpass for the shooter by writing "WRONG" in an FBI memo on a column Kilgallen wrote about the account.

Immediately ordering JFK's body to be flown to Washington, DC, where the autopsy would be performed when it should have happened at Parkland Hospital. (Addressing the autopsy conducted, Dr. Cyril Wecht called it "botched, a terrible piece of medicolegal investigation. The people who did the autopsy were career military officers who had no forensic pathology experience. It was incredibly orchestrated incompetence.")

Preventing Captain Will Fritz, described by Curry as "one of the most skilled investigators in law enforcement," from "being allowed to carry out an orderly private interview with Oswald." Curry added, "The Dallas Homicide Bureau was caught in a politically motivated crossfire from... other government agencies (FBI). The interrogation was a three ring circus."

Developing an immediate strategy once his agents failed to secure a "confession" from Oswald on his death bed per a bureau memo as exposed in government documents October 2017, to convince the American people and the world that a "lone nut" killed JFK. (Motive: if there is no conspiracy, he and the Bureau cannot be held responsible for JFK's death since they could never have targeted a "lone nut" as a suspect. Later it will be proven that Oswald was on the bureau's "radar.")

The memo, issued just a few hours after the failed confession try on November 24, 1963, directed the Bureau to "have something issued so that we can convince the public that Oswald is the real assassin."

Calling White House aide Walter Jenkins and telling him, "The thing I am most concerned about and so is Mr. Katzenbach [deputy attorney general] is having something issued so we can convince the public that Oswald is the real assassin."

Instructing FBI aide Clyde Tolson to "prepare a memorandum to the Attorney General setting out the evidence that Oswald was responsible for the shooting that killed the president."

Informing the media that "not a shred of evidence has been developed to link any other person in a conspiracy with Oswald to assassinate President Kennedy."

One day after Ruby shot Oswald, ordering the Dallas Police Department to forward all the investigation files to the Bureau in Washington, a decision infuriating Jesse Curry according to his book, *Retired Dallas Police Chief Jesse Curry Reveals His Personal JFK Assassination File.*

Ignoring Dorothy Kilgallen's columns such as "The Oswald File Must Not Close" where she criticized the assassination investigation and closed with a warning: "Justice is a big rug. When you pull it out from under one man, a lot of others fall too."

Proclaiming that the convening of a grand jury was in fact illegal because as Hoover explained, "Killing the president is not a Federal crime *unless* a conspiracy exists, and none does here." (This was not true as explained in the House Select Committee Report.)

Per an FBI memo, investigating whether Ruby co-counsel Joe Tonahill met Dorothy Kilgallen during her stay in Dallas, February/March 1964, during Ruby trial, whether he had known her before, how long, whether he has seen or corresponded with her since, if so, the nature of the conversations and correspondence, whether she solicited him for any documents regarding Ruby, if so, when, where, and how, and specifically whether he furnished a copy of the Ruby interview with the Warren Commission on June 7, 1964, to her, and if so, when, where and how?

Chastising Kilgallen's column, "My Reaction to the Warren Report," which she called "laughable" (more about this column to come).

* * *

This all said, based on this author's recent discovery of the new evidence sent through an improbable source, the FBI director secured a new "partner" in his "Oswald Alone" obsession, none other than President Lyndon Johnson, who had his own self-interest, his own personal agenda for doing so.

How do we know? Because apparently hiding in plain sight for years on end, and intentionally ignored or missed by the authors and so-called "experts" who continue to perpetuate the bogus "Oswald Alone" theory, there has existed a YouTube audio version of conversations between Hoover and President Lyndon Johnson about a commission to investigate JFK's death.

The ruse had begun when, by Executive Order No. 11130, signed by President Johnson, as noted, on November 29, 1963, the infamous Warren Commission was established "to investigate the assassination on November 22, 1963 of John Fitzgerald Kennedy, the 35th President of the United States." The commission was directed to "evaluate all of the facts and circumstances surrounding the assassination and the subsequent killing of the alleged assassin and to report its findings and conclusions to the President." Further, on December 12, 1963, Congress passed a Senate resolution authorizing the commission to subpoena witnesses and obtain evidence concerning any matter pertaining to the investigation.

The seven members of the commission included United States Supreme Court chief justice Earl Warren, Republican congressman and future president Gerald R. Ford of Michigan, former CIA director Allen W. Dulles, Georgia senator Richard Russell Jr., Representative Hale Boggs of Louisiana, former presidential advisor John J. McCloy, and Kentucky senator John Sherman Cooper, each known, despite political party affiliation, for their conservative political views. The work of federal agencies bolstered their efforts, including the Federal Bureau of Investigation and the Secret Service, with the former conducting, according to the report, more than "25,000 interviews and re-interviews of persons having information of possible relevance to the investigation."

These men being chosen took on a new, disturbing light when I began closely examining the substance of a recorded conversation between President Lyndon Johnson and J. Edgar Hoover on the aforementioned date, November 29, 1963, posted at https://www.youtube.com/watch?v=NVj1sF0Hw3w under the title: LBJ and J. Edgar Hoover 11/29/63 1:40P. Without question, this primary source evidence proves that one of the, if not *the*, most important investigations in United State history was a whitewash designed with one purpose, and only one purpose in mind—to cover up the truth about who assassinated John Fitzgerald Kennedy and why.

Warren Commission: Telephone conversation between LBJ and J. Edgar Hoover, 11/29/1963.

Readers are encouraged to listen to the entire audio recording and inspect the photographs posted on the YouTube site to experience the full impact of the conversation, but among the disturbing aspects of this exchange, held in secret, never divulged at that time, and barely known today, are the following excerpts. The conversation begins with LBJ's secretary, Geraldine Whittington, notifying the president that Hoover is on the line (main points of interest in bold font):

LBJ: Yes.

Secretary: J. Edgar Hoover on [extension] 2192.

LBJ: **Are you familiar with this proposed group that they are trying to put together on this study of your report and other things, two from the House, two from the Senate, somebody from the court, uh, a couple of outsiders?**

JEH: **No, I haven't heard of that. I've seen the reports on the Senate Investigating Committee that they've been talking about.**

LBJ: **Well, we think if we don't have to, I want to get by just with your filing your report.**

JEH: **I think it would be very, very bad to have a rash of investigations.**

LBJ: **Well, the only way we can stop 'em is probably to appoint a high-level one [investigation] to evaluate your report and put somebody that is pretty good on it, that I can select, uh, out of the government, and tell the House and the Senate not to go ahead with the investigation.**

JEH: **Yes.**

LBJ: **'Cause we get a bunch of television going and I thought it'd be bad.**

JEH: **It'd be a three-ring circus.**

LBJ: What do you think about **Alan Dulles?**

JEH: **Uh, I think he'd be a good man.**

LBJ: What about **John McCloy?** [American lawyer, diplomat, banker, and a presidential advisor]

JEH: Uh, I am not as enthusiastic about McCloy. I knew him back in the Patterson, the Pattersons, down here, the secretary thing. He's a good man, but uh, I'm not so certain as to the matter of the publicity he might seek on it.

LBJ: What about [indistinguishable]

JEH: Uh, good man.

LBJ: Alright. I guess **Bob** [?] has started it in the House and I felt I might try to get **Bob** and **Gerry Ford** in the House, try to get **Dick Russell**, and uh, maybe **Cooper** in the Senate. [Rep. Gerald Ford, Sen. Richard Russell, Sen. John Sherman Cooper]

JEH: **Yes, I think so.**

LBJ: I don't know, you know anything, any reason I just talked, me and him talk like brothers, you know. By the way, is there any reason, anyway, I thought Russell could kind of look after the general situation and see that, uh, the state's, uh, and their relations.

JEH: Russell's an excellent man.

LBJ: **I thought that Cooper might look after the liberal group.**

JEH: That—

LBJ: **Cooper can—**

JEH: Oh yeah.

LBJ: **So they wouldn't think, he is pretty judicious fellow.**

JEH: Yeah.

LBJ: **He's a pretty liberal fellow.**

JEH: Yes.

LBJ: I wouldn't want **Javits** [Sen. Jacob Javits] or…

JEH: No, no.

LBJ: Some of those [indistinguishable]

JEH: Javits plays the front page.

LBJ: **Cooper's** kind of border state. It's not South, it's not North.

JEH: That's right.

LBJ: Do you know **Ford** from MI?

JEH: I know of him, but I don't know him.

LBJ: Alright.

JEH: I saw him on TV the other night for the first time he handled himself well on that.

LBJ: Do you know **Boggs**? [Sen. Hale Boggs]

JEH: Uh, oh yes, I know Boggs.

LBJ: He offered the resolution.

JEH: Yes, yes, yes I know him.

LBJ: Now Walter tells me, I know **Walter Jenkins** [longtime aide to Johnson] that you designated to work with us like he did on [indistinguishable]

JEH: Oh, yeah.

LBJ: I tell you I appreciate that. I didn't ask for it 'cause **I knew you know how to run your business better than anybody else** and I just want to tell you, though, that we consider him as high class as you do and it is a mighty gracious thing to do and we might be happy and we salute you on knowing how to pick good men.

JEH: Well, that is mighty nice of you, Mr. President, see, we, we hope to have this thing wrapped up today, but we, we probably won't have it until the first of the week. This angle in Mexico is giving us a great deal of trouble. **Because the story there, this man, Oswald getting 6500 dollars from the Cuban Embassy and getting back to this country with it. Uh, they, were not able to prove that fact or the information was, was that he was there on eighteenth of September in Mexico City and we had, we are able to prove conclusively he was in New Orleans that day.** Now then they moved, they changed the date to the twenty-eighth of September and he was in Mexico City on the twenty-eighth. Now the Mexican police again arrested this woman, Doran, who's a member of the Cuban Embassy and will hold her for two or three more days. And we're going to confront her with the original informant that saw the money passed, so he says, and we also are going to put the lie detector test on him. Meantime, because Castro is hollering his head off—

LBJ: **Can you pay any attention to those lie detector tests?**

JEH: I would not say I would pay one hundred percent attention to them. All they are is a psychological asset in an investigation. I wouldn't want to be a part of sending a man to the [electric] chair on a lie detector, uh, they, we have found many cases where we have used them, and, in a bank where there's been an embezzlement and a person will confess before the lie detector test is finished. More or less fearful of the fact that the lie detector test will show them guilty. Psychologically they are at a disadvantage because it's a misnomer to call it a lie detector because what it really is, is an evaluation of the chart made by this machine and that evaluation is made by a human being. And any human being can be apt to make a wrong interpretation. So I would not, myself, go on that alone.

On the other hand, if this Oswald had lived and had taken the lie detector test and it had shown definitely that he had done these various things together with the evidence that we very definitely have, they uh, it would have just added that much more strength to it. There is no question that he is the man, now the fingerprints and things that we have.

This, uh, this fellow Rubenstein [Ruby] down there, he has offered to take the lie detector test, but his lawyer's gotta be cross consulted first. And I doubt the lawyer is going to allow him. He is one of those criminal lawyers from the West Coast and somewhat like an Edward Bennett Williams type, and almost as much of a shyster.

LBJ: **Uh, have you got any, uh, relationship between the two?**

JEH: **Between, uh, Rubenstein?**

LBJ: Yeah

JEH: **No.**

LBJ: Yeah

JEH: At the present time we have not. There is a story down there.

LBJ: Was he ever in his bar and stuff like…

JEH: **There was a story that this fellow had been in this nightclub, that is a striptease joint that he had, but that has not been able to be confirmed. Now this fellow Rubenstein is a, is a very shady character. Has a bad record, street brawler, fighter, and that sort of thing** and in the place in Dallas if a fellow couldn't pay his bill completely, Rubenstein would beat the very devil out of him and throw him out of the place. He was that kind of a fellow. He didn't drink. He didn't smoke. Boasted about that.

He was, was what I would have put in the category of one of the ego maniacs. He likes to be in the limelight. He knew all the police in that white light district where the joints are in there. And he also, uh, let them come in to see the show, get food and get liquor and so forth. That's how I think he got in to police headquarters. Uh, because they accepted him as kind of a police character hanging around police headquarters. And for that reason raised no question. Of course he never made any moves past the picture show [movies being made] even when they saw him approaching this fellow, got up right to him and pressed the pistol against Oswald's stomach.

I, uh, neither one of the police officers on either side made any move to push him away or to grab him. Wasn't until after the gun was fired that they then moved. Of course, that is not the highest degree of efficiency, such as it is to say. Secondly, the chief of police admits that he moved him [Oswald] in the morning as a convenience at the request of the motion picture people who wanted to have daylight. He should have moved him at night, but he didn't. And, uh, they, I mean, those derelicts in that phase, **but so far as time Rubenstein and Oswald together we haven't, as yet, done so.**

There have been a number of stories come in. We have tied Oswald into the Civil Liberties Union in New York, membership into that. And, of course, into this thing, this Cuban fair play commission—committee—which is pro-Castro and dominated by Communism and financed to some extent by the Castro government.

LBJ: How many, how many, how many shots were fired?

JEH: Three.

LBJ: Any of them fired at me?

JEH: Uh, no.

LBJ: All three at the president.

JEH: All three at the president and two of the shots fired at the president were splintered. But they had characteristics on them so that our ballistics expert was able to prove that they were fired by this gun.

LBJ: Ah.

JEH: The third shot which, uh, which hit the president. He was hit by the first and the third. The second shot hit the governor. The third shot is a, completely, is a complete bullet that wasn't shattered, and that rolled out of the president's head and tore a large part of the president's head off. And in trying to massage his heart, on, at the hospital—on the way to the hospital—they apparently loosened that and it fell onto the stretcher and we recovered that, and we have that. And we have the gun here also.

LBJ: Were **they** aiming at the president?

JEH: **They** were aiming directly at the president. There, there is no question about that. This, this telescopic lens which I have looked through it brings a person as close to you as if they were sitting right beside you. And, we also have kept it. The fact that you can fire, those three shots that were fired, uh, within three seconds. There been some stories going around the papers and so forth that there must have been more than one man because no one man could fire those shots in the time they were fired. We have just proved that by actual tests we have made.

LBJ: How did it happen they hit Connelly? As Connelly turned?

JEH: As Connelly turned, as Connelly turned to the president when the first shot was fired, and I think in that turning was where he got hit.

LBJ: If he hadn't turned he probably wouldn't have got hit.

JEH: I think that is very likely.

LBJ: The president got hit second.

JEH: No, the president wasn't hit with the second one.

LBJ: I am saying if he, if Connelly, hadn't been in his way.

JEH: Oh yes, yes. I think president, no doubt would have been hit.

LBJ: He would have been hit three times.

JEH: He would have been hit three times, yep.

Hoover then launches into evidence against Oswald regarding the gun and wrapping paper they found on the sixth floor of the depository as well as fingerprints on the gun and three empty shells and one shell that had not been fired. Hoover told LBJ that Oswald "threw the gun aside and came down [and went to] the entrance" and a police officer and manager talked to him, and he said he worked there and they let him go. "That's how he got out." Hoover added, "And then he got on a bus…and went out to his home. Got hold of a jacket and came back downtown, walking, and the police officer who was killed stopped him not knowing who he was…and he fired, of course, and killed the police officer."

Continuing the conversation, the president says:

LBJ: **Your conclusion is that he is the one who did it…. No connection between he and Ruby.**

JEH: **Yes.**

JEH: There was no Secret Service man standing on the back of the car. Usually the presidential car has had steps on the back next to the bumpers and usually there had been one [agent] on either side standing on those steps at the back bumper. Whether the president asked that that not be done, we don't know. And the bubble top was not up but the bubble top wasn't worth a damn anyway 'cause it's made entirely of plastic.

And much to my surprise, the Secret Service do not have any armored cars.

LBJ: Do you have a bulletproof car?

JEH: Yes, I do.

LBJ: Do you think I oughta have one?

JEH: Most certainly, Sir…. The top was down. The president had insisted upon that so he could stand up and wave to the crowd. [Hoover proceeds to explain his thinking that the president should use a bulletproof car going forward.]

LBJ: You mean when I ride around my ranch I oughta be in a bulletproof car?

JEH: I would certainly think so…I think you need that car down at your ranch…. It's perfectly easy for somebody to get onto the ranch.

LBJ: Those entrances all oughta be guarded, don't you think?

JEH: By all means. You've got to recognize, you've got to really almost be in the capacity of a so-called prisoner because without that security anything can be done. We've gotten a lot of letters and phone calls over the last three, four, five days; we've got one about this parade where they were going to kill you there. [The parade meant one in DC for JFK's funeral.]

LBJ: I want your thoughts on all that. I want to talk to you, you're more than the head of the federal bureau as far as I'm concerned, **you're my brother and personal friend, and you have been for twenty-five, thirty years…. I've got more confidence in your judgment than anybody in town.**

JEH: I certainly appreciate your confidence.

Of main interest are the comments about, as will be seen, Senator Cooper, Hoover's insistence that Oswald is "the man" who killed the president, that Ruby knew "all the police" and let them into his bar (Carousel), and that LBJ considers Hoover to be his "brother."

Also of note is that at no time during the conversation is there any remorse indicated by either LBJ or Hoover that JFK had been assassinated.

* * *

In addition, another conversation between the twin powerhouses, dated October 31, 1964, two-months-plus after the Warren Commission report had been issued, is available at https://www.youtube.com/watch?v=cMl1oSJmwcU with the title, LBJ and J. Edgar Hoover, 10/31/64, 10.35A.

Readers are encouraged to watch the video and determine what is important historically. Of great interest in light of my research regarding Dorothy Kilgallen is both men attempting to figure out who a "source" is, apparently the one who leaked Jack Ruby's Warren Commission testimony to Kilgallen. These passages read:

JEH: Well, you know, you know I often wonder what the next crisis is going to be.

LBJ: I swear I can't recognize 'em. I don't know nothing about...

JEH: Uh, but to the nearest one they said that this particular man had been under surveillance, and that, uh, **that they were going to explode this bomb today.** [News story?] Now the only person I know of who's been under surveillance by any agency has been this man over in the navy department. Uh, we had no one under surveillance and I don't know of any other intelligence agency that has had one, except the naval intelligence.

LBJ: No, I read that. What they said was, that they had raised the question of the way he combed his hair, or the way he did something else, but they—they had no act of his, uh, or that he had done nothing.

JEH: It's a thing you just can't tell sometimes, just like in the case of this fellow [indistinguishable], there was no indication in any way, and I knew him pretty well, and he looks good also, and there was no suspicion, no indication. **And there are some people who walk kind of funny and so forth and you might kind of think are a little bit off, or maybe queer**, but there was no indication of that. [Inaudible few words.] I have never seen this fellow [intentional beep to cover up words]. We had so much of these things, uh, news stories for instance, that story uh, I think Pierson had information for ya. We got an affidavit from that source saying it was saying absolutely untrue and it was just said as a gag. We got that yesterday.

LBJ: And what was that?

JEH: That was the story of a, uh, this man being planted in the Republican National Committee and the frame-up of Jenkins, and I think that Pierson had an affidavit, from this particular person who gave us the story and consulted with Abe Fortas as to whether he should use it or should print it for if it drives him, or lose his livelihood it should not be printed. Then we received word to make the investigation, and we did, we introduced this body, got an affidavit completely denying the former affidavit saying it was just a gag. **It's not a very funny gag, but I mean, that's the kind of tricks and rumors that are going around.**

LBJ: **Yeah.**

JEH: **And I think that, of course, as we get nearer to next Tuesday, I think the likelihood of this rumoring going along that they can't prove and will not be able to prove, unless of course,**

somebody, someone, one of these dirty columnists, is very apt to carry something in her column.

LBJ: **Yeah.**

JEH: Uh, so far I haven't, I haven't been able to get any more details than was given to me yesterday naming that this man was a cabinet officer, and would be exposed today. I've thought of all the cabinet officers that we have and, uh, whom I don't know personally, but there're none of them that create any suspicion in my mind.

LBJ: None in mine. You might do this, if this thing comes down on Tuesday, you might give some thought to what we ought to do with all secretaries, and undersecretaries, and assistant secretaries. You'll need give a little thought to it from my standpoint, kind of represent me, and uh, I don't want to run you crazy over there, but I rather think that you ought to protect everybody—from me right on down.

[Hoover agrees.]

LBJ: Well, you give some thought to that 'cause I have implicit confidence, and whatever you say we'll do.

JEH: Alright, I'll be very glad, Mr. President.

LBJ: Thank you.

What LBJ and Hoover were talking about regarding whatever "bomb," apparently something newsworthy, that might have been released "next Tuesday," damaging to the president, has not become clear based on this author's research. This said, several points of interest are possible regarding this phone conversation.

The first is Hoover, speculating on what was transpiring and who was involved, stating, "It's a thing you just can't tell sometimes, just like in the case of this fellow [indistinguishable], there was no indication in any way, and I knew him pretty well, and he looks good also, and there was no suspicion, no indication. And there are some people who walk kind of funny and so forth and you might kind of think are a little bit off, or maybe queer." For Hoover, who had covered up his sexual preference for men (his relationship with second-command FBI agent Clyde Tolson), to criticize someone for being "queer" is quite hypocritical but in keeping with the sleaziness of the FBI director.

Hoover and his lover
Clyde Tolson relaxing
in Miami

The second excerpt from the conversation of interest is this one:

> JEH: And I think that, of course, as we get nearer to next Tuesday, I
> think the likelihood of this rumoring going along that they can't
> prove and will not be able to prove, unless of course, somebody,
> **someone, one of these dirty columnists, is very apt to carry
> something in her column.**

Who might that "dirty columnist" be who would "carry something in
her column?" No absolute proof exists, but since Dorothy Kilgallen had been
a thorn in the side of Hoover for months/years on end, it is not a stretch to
believe the director was pointing the finger at her.

Regarding LBJ and Hoover, noted historian and author Morris Wolff
(more about him to follow) explained to me on February 18, 2022, that:

> LBJ was very crafty when it came to strangling or "milking information"
> from various sources. [And] LBJ and Hoover had a bad habit and practice
> of side-stepping Attorney General Kennedy. The attorney general was to
> have been, according to protocol, the first point of contact for any president
> to make in the Justice Department. Hoover technically was under Bobby
> Kennedy [but] a practice of constant circumvention existed, and Bobby
> knew all about it. He was peeved, pissed, and angry about the practice.

Robert Kennedy and J. Edgar Hoover, enemies face to face

Another point of interest during the LBJ/Hoover conversations on November 29, 1963, is the following:

> This, uh, this fellow Rubenstein [Ruby] down there, he has offered to take the lie detector test, but his lawyer's gotta be cross consulted first. And I doubt the lawyer is going to allow him. He is one of those criminal lawyers from the West Coast and somewhat like an Edward Bennett Williams type, and almost as much of a shyster.

Common sense dictates the "shyster" Hoover refers to is Ruby's attorney Melvin Belli, and Bennett Williams, to whom he is compared, was a high-profile Washington, DC, defense lawyer at the time.

Of even more interest is the excerpt regarding Ruby and Dallas police officers:

> [Ruby] was, was what I would have put in the category of one of the ego maniacs. He likes to be in the limelight. He knew all the police in that white light district where the joints are in there. And he also, uh, let them come in to see the show, get food and get liquor and so forth. That's how I think he got in to police headquarters. Uh, because they accepted him as kind of a police character hanging around police headquarters.

Hoover's proclamation to LBJ about the Ruby/Dallas Police Department connection causes one to recall Dorothy Kilgallen's column about this subject:

A close reading of the first paragraph reveals Kilgallen's savvy interviews with "variety acts" in New York City. It reads:

Note that Kilgallen called the Ruby/cops relationship "chummy," pointing to confirmation not only of her quite credible continuing investigation of the JFK and Oswald assassinations, but also evidence that Ruby was permitted to "hang around [police] headquarters when they [the police] were questioning Lee Harvey Oswald." While it is not known for certain, although common sense indicates knowledge based on Kilgallen's numerous columns, is whether commission members were actually aware of any of those columns, despite my researching the matter (they are not included in the WC Report). It is important to understand the Ruby/cops "friendship" to the extent of Hoover saying, "[Ruby] let them come in to see the show, get food and get liquor and so forth. That's how I think he got in to police headquarters." This Hoover statement jives with Kilgallen's last line of the column: "[The acts] also report that the town's gendarmes made Ruby's place their late hangout, enjoying parties with the strippers and [his] men friends long after the official closing time."

To supplement what Kilgallen wrote, in 2017, as part of the government's release of JFK assassination files, a memo dated 11/29/1963 surfaced regarding Ruby's relations with Dallas Police officers.

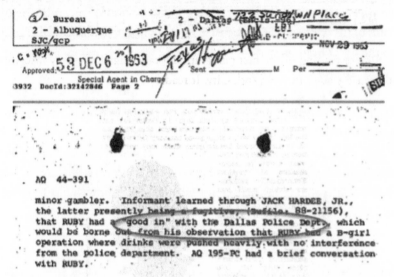

A close reading of the document reveals that "Ruby had a 'good in' with the Dallas Police Dept." It also stated he had a "B-girl operation where drinks were pushed heavily with no interference from the police department."

In Kilgallen's close friend Mark Lane's groundbreaking book, *Rush to Judgment*, Lane devoted an entire chapter (18) to exposing in great detail Ruby's close friendships with more than a hundred Dallas Police officers. Two of Lane's interviews among the several he conducted tell the story, one being from William O'Donnell, "who knew Ruby for 16 years and worked with him at the Carousel." O'Donnell told Lane, "Ruby was on speaking terms with about 700 of the 1200 men on the police force," and that he thus was "not at all surprised to learn of Ruby's admittance to the DPD basement."

Further, Edward H. McBee, one of Ruby's bartenders, told Lane, "Ruby knew many, and probably most, of the DPD officers," a statement he also made to the FBI, one ignored by the Warren Commission according to Lane.

No wonder that seconds after Ruby, who, it may be recalled said "several times he loved police," a reference to the Dallas force, during his psychiatric examination, shot Oswald, Ruby exclaimed, "You know me, I'm Jack Ruby," while the flood of police officers restrained him and then planted Ruby on the cement floor. His outburst substantiates the information in the Ruby trial transcripts to the effect that Ruby had been able to enter the Dallas Police Department basement by "making like a reporter," with the help of friends of his on the DPD force just as he had done when he gained entrance into the DPD headquarters on November 22 after JFK was assassinated and Oswald arrested.

Based on these observations, one may ask this question: Where is Kilgallen's explosive column disclosure and the Ruby trial transcript exposures about the police and Ruby in the Warren Commission report? The answer is "nowhere," leading to the logical conclusion that what she knew caused the report to be, in her eyes: "A fascinating document, fascinating for what it leaves out as well as fascinating for what it says," since she had firsthand proof of the former.

* * *

With the exception of Supreme Court chief justice Earl Warren, each of those chosen to serve on the Warren Commission was discussed by LBJ and J. Edgar Hoover on November 29, 1963. It was apparently LBJ who convinced Warren to serve as the head of what's called a "bipartisan commission" tasked with investigating the assassination and to avoid the confusion and duplication of parallel investigations including the one being planned in Congress. The chief justice did his part by convincing Texas authorities to defer any local inquiry into the assassination to the commission, thus ruling out another of the investigations LBJ and Hoover wanted to avoid happening.

Following issuance of the report, Warren told the commission staff not to worry about conspiracy theories and other criticism of the report because "history will prove us right." In fact, history proved them "dead wrong" due to the tons of evidence presented by credible researchers like me to the contrary for several decades and counting and for sure, the new evidence that follows.

Certainly of note, then, is that the panel was not independently chosen but instead hand-picked to do what LBJ wanted in the first place: to follow, basically "rubber stamp," the "report" Hoover and the FBI filed that the president mentioned. Recall this excerpt from their first conversation:

LBJ: Well, we think if we don't have to, I want to get by just with your filing your report.
JEH: I think it would be very, very bad to have a rash of investigations.

Based on the November 24, 1963, FBI memo in which Hoover directed his staff to convince the public Oswald was the only assassin, Hoover's report would have, word for word, determined that Oswald did act alone. Confirmation is Hoover having told LBJ during their conversation, "There is no question that he is the man, now [with] the fingerprints and things that we have." End of story, or so Hoover hoped would be the case.

As noted, recall that Hoover had taken over the investigation and ordered his agents and the Justice Department to only release information targeting Oswald as the lone gunman. With Hoover leading the way with commission members LBJ had approved trusting Hoover's "report" like lap dogs, the report "conclusions" were a sure thing. In LBJ's eyes, the FBI director was a hero, as indicated by the praise the president gave him during the conversations, and both men were saved from any other investigations in the House of Representatives, the Senate, or "someone from the court," which the conversations show they did not want to happen.

LBJ: Well, the only way we can stop 'em is probably to appoint a high-level one [investigation] to evaluate your report and put somebody that is pretty good on it, that I can select, uh, out of the government, and tell the House and the Senate not to go ahead with the investigation.
JEH: Yes.

The key words from LBJ are "a high-level one" (investigation), "put somebody that is pretty good on it," and "that I can select." This will, the president knows, stop Congress from meddling in any investigation.

Passages where certain individuals of stature are mentioned in the telephone conversation indicate LBJ's preferences and ones he does not prefer as members of the commission. The first category includes Allen Dulles, Gerald Ford, Richard Russell Jr., John Sherman Cooper, Hale Boggs, and John McCloy, and the latter, Jacob Javits, whom the president didn't favor. Chief Justice Warren is not mentioned. Note that LBJ got his wish: each of the ones he wanted on the commission ended up serving, and Javits was not chosen to do so.

Of special interest is the inclusion of Allen Dulles, wearing a bowtie and standing to the left of the president in the photo taken when the report was given to LBJ. According to several sources, Dulles was one of the prime movers in the "Oswald Alone" conclusion reached by the commission, and his being selected by LBJ is no surprise, since he'd cared little for JFK since the then-president had fired Dulles as CIA director in 1961.

That the two men, LBJ and Dulles, were at least acquaintances if not friends, is proven through this photograph depicting the president and him side by side at the LBJ ranch during the summer of 1963, just months before the assassination. No account this author has uncovered provides an explanation as to why Dulles visited LBJ, attired in western wear and his cowboy boots, or what they discussed, but the somber look on both men's faces is telling.

Allen Dulles and President Lyndon Johnson

Before shocking new evidence is presented regarding Senator Cooper that rocks any conception that the Warren Commission provided the public with an unbiased investigation, it is important to consider the final report presented on September 24, 1964, six months after completion of the Jack

Ruby trial. During that time, the commission, according to its records, received the testimony of 552 witnesses, including 94 appearing before them, 395 questioned by commission staff, 61 supplying sworn affidavits, and 2 providing statements. Summing up their duties, the commission reported that it "has functioned neither as a court presiding over an adversary proceeding nor as a prosecutor determined to prove a case, but as a fact-finding agency committed to the ascertainment of the truth."

Based on this statement and the final 888-page report, which I read page by page utilizing my legal acumen, the commission concluded:

> That there was (1) "no evidence that anyone assisted Oswald in planning or carrying out the assassination," (2) "no evidence that Oswald was involved with any person or group in a conspiracy to assassinate the President," (3) "no evidence to show that Oswald was employed, persuaded, or encouraged by any foreign government to assassinate President Kennedy," (4) "no evidence to support the speculation that Oswald was an agent, employee, or informant of the FBI, the CIA, or any governmental agency," (5) "no direct relationship between Lee Harvey Oswald and Jack Ruby," and (6) "no evidence that Jack Ruby acted with any other person in the killing of Lee Harvey Oswald."

This said, as will be proven beyond any doubt for the first time, the commission statement that it "functioned neither as a court presiding over an adversary proceeding nor as a prosecutor determined to prove a case, but as a fact-finding agency committed to the ascertainment of the truth," is blatantly and wholeheartedly false, amounting to distortions of history unlike any ever witnessed in the history of the United States of America.

CHAPTER 21

Without question, the most positive assessment of any potential commission members was showered on Senator John Sherman Cooper of Kentucky. The words of note include:

LBJ: I thought that **Cooper** might look after the **liberal group**.
JEH: That—
LBJ: **Cooper** can—
JEH: Oh yeah.
LBJ: **So they wouldn't think, he is pretty judicious fellow.**
JEH: Yeah.
LBJ: **He's a pretty liberal fellow.**
LBJ: **Cooper's** kind of border state. It's not South, it's not North.
JEH: Right.

With this favorable praise in mind ("judicious" means "showing good judgment"), Senator Cooper was appointed to the commission, and no credible evidence had ever surfaced regarding his participation until this author dove once again into the matters surrounding how Dorothy Kilgallen ended up publishing Jack Ruby's testimony before the commission report's release date. Recall that J. Edgar Hoover sent FBI agents to her Manhattan townhouse on August 24, 1964, demanding she reveal the source at the behest of commission legal counsel J. Lee Rankin.

Before visiting Senator Cooper's importance in unveiling the disturbing inner workings of the commission for the first time, one should note that the famous reporter and Cooper were credible primary-source eyewitnesses to history. To aid in realizing how Kilgallen's devotion to the truth since her early days as a reporter put her square in the eyes of Hoover and the FBI (she also warranted a CIA file), a listing of the lethal columns (anti-"Oswald Alone" in tone) she wrote about the assassination and events occurring during her interaction with the FBI, LBJ, Ruby's Warren Commission testimony she released ahead of time, and the FBI's actions on the day she died is warranted. When this is examined, it becomes clear that J. Edgar Hoover was obsessed with the reporter, in effect had "birddogged her" from as early as the 1950s up to and including the day when she died.

- In the early 1950s, Dorothy Kilgallen and husband Richard Koll-mar discussed Russian movies appearing at New York theater during their *Breakfast with Dorothy and Dick* radio program. Richard said he believed many of the Communist-front organizations were allowed to continue operation so the FBI could root out subversives. He surmised that "in about an hour [after the Communist meetings], the FBI comes in and they pick up every little scrap of paper, cigarette butts, anything that could be used as evidence."

  Adding her thoughts, Kilgallen told the radio audience, "They probably take little candid snaps. Now they have cameras the size of cigarette lighters. They can take pictures under all circumstances."

  Such banter caught the attention of an FBI informant, who quickly called bureau agents in the New York office. He described the twosome as "idiot-type people" and the program as "chatter and comments." Immediately, Hoover received a complete transcript of the show under the title: "Kollmars Tell How FBI Operates at Radical Meetings." Monitoring *Breakfast with Dorothy and Dick* became a continuing FBI operation.

- FBI memo regarding surveillance of Kilgallen including planting an informant in her "Science Club" meetings.

Most disturbing is that according to this difficult-to-read memo sent to Hoover, Kilgallen had been under close surveillance since September 17, 1959. It was obtained by this author under the Freedom of Information Act and depicted a clandestine operation since an informant was assigned to infiltrate the lives of both Kilgallen and husband Richard. Regarding him, the memo stated:

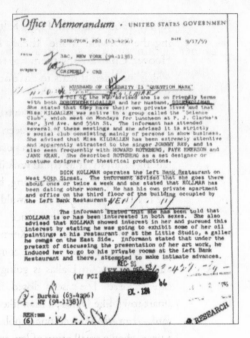

DICK KOLLMAR operates the Left Bank Restaurant on West 50th Street. The informant advised [Kilgallen] goes there about once or twice a week and that KOLLMAR has been dating other women. He has his own private apartment on the third floor of the building... KOLLMAR is or has been interested in both sexes...KOLLMAR showed interest in the informant.... Informant stated under the pretext of discussing the presentation of her art work [in the Left Bank], he induced her to go to his private room at the Left Bank and there, attempted to make intimate advances.

Concerning Kilgallen, the memo stated:

DOROTHY KILGALLEN and her husband RICHARD KOLLMAR... have their own private lives...KILGALLEN is active in a group called the "Science Club," which meets on Mondays for luncheon at P. J. Clarke's Bar. The informant has attended several of these meetings...[the informant] advised that Miss KILGALLEN has been extremely attracted to the singer JOHNNY [sic] RAY....

[Author's note: The "Science Club" noted is the same one that Howard Rothberg, the Kilgallen friend who is the subject of wiretapped conversations between Dorothy and him, included in the Atherton CIA document referred to before.]

244

- In late 1963 and early 1964, Kilgallen published several columns assaulting the "Oswald Alone" theory being shouted to the world by J. Edgar Hoover. Chief among them was the "Oswald File Must Not Close" article, which included threats to anyone connected to a cover-up including LBJ. Kilgallen wrote:

    President Lyndon Johnson has been elevated so swiftly to his new high post that in one sense, he has been snatched up into an ivory tower. As Chief Executive, he is no longer in a position to hear the voices of ordinary people talking candidly. If he could walk invisible along the streets of the nation and listen to ordinary people talking, he would realize that he must be sure that the mystery of Lee Harvey Oswald is solved and laid before the nation down to the smallest shred of evidence.

    If Oswald is President Kennedy's assassin, he is the most important prisoner the police in this country had in 100 years and no blithe announcement in Dallas is going to satisfy the American public that the case is closed. The case is closed, is it? Well, I'd like to know how, in a big, smart town like Dallas, a man like Jack Ruby—owner of a strip tease honky tonk—can stroll in and out of police headquarters as if it was a health club at a time when a small army of law enforcers is keeping a "tight security guard" on Oswald. Security! What a word for it. **"Justice is a big rug. When you pull it out from under one man, a lot of others fall too."**

- Continuing her prowl for the truth, Kilgallen focused on Dallas Police Department (DPD) chief Jesse Curry and garnered an exclusive interview. He told her that his first instinct after JFK was shot was to send officers not to the Book Depository building but to the Dealey Plaza overpass. This account is confirmed in Curry's autobiography *JFK Assassination File*.

- An FBI document secured from the National Archives indicates J. Edgar Hoover was certainly monitoring Kilgallen's movements since he twice wrote in longhand across a copy of the article she wrote about Curry's admission: "WRONG, WRONG."

...order to surround and search the building.

But actually, as we see from the Police Department's official version of events, Chief Curry's immediate concern was not the Depository, but the triple-tiered overpass towards which the Presidential car was moving at about eight miles-an-hour when the fatal shots were fired.

Two-Sniper Theory Out

One of the two bullets that struck Mr. Kennedy pierced his throat. This fact resulted in speculation that two snipers had fired on him—one from the overpass and the other, Lee Harvey Oswald, from the Depository's sixth floor.

Dallas police and Federal agencies probing the assassination of the President have dismissed this theory.

Yet, why did Chief Curry order "a man" to the overpass—which the "pilot car" had passed beneath perhaps a half-minute earlier—rather than to the Depository? How much time elapsed before a policeman reached the overpass? What—if anything—did he find?

From Chief Curry's immediate response to the assassination crisis, we can also conclude that the overpass was unguarded. And this too is strange. (is st 1 x 6)

According to the report, Dallas police officials had decided on Nov. 18 — four days before the assassination — to station either two or four officers on every overpass along the motorcade route.

I find the report — which was submitted to Chief Curry by three of his top assistants last Nov. 30 — almost as fascinating as the transcript of Jack Ruby's Warren Commission testimony, which was published in full last week in The New York Journal-American.

Report Bares More Details

For the document—known officially as "a chronological report of events prior to, during and after the assassination of President John F. Kennedy"—also bares this additional information:

• Five hours before Oswald was slain by Ruby, Dallas police received a telephone warning that "about 100 men are going to take the prisoner Oswald and we don't want any policemen to be hurt."

• On the basis of this threat, Dallas police laid out an elaborate security system to safeguard Oswald. This even included bringing in two armored "decoy" cars. Ruby, however, had no trouble piercing the security screen.

• The order to seal off the Depository building on the day of the assassination was given by Deputy Police Chief George L. Lumpkin, but only after a trip to and from Parkland Memorial Hospital. So perhaps 20 minutes passed between the shooting and the order. Quite a far cry from the statements by Dallas police officials that the building was buttoned up "immediately."

• Two anti-Kennedy pickets and three men who came to their aid were arrested during a dispute with a crowd soon after the assassination.

The five were charged initially with conspiracy to commit murder. Later this was changed to trespassing. But it seems apparent that Dallas cops believed at first that Mr. Kennedy was the victim of a plot.

Account Covers Critical 2 Days

The chronological report spans a 12-day period. It begins with an early morning meeting Nov. 12 between city and Federal officials involved in planning the President's visit. It ends with Ruby's arraignment for murder Nov. 25.

The key days, of course, are Nov. 22—the day of the assassination—and Nov. 24—when Ruby shot and killed Oswald. Both days are covered completely in the Dallas police document. Some excerpts from the report:

"... Deputy Chief Lumpkin turned into Main st. to Houston st., stopped momentarily at the corner of Houston and Elm st. (location of the Depository) and notified the men—working traffic at that corner that

Kilgallen column on Jesse Curry
including J. Edgar Hoover comments

- LBJ/Hoover telephone conversation, 1:40 pm—11/29/1963

- Warren Commission members selected—11/29/1963 (same day)

- Congress passes Senate resolution authorizing the commission to subpoena witnesses and obtain evidence concerning any matter pertaining to the investigation—12/13/1963

- Ruby Warren Commission (WC) testimony—6/7/1964

- Kilgallen given Ruby WC testimony—6/7/1964

- *NY Journal-American* publisher Kingsbury-Smith requests Kilgallen Ruby/Warren Commission sources, she refuses—8/15/1964

- Kilgallen WC Ruby testimony release—8/18–8/20, 1964 ("It is a fascinating document, fascinating for what it leaves out as well as fascinating for what it says.")

- Hoover sends agents to Kilgallen townhouse to discover her sources—"I would rather die than reveal my sources."—8/21/1964

- Hoover letter to WC counsel Rankin about Kilgallen investigation— 8/26/1964

- FBI memo regarding Joe Tonahill, Melvin Belli, and Kilgallen concerning her source for Ruby WC testimony—9/23/1964

- Memo secured by this author through the Freedom of Information Act included several questions about Kilgallen's whereabouts and behavior and how she ended up with Ruby's testimony before the Warren Commission. Joe Tonahill and Melvin Belli are discussed in addition to Kilgallen.

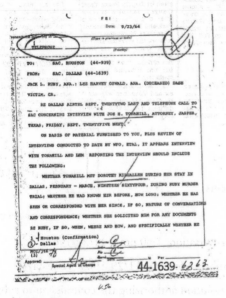

- Excerpts include:

  Whether Tonahill met Dorothy Kilgallen during her stay in Dallas, February–March 1964, during Ruby trial, whether he had known her before, how long, whether he has seen or corresponded with her since, if so, the nature of the conversations and correspondence, whether she solicited him for any documents re Ruby, if so, when, where and how, and specifically whether he furnished copy of Ruby interview on June 7, 1964 to her, if so, when where and how?

  Does [Tonahill] have any info as to who furnished the [Ruby WC] info to Kilgallen if he did not do same?

  Whether Tonahill has reproduced any copy from the copy furnished by the Commission. If so, why, to whom it was published, when, where and how did he furnish a copy to Melvin Belli, former defense attorney [for Ruby]? … Does he have any info as to who furnished the material to Kilgallen if he did not do the same.

- Warren Commission report published—9/24/1964

- FBI Memo regarding Kilgallen and Ruby WC testimony—9/30/1964

- According to the memo, FBI agents were acting "in connection with our inquiry regarding Kilgallen specifically requested by the President's Commission to determine where she obtained the verbatim testimony of Jack Ruby's interview in Dallas." Proof Kilgallen knew the FBI represented the commission is a given, with a further post reading, "Kilgallen is fully aware that our inquiry is based on a specific Commission request."

- "Maybe You Didn't Know" Kilgallen column—10/4/1964:

  "I'm inclined to believe that the FBI might be more profitably employed in probing the facts of the case [JFK assassination] rather than how I got them which does seem a waste of time to me."

- LBJ/Hoover conversation—10/31/1964 ("dirty columnist")

- Summer months to early November 1965—Kilgallen tells *What's My Line?* makeup man Carmen Gebbia, "I am going to crack the [assassination] case wide open," hairdresser Marc Sinclaire, "I'm afraid for my life and my family. I bought a gun," and hairdresser Charles Simpson, "If the wrong people knew what I know about the assassination, it would cost me my life."

- Dorothy Kilgallen dead—11/8/1965 (FBI agents or those posing as agents invade her townhouse and confiscate her JFK assassination files.)

- Butler James Clement's recollections according to his daughter Brenda DeJourdan:

- A flood of FBI agents, or those stating they were FBI agents, swarmed into the hallway. Dad's voice, tempered with a bit of fear, inquired as to why they were there but received no explanation.

- The agents headed for the third floor. Dad said there were people coming in taking boxes out. All of Dorothy's papers, things she had, all gone. The family didn't take them. The FBI did. When the FBI took things out, my father asked, "Why are you doing this?" He went at the agents so hard that he was finally told to keep his mouth shut.

* * *

J. Edgar Hoover's obsession with Kilgallen for years on end, to the extent of labeling her a "dirty columnist" during his conversation with LBJ late 1963, (who else could it be?) had caused me, as I believed it would have Dorothy if this were a different journalist, to delve deeper into Hoover's hatred for the celebrated reporter. He must have been quite offended when she called the commission report "laughable."[15] To add to the FBI director's torment, her columns such as "The Oswald File Must Not Close" basically called him a liar.

With all this in mind, I was set to conduct a more intensive investigation of the Warren Commission, something I had not done in previous books. The starting point was that the LBJ/Hoover conversations had proven the

---

15 Regarding the conclusions presented in the commission's report, Dr. Cyril Wecht, in his bestselling book, *Cause of Death*, stated, "It is absolute nonsense. Libraries should move the report to the fiction section." He then added, "It is quite possibly the worst investigation of a homicide I have ever come across. Putting science aside and simply using reasonable common sense, much of the panel's rationalizations are downright silly."

commission members were, in effect, "stacked" by the president to rubber-stamp Hoover's "Oswald Alone" nonsense.

Like other leads that had come my way leading to further evidence in the criminal cases I'd handled many years before, or when investigating Dorothy and Marilyn's deaths, the commission's behavior under the control of LBJ and Hoover made me wonder whether I could discover comments by any of those members providing insight as to how the commission functioned and the worthiness of the report. It was apparent that the HSCA had not done so nor had any authors or so-called assassination "experts" but having discovered the LBJ/Hoover audio tapes caused me to decide that reviewing what I had published in previous books made it imperative that I once again consider who had given Dorothy the Ruby Warren Commission testimony, a mystery for nearly sixty years.

Like LBJ and Hoover had done during their conversations, I tried to pinpoint who the suspects might be in view of Kilgallen's comments, or lack thereof, about her source. What struck me was that while she had absolutely refused to answer questions about the identity of the source despite the strong-arm tactics by the FBI agents, one remark she made stood out: that it was "a friend of longstanding."

As had happened many times during my literary journey, the improbable took place when the aforementioned Morris Wolff, the distinguished historian and author, contacted me in early 2022 after he watched the YouTube presentation on *Denial of Justice* at the Allen Library near Dallas (https://www.youtube.com/watch?v=lc2jGQFjVFs). Checking his credentials more seriously as I believed Dorothy would have done, I discovered that not only was he working for Robert Kennedy fresh out of Yale Law School in January 1963 on civil rights issues, an agenda that is the crowning point of RFK's career along with his wisdom during the Cuban missile crisis, but that Wolff had actually written the first draft of one of the most important pieces of legislation ever passed, Title II of the Civil Rights Act of 1964.

Morris Wolff

In addition, Wolff, a man of the truth at age eighty-six, had written the book *Lucky Conversations: Visits with the Most Prominent People of the 20th Century* that included his speaking with JFK, RFK, Moshe Dayan, Representative John Lewis, Dwight Eisenhower, and Eleanor Roosevelt. Even more impressive was that Wolff published *Whatever Happened to Raoul Wallenberg?* based on his tireless, courageous efforts to free the Swede, who saved the lives of more than one hundred thousand Jews during the Holocaust from Russian prisons and certain death.

As we conversed, Wolff, whose outstanding career is highlighted by his alma mater Amherst fraternity Psi Upsilon fraternity at https://psiu.org/a-lifetime-of-serving-society-morris-wolff-gamma-58-amherst/ shared with me the reasons he had been in contact, including his having been the then-trusted legislative assistant to Senator John Sherman Cooper, as noted, one of the members of the Warren Commission. Recall this is the same senator whose wife Lorraine had been mentioned by Maxine Cheshire, a society reporter for the *Washington Post*, regarding evidence that JFK had married Durie Malcolm before he married Jackie.

One may ask, what do we know about Senator Cooper's background? My research has indicated that he attended Centre College in Danville, Kentucky, before graduating from Yale University and then Harvard University Law School. Following military service during World War II, he was first elected to the Senate in 1956. He was reelected to two terms and served for twenty years. He was an early sponsor of civil rights legislation and opposed intervention in the Vietnam War. Amazingly enough, in another one of the serendipitous connections pockmarking my life, out of all of the fraternities Cooper could have joined at Centre College, he was a member of Beta Theta Pi, my fraternity at Purdue. Go figure!

When the shocking news, to say the least, about Senator Cooper, and more of interest as will be explained, hit me against all odds, I knew that whatever spirit was guiding my life had caused Wolff to not only watch that presentation video but also take the time to send an email introducing himself. And the moment he did, my eyes lit up as I had the feeling this might be another one of those "ah-ha" moments occurring so many times along not only my literary journey but my life journey as well.

This defining moment began with Wolff telling me that not only had he worked with Robert Kennedy but he had access to JFK in the White House as well. With this in mind, Wolff provided an eyewitness account of the brothers' relationship as being "playful" but although one where "jealousy" was an issue with the president when he became concerned that Bobby might "one upmanship" JFK by gaining too much media attention. It was, Wolff told me, "a complex relationship," and he should have known, since at one point, JFK selected Wolff to be the go-between for the two brothers and deliver documents of national and international security by actually either bicycling or walking between the White House and the Justice Department. This was necessary, Wolff said, because "neither Kennedy trusted J. Edgar Hoover to not intercept their phone call through wiretaps."

Wolff then trusted me with a secret: that Senator Cooper, who called himself a "maverick" politician and was what Wolff called a "man of the truth," became "very skeptical of the slipshod job being done by the commission staff and its rush to judgment" regarding the final report issued.

Further, Wolff disclosed that Cooper, a staunch civil-rights activist despite being a Republican senator from the conservative state of Kentucky, uttered strong words during the times Wolff actually rode with him in the senator's car to the hearings. Those words included "[the Commission] doesn't get it, it's more than Oswald, but Warren [Chief Justice Earl Warren] keeps pushing the Oswald alone idea."

Asked why Senator Cooper was chosen to be on the commission, Wolff said, "LBJ had the idea to put him on there since he was such a distinguished senator, admired by so many due to his integrity, and thus due to his participation the Commission would be beyond reproach."

Senator Cooper

Regardless, Wolff recalled the senator telling him, "There's something very wrong going on with the Commission."

Among the other recollections Wolff divulged to this author were that Cooper told him, "My own views are different than the Report conclusion." The senator then added, "They say this [Oswald alone business] is good for God and the country, but there is internal corruption, and I don't know why." Cooper also told Wolff, "They [the Commission] knew about the Ruby connection to organized crime, but they don't want to touch it but instead stick to the single bullet theory."

Wolff pointed out that if one views the photograph taken when the commission report was issued, "The senator is way in the back, almost out of eyesight." In the photo, it appears that Cooper (second from the right) is standing behind Representative Hale Boggs with a very nonplussed, even disgusted, look on his face.

Left to right: John J. McCloy, legal counsel Lee Rankin, Sen. Richard Russell Jr., Rep. Gerald Ford, Chief Justice Earl Warren, LBJ, Allen Dulles, Sen. John Sherman Cooper, Rep. Hale Boggs

Confirmation of Morris Wolff's account that Cooper was dissatisfied with the Warren Commission investigation is proven through an oral history the senator provided for the University of Georgia archives (also available at https://tinyurl.com/2p922t5a). During an interview by Hugh Cates, Cooper disclosed that he had joined commission member Richard Russell in demanding that a "dissent" or "minority report" be added to the final commission report specifically rejecting the "single bullet" theory, that one bullet had struck both JFK and Governor Connally, based on Connally's own commission testimony.

Cooper admitted that Russell's well-reasoned opinions had "great influence" on Cooper's own conclusions. In the end, despite his joining Russell in the dissent/minority report with the promise that it would be included in the final report, it was not mentioned. It is thus no wonder that Cooper told Morris Wolff, as noted, "My own views are different than the Report conclusion."

Bolstering Cooper's continuing dissatisfaction with the commission inquiry, the senator at one point wrote a memo in longhand on Senate stationary (included in the oral history). He stated, "W. [Chief Justice Warren] and Katzenbach [Deputy Attorney General Nicholas Katzenbach— RFK's "spy" who greatly influenced the commission to dismiss any potential investigation of the Kennedy family] know all about F.B.I. and they are apparently [illegible] and others planning to show Oswald only one to be considered [regarding JFK death]. This to me is an untenable position..."

Cooper also joined Russell in believing there were "some aspects of this case [assassination] I cannot decide with absolute certainty," while stating his opinion that:

> The inability to gather all evidence in certain areas as well as a number of suspicious circumstances deduced from the record has made [me] preclude the conclusive determination that Oswald and Oswald alone, without the knowledge, encouragement or assistance of any person, planned and perpetrated the assassination.

Following JFK's death, Jackie Onassis, while being interviewed for a May 13, 1981 University of Kentucky oral history interview by UK Libraries' Terry Birdwhistell, described Sherman, whom she met many times during the presidency, as "a man of great character." She even compared him to another beloved Kentucky leader, Abraham Lincoln, noting his ability to connect with individuals from small-town Kentucky to communities abroad.

President Kennedy and Senator Cooper circa 1962

"It's a question of character, really," she said. "If the man seems to you wise, profound, compassionate, intelligent, learned-well, you're going to look up to him. And then he was also loved. He couldn't help but be loved, if you just spend 15 minutes with him, you're going to like him." (https://tinyurl.com/bdd889cp)

If Wolff's account regarding Cooper's distaste for the commission report wasn't enough, my ears perked up when, again, against all odds, Wolff, his memory as sharp as a man half his age, said Senator Cooper and Dorothy Kilgallen were "good friends." To that end, Wolff told me, "The senator used to have soirees [evening parties] at his home at Twenty-Ninth and North Street in Georgetown, and Dorothy was often a guest. I was invited as well, and I recall talking to Dorothy. She was a bright lightbulb and what I would call 'investigative by nature' since she kind of interviewed me since I was working for the senator and there might be a story in what I said."

Predictably, now realizing that Kilgallen and Senator Cooper were good friends and that he was, at the very least, disgruntled with the Warren Commission's inner workings and the report, I had to ask whether the senator could be the "longstanding friend" who provided Dorothy with Ruby's commission testimony. To that question, Wolff readily replied, "Dorothy was very congenial and a woman of integrity who pursued the truth, characteristics of the senator as well, and I thus have no problem stating that because of his problems with the Commission taking what he called a 'shortcut' and 'rush to judgment,' and his admiration for Dorothy, it makes good sense that he was instrumental in secreting the Ruby Commission testimony to her knowing that she would go forward with the truth." Summing up, Wolff said, "Senator Cooper hated misinformation, hated cover-ups, and I believe he thought the Warren Commission was covering up the truth."

With this in mind, the obstacle to considering Senator Cooper as being, in essence, a whistleblower of sorts within the commission, was Kilgallen refusing to answer the FBI agents' questions about her source. Recalling exactly what she did say assists with better understanding the difficulty of pinpointing that source.

Important to note is that twice Kilgallen "refused to answer" questions, the first dealing with "whether or not the source was a member of the

President's Commission itself or a staff member or employee," and the second when asked the question as to whether "the source was someone not on the Commission, such as Ruby's defense counsel or someone else who was present during the interview or who might legally have retrieved a copy of the transcript." Important

Miss Kilgallen stated that she refused to reveal the source who gave her the transcript of the Jack Ruby interview by the President's Commission on the Assassination of President Kennedy.

Miss Kilgallen stated that she would identify the source only as a "responsible person who had a legal right to the transcript." She stated that she was the only person who knew the identity of the source and that she "would die" rather than reveal his identity. Miss Kilgallen said that she based her refusal to identify her source on the right of a newspaper reporter to protect his sources of information.

Miss Kilgallen specifically was asked whether or not the source was a member of the President's Commission itself or a staff member or employee. She refused to answer.

Miss Kilgallen specifically was asked if the source was someone not on the Commission, such as Ruby's defense counsel or someone else who was present during the interview or who might legally have received a copy of the transcript. She refused to answer.

Miss Kilgallen also said that she would refuse to give the date on which she received the Ruby transcript and would refuse to identify the city in which she obtained it.

Miss Kilgallen did state that her source was a man and not a woman. She said her source is a friend of hers of long standing. She stated that the source gave her the transcript as a "friendly gesture."

to note is that Dorothy, by refusing to answer, did not deny that the person who gave her the transcripts wasn't someone on the commission, leaving the possibility open that it could have been a member such as Senator Cooper.

Kilgallen did tell the agents that the source was a "responsible person who had a legal right to the transcript." She refused to provide a date when she received the transcript as well as the city where "she obtained it," but did admit that "her source was a man not a woman," and that the source "is a friend of hers of long standing" who "gave her the transcript as a friendly gesture."

Exhibiting courage in the face of possible prosecution by Hoover's FBI, Dorothy said, according to the FBI memo, that would define her character, her career, her courage—she "would die" rather than reveal his identity.

Since the evidence appears so compelling regarding Senator Cooper trusting Dorothy with the Ruby testimony as not only a "responsible person who had a legal right to the transcript," but a "friend of hers of long standing," it is not a stretch to believe that to avoid any possible connection to him, Cooper would not have dealt directly with Kilgallen. Instead, it appears likely that he used an "intermediary," a "go-between," someone he knew with access to the famed reporter.

Due to Senator Cooper's prominence, it is no wonder that Kilgallen protected him from being exposed as the one who provided Ruby's testimony. It may be noticed that she avoided even coming close to arousing suspicion about the senator by refusing to answer specific questions to avoid even a speck of potential that he could be implicated.[16]

That Cooper trusted Kilgallen with the Ruby testimony (no question that this honorable man shared the Ruby testimony out of a sense of duty to the truth) is a testament to not only her stature but her integrity, since he apparently chose her instead of any other journalist. Based on her reputation and friendship to the extent of inviting her to his home, the senator knew he could rely on Kilgallen's keeping a secret. He was right, since she never exposed her "source" to the very day she died.

To be certain, the final commission report ignored, as noted, the Ruby/Dallas cops connection completely, including what Hoover had told LBJ regarding police being at the Carousel and them helping Ruby enter police headquarters, as well as the information that Oswald was seen in New Orleans in September 1963, a definite reason for the FBI to check out any possible Oswald/New Orleans Mafia don Carlos Marcello association. Hoover also must have directed the commission members away from Marcello's obvious motive to kill JFK so Bobby would be powerless, which Hoover had to have been aware of for certain. And, of course, RFK's complicity in Marilyn's death, which as mentioned, the director must have known about (recall that when actress Veronica Hamel purchased Marilyn's home, it was wiretapped with what appeared to be FBI apparatus) but had to ignore due to his close friendship, as will be explained, with Joseph Kennedy.

In effect, it was J. Edgar Hoover who masterminded (along with LBJ) the most devastating cover-up in US history. Hopefully one day, the FBI building in Washington, DC, named for him will remove that name and throw it into a toilet.

With this in mind, it is no wonder that a man of integrity like Senator Cooper told Morris Wolff that among other issues he had with the

---

16 Recall the earlier mention that Kilgallen told no one of her secret source, but when she ran into Howard Rothberg, an interior designer and friend who was a founding member of her P. J. Clarke's "Science Club," she showed him a thick grouping of papers hidden inside the *Life* magazine cover depicting Lee Harvey Oswald holding the Mannlicher-Carcano rifle the authorities swore he used to assassinate John F. Kennedy. When Rothberg asked, "What's this?" Kilgallen calmly replied, "It's just part of the Warren Commission report." No evidence exists that she ever confided in Rothberg as to who passed the Ruby WC testimony to her.

commission, "corruption" was one of them. "Obstruction of justice" might be a better description, since the report denied JFK, who I had taken on as a "client," the justice he deserved.

One point of interest that may have been why Senator Cooper was disgusted with the Warren Commission proceedings and why Dorothy Kilgallen called the report "laughable" may be learned from the report itself. Recall parking garage manager Garnett Hallmark testified at the Ruby trial that Ruby, when he visited the parking facility at about one thirty in the afternoon the day before he shot Oswald, said over the telephone that "he would be there" when Oswald was transferred.

With this in mind, it is quite noticeable that on page 346 in *The Official Complete and Unabridged Edition of the Warren Commission Report*, the following account of the Ruby phone call appears. It reads: "Hallmark said Ruby never called Oswald by name, but used the pronoun, 'he' and remarked to the recipient of the call, 'You know I'll be there.'"

The report even identifies the man whom Ruby was speaking to as Ken Dowe, a KLIF (radio) announcer "to whom Ruby made at least two telephone calls within a short span of time Saturday afternoon."

Common sense, any at all, dictates that when Senator Cooper heard this evidence, he must have asked himself, "Wait a minute, why did Ruby say he just happened to visit the Dallas Police Department basement on the Sunday morning (Report page 354) when he shot Oswald?" Nonsense, Cooper would have surmised, just as he would have questioned why Ruby "placed his keys and billfold in the trunk of the car, then locked the trunk... and placed the trunk key in the glove compartment." In addition, the senator would have wondered why Ruby left his dachshund, a dog he dearly loved, in the unlocked car (page 354).

Recalling what appears to be Senator Cooper's most telling remarks to Morris Wolff for emphasis, the senator's having said he was "very skeptical of the slipshod job done by the Commission staff and its rush to judgment" regarding the final report and that "they [the Commission] say this [Oswald Alone result] is good for God and the country, but there is internal corruption and I don't know why" causes one to shiver at the distortions of history. For a man who "hated misinformation, hated cover-ups," one who also had told

Wolff, "[The Commission] doesn't get it, it's more than Oswald, but Warren [Chief Justice Earl Warren] keeps pushing the Oswald alone idea," and "They [the Commission] already knew about the Ruby connection to organized crime, but they didn't want to touch it but instead stick to the single bullet theory," being a member of that commission must have been an excruciating experience. No doubt exists, it would appear, that at some points in time Senator Cooper must have wanted to shout to the world, "This commission is corrupted," just as I was tempted to do at the Mike Tyson trial when he was being denied justice.

Only, it would seem likely, to calm his conscience, the courageous senator from Kentucky passed Ruby's commission testimony to his "longtime" friend Dorothy Kilgallen through the intermediary. Further, if somehow Cooper also let Kilgallen know, through that same intermediary, of his disgust for the inner workings of the Warren Commission including the "corruption" therein and she told her friend-turned-Judas Ron Pataky who then informed the aforementioned "wrong people" of that information, which she intended to include in the book she was writing for Random House, the motive for eliminating the dogged journalist before she could publish what Cooper, through the intermediary, had revealed was increased a hundred-fold.

Regardless, while the Ruby trial testimony appears to be the most credible evidence about the JFK assassination, Cooper's firsthand account of the corruption involved with the Warren Commission is arguably the most explosive, breakthrough evidence exposed about that assassination for nearly sixty years and counting. Historians hopefully will not water down its importance since the senator's shocking revelations permit you the reader, and those who will learn about Cooper's disgust for the commission's deliberate exclusion of the truth about JFK's death, a seat at the table just as if all of you attended the commission hearings.

* * *

Adding to the curious nature of LBJ and Hoover's "buddy/buddy" friendship ("like brothers"), as proven by the audio-taped conversations, is the relationship between Hoover and Joseph Kennedy first exposed, in part, in *The Poison Patriarch*. Regarding the flawed man who "poured into his sons everything he learned and wished for himself," Joe's 738-page FBI file acquired by this author under the Freedom of Information Act provided more information about who he was, and how he was clearly a clever, deceitful man who played on both sides of the street.

Little known is the fact that as early as 1937, Joe was under scrutiny by the bureau. Even less known is that Joe and future FBI director J. Edgar Hoover became friends during a time when both interacted with the National Maritime Union. When Hoover was appointed head of the Bureau, there was an obscure posting in Kennedy's FBI file indicating that in October 1944 "[Joe Kennedy] was enlisted in this office [Boston] in the case entitled Bureau File #1–8039." The reference, based on further file notations, was to Joe becoming a "Special Service Contact." Nine years later, a file memo, one commenting on Joe's qualifications to be appointed to the Commission on Governmental Reorganization, the notations included, "The Bureau's relations with Kennedy over the past years have been very cordial."

This apparently meant Joe could be helpful based on, as a November 1954 memo mentioned, his position as "an outstanding financier and industrialist and [being] highly regarded in business, governmental and professional circles." A previous memo in January 1954 called him "a Special Services Contact of the Boston Division for many years," one who was "valued." The November memo noted that Joe was "a close personal friend of the Director and the Bureau."

Whatever had attracted Hoover and Joe Kennedy to become close friends continued through the years according to the FBI file. On October 30, 1959, Joe, acting in the ilk of a sycophant by heaping overwhelming praise on Hoover to gain influence,[17] wrote to the FBI director regarding what Joe referred to as a "real masterpiece" article written by Hoover, "Communist Illusion and Democratic Reality." Joe liked the piece so much he mentioned to his friend that his son John might use excerpts in stump speeches to "audiences who are completely sympathetic to your ideas but

---

17 According to Curt Gentry's excellent book, *J. Edgar Hoover: The Man and the Secrets*, "Kennedy Senior went out of his way to court the FBI director, making sure cards were sent on all the right anniversaries." Gentry added that "in addition to a case of Jack Daniels's Black Label, the former bootlegger added a case of Haig & Haig scotch."

lack the imagination as to how to put them into effect." Edgar responded, "my thanks for your thoughtfulness and compliments."

When John Kennedy won the White House, Hoover wrote a November 9, 1960, letter to the "Honorable Joseph P. Kennedy" stating, "I do want to let you know how pleased I am with his election as President of the United States" while ending the letter with "Warm personal regards, Edgar." After Joe died in 1969, Hoover sent a letter, the file noted, to Ted Kennedy, with the final paragraph including the words, "I am grateful for the close friendship I shared with [Joe] over the years…. I have lost a dear friend and my thoughts are with you during this time of grief."

Two file notations indicated how the clever Joe had ingratiated himself to the Bureau and to Hoover with the first indicating how Joe was polishing the apple with Hoover and the second how he lured his son John into the same sort of lovely compliments. In March 1953, Joe wrote Hoover, "I want to tell you that I am very grateful to you…. Again it makes me feel how privileged we all are to have a man like yourself giving his life to the service of his country." Later, Joe met with Special Agent J. J. Kelly but brought along JFK. Kelly later wrote, "Senator Kennedy expressed to him [Joe] as believing the FBI to be the only real government agency worthy of its salt and expressed his admiration for your accomplishments."

To my surprise, evidence appeared before me in yet another improbable fashion. This happened when the Edward Kennedy FBI files were released in 2010 and Joe Kennedy's high admiration for Hoover was apparent throughout. The file divulged that Joe, according to the FBI director, had in 1955 written to Hoover "that he [Joe] understood I [Hoover] was interested in becoming a candidate for the Presidency. He urged me to run for this position either on a Republican or Democratic ticket, guaranteeing me the largest campaign contribution I would ever get from anyone, and his personal services as the hardest campaign worker in history." Hoover declined the suggestion, but the file noted that he "was deeply touched by the wonderful confidence implicit in his offer."

This disturbing evidence causes me to wonder whether Joe may have influenced both the composition of, and the direction taken by, Hoover's Warren Commission—his and really not LBJ's. Could Joe, protective of the Kennedy name at all costs, have, on his own since Hoover and Bobby Kennedy hated each other, "persuaded" the very man he intended to support for president to pack the commission with those who would never peek into any matters involved with dirty laundry regarding JFK, RFK, or himself that could be damaging to any of them?

When one considers this potential, that Joe, all-powerful with his millions in wealth, was in on the Warren Commission cover-up, it makes sense to understand that the last thing he would have wanted uncovered was that his ordering JFK to appoint Bobby attorney general triggered RFK's illegal actions toward the Mafia, specifically Carlos Marcello, causing the president's assassination. Further, Joe would certainly not have wanted any investigation of RFK's potential complicity in Marilyn Monroe's death just a year and change earlier. Due to Joe being as crafty as any politician as ever lived, the one who dreamed of a Kennedy dynasty in the White House for twenty-four straight years, first JFK, then RFK, then Ted, it is certainly possible that Joe, who counted as his friend NYC crime boss Frank Costello, an "associate" of Carlos Marcello, used his power to influence the very commission investigating the assassination of his son, the president.

* * *

Though Joe Kennedy attempted to keep his image squeaky clean, he was, among other disturbing qualities, down-and-dirty Joe, the one who was a serial philanderer to poor Rose, the one who pacified Adolf Hitler, and the one whom Breckinridge Long, former ambassador to Italy, said was "terribly explosive and dangerous." As ambassador to Great Britain, Papa Joe, Long said, "was looked upon not as a hero but a troublesome publicity hound who made impossible demands and then blamed Washington when they could not be met."

With all of this new evidence in mind, who "wins" when the commission report nailed Lee Harvey Oswald, who called himself a "patsy" and rightfully so when arrested, as being the lone gunman for JFK's death? Certainly LBJ, who became some sort of a hero in his own mind for "protecting" what Senator Cooper called "god and country," wins since the president wanted no investigation of his private affairs. Proof: In 2017, as part of the 2,981 previously secret JFK assassination documents released by the US government, a 1966 memo forwarded to the White House by Hoover alleged: "The KGB had 'data' indicating Vice President Lyndon Johnson was behind the assassination, JFK's murder" and that there was "a well-organized conspiracy on the part of the 'ultraright' in the United States to effect a coup."

With no apparent investigation among the Warren Commission documents, it appears LBJ was saved from the FBI, or arguably worse for the president, the CIA, probing the KGB account. If that had happened, the president, who most benefited from JFK's death, could have himself been implicated.

Of course, another winner is Director Hoover, the man who covered up his sexual preferences from the public so he could continue to be a macho man, the "G-man" keeper of America's safety, since there were no assassins due to his outlandish proclamations to the world that Oswald had acted alone, walking around the streets of America, and the FBI could not be held responsible for a "lone nut" killing JFK. Ramrodding the commission in his favor in the ilk of a bully was his ticket to never being indicted himself for the cover-up, that is, unless Dorothy Kilgallen published her Random House book, and evidence certainly points to his making certain that did not happen.

Joseph and Robert Kennedy also win since the "Oswald Alone" "verdict" terminated any further investigations including the ones in Congress and others that LBJ and Hoover conversed about that neither wanted. If those investigations had happened instead of, or even in addition to, the Warren Commission probe, perhaps those who really cared about the truth, as did the House Select Committee later on, could have stretched to the fixing of the 1960 election by Joe Kennedy via Mafia intervention. And even to Bobby's involvement in Marilyn Monroe's death, covered up as it was by the Kennedys one year and change before JFK was killed.

Spearheading the Kennedys' effort to suffocate any investigation of these matters was Deputy Attorney General Nicholas Katzenbach, a close ally of RFK. While Hoover had instructed his right-hand man, Clyde Tolson, as noted, to "prepare a memorandum to the Attorney General setting out the evidence that Oswald was responsible for the shooting that killed the president," proof of Katzenbach's attempts to protect the Kennedys from any investigation, surely at RFK's behest, is based on this quote from the April 1976 Church Committee Report (investigated US intelligence operations) at page 10. It read: "On December 10, 1963, Deputy Attorney General Katzenbach wrote each member of the Commission recommending that the Commission immediately issue a press release stating that the FBI report clearly shows there was no international conspiracy, and that Oswald was a loner [when he killed the president]." Katzenbach's mission—to blunt any investigation at all, exactly what the Kennedys hoped for, by issuing the press release, one that would put a stop to the commission's probe since Katzenbach's letter to the members happened only five days after the commission initially met and *before* it even began its investigation!

Ultimately, based apparently on blowback from commission members and staff, the press release was not issued, but Katzenbach continued to push the commission toward the "Oswald Alone" conclusion despite no definitive motive being established then, or since, as noted in the church report, that Oswald acted alone. More about Katzenbach's commission interference and its malfeasance, and J. Edgar Hoover's obsession with "protecting the Bureau's image" by excluding any evidence contrary to the "Oswald Alone" theory, is included in the church report as provided at https://www.maryferrell.org/pages/Church_Committee.html. Committee report excerpts are available at www.markshawbooks.com.

Finally, none other than Frank Sinatra was a winner, since without any probe by an investigative committee, his part in the fix of the 1960 election, possible only because of his close friendship with mobster Sam Giancana and others like him in the underworld, was covered up as well. Frank could thus keep singing his heart out and womanizing his way through some of the beauties that he used for sex and then threw to the sidelines.

With this in mind, who could be labeled a "loser" through the Warren Commission's fraudulent investigation and report? Certainly the public, one that had been bamboozled into believing the "Oswald Alone" nonsense, lied to from the moment the commission was formed. And there was no bigger liar than President Lyndon Baines Johnson.

How do we know—by reading portions of his letter to Chief Justice Earl Warren, another liar of the first degree, on the day Johnson received the Warren Commission report (emphasis added):

Letter to the Chief Justice Upon Receipt of the Warren Commission Report

September 24, 1964

Dear Mr. Chief Justice:

You have today submitted to me the report of the Commission which I appointed on November 29 last to report on the assassination of President John F. Kennedy. The submission of this report fulfills the assignment which I gave to the Commission, and accordingly I now discharge the Commission with my heartfelt thanks.

In my service as President, nothing has impressed me more than the readiness of outstanding Americans to respond to calls for service to their country. There has been no more striking example of this great American strength than the service of the seven extraordinarily distinguished members of your Commission. I send thanks to you all, as I also send thanks to your General Counsel, Mr. Lee Rankin, and to all those who have assisted in your work.

Your Commission, I know, has been guided throughout by a determination to find and to tell the whole truth of these terrible events. This is our obligation to the good name of the United States of America and to all men everywhere who respect our nation—and above all to the memory of President Kennedy.

I have given instructions for the prompt publication of this report to the American people and to the world. I myself shall give it the most careful study. I commend it to the attention of all Americans and all our friends everywhere.

Let me thank you again for all that you have done. You have earned the gratitude of your countrymen.

Sincerely,

LYNDON B. JOHNSON

Having stacked the deck along with Hoover to make certain only pro "Oswald Alone" believers were members of the commission, and then committed the sins of untruth described so aptly by Senator John Sherman Cooper, Johnson became the chief purveyor of arguably, as mentioned, the "biggest lie" in American history to millions of people around the world. The proof—Johnson writing in the letter to the chief justice, "Your Commission, I know, has been guided throughout by a determination to find and tell the truth of these terrible events." He then had the audacity to add, "and above all to the memory of president Kennedy," a man he detested along with his brother Bobby. By Johnson's lies, and that of the commission, the American public and beyond lost any chance to know that truth, a public that believed it could trust its government, trust the commission—one that thirsted for the truth and, when the commission issued its report, bought the lies because they did not want to believe there was any plot to kill the president. In the coming years, the big lie that Oswald acted alone would trigger a countless number of books packed with distortions of history solely focused on that ludicrous theory, published by authors who became and are enablers of the big lie to this very day.

As will be noted in subsequent pages, these lies also birthed the 6th Floor Museum at Dealey Plaza, a museum of lies since it is, for practical purposes, a shrine to Oswald, as will be explained. The end result, based on the shocking new evidence, is to hold those responsible, ones who somehow adhered to an unworthy "code of silence" through the years, accountable for the first time based on proof that cannot be questioned. Each of the commission members' legacies, including Cooper's, as well as Johnson's and Hoover's, are tarnished forever, but it is the commission members who must take the brunt of the criticism. Apparently they never spoke up with even a hint of possible fallacies with their "Oswald Alone" conclusion during the ensuing some six decades and counting following Chief Justice Warren's warning at a farewell dinner. He told the members as well as staff, according to an official record of the proceedings, that each had a relationship to the government "analogous to a lawyer-client relationship" and thus "the investigation was privileged information."[18]

---

18 A book worth reading about the Warren Commission is *Inquest* by Edward Jay Epstein published June 1966 by Viking Press. Based on in-depth research, Epstein proves how obsessed the members were with Lee Harvey Oswald since, for instance, fifty-one pages deal with him as compared to nineteen about Jack Ruby. Further, there is no mention of Melvin Belli, Dorothy Kilgallen, Carlos Marcello, or Robert Kennedy. Epstein also points out that very limited time was actually spent by the members investigating JFK's death with the brunt of the work done by unqualified staffers.

This said, certainly no one could ever label Dorothy Kilgallen, without question "the dirty columnist" referred to the LBJ/Hoover recordings, as a "loser," but due to the commission's distortions of history, she was never called as a witness, depriving her of changing the course of history for the better through the results of her eighteen-month JFK assassination investigation— the most credible in history. Why was she deprived of her chance to testify before the Warren Commission? Because the mother of three children truly was the reporter who knew too much and what she had learned through that investigation would have suffocated any of the conclusions reached by the commission. Without question, Dorothy was a threat to the truth as the "bright lightbulb" Morris Wolff so aptly described her as to me during our interviews. Just two years later, that lightbulb was turned off when she was murdered, but based on thousands of emails over the years from those who have grown to love her, this courageous woman will never be forgotten.

One final insight is important to consider: at the very genesis of Marilyn Monroe's murder, JFK's assassination and Dorothy Kilgallen's homicide, each a tragedy for sure, lies the Kennedy family name and the condition of neurosis, which infected that family's men as aptly described in Nancy Gager Clinch's book, *The Kennedy Neurosis: A Psychological Portrait of an American Dynasty*. Close scrutiny of her no-holds-barred analysis discloses her perspective that Papa Joe projected, as noted—"mental, emotional, or physical reactions that are drastic and irrational," into his sons' behavior up and down the line, especially by their having few ethics or morals. Instead of blaming any misfortune in the family on a "curse" of some sort, Clinch believed the personal disasters, as noted, were due to what she called, "the fate of all mortals who aspire too high—they are punished. This is the ancient Greek concept of *hubris*—or excessive pride and arrogance, which offends the gods," with the emphasis on the family's, especially the sons' "excessive pride and arrogance."

Clinch's observation of singling out Papa Joe for his overwhelming dominance causing him to "not only set neurotically perfectionist goals in his off-springs' childhood, but to do so continuing through the sons' adult years," is right on point as is his imprinting on their very souls that they were "superior in nature" to others expecting to always "win." Joe's influence was especially disturbing when it came to the treatment of women, causing the sons to be male chauvinists of the first degree, womanizers like him. In effect, the patriarch was a true failure as a father due to his not being a role model who respected women and lived by a code of proper ethical and moral values. This is the single greatest reason why John and even more so, Robert, became as immoral and unethical as Joe was during his lifetime.

What was Papa Joe best at—not any real contributions to history but covering up the sins of his sons from John to Bobby to Ted. And the result was each of them paying the price, two by assassination and one by being disgraced after he left a young woman in the Chesapeake Bay to die.

Certainly author Seymour Hersh nailed it when he titled his bestselling book, *The Dark Side of Camelot*. If not for that dark side, Marilyn Monroe, JFK, and Dorothy Kilgallen may have very well lived a long and blessed life.

CHAPTER 22

On November 11, 1965, nearly three thousand mourners gathered inside the St. Vincent Ferrer Roman Catholic Church on New York City's Upper East Side. Another fifteen hundred huddled outside to pay respects to the famous *What's My Line?* television star, radio personality, celebrated journalist, revered investigative reporter, and author Dorothy Kilgallen. Those present and millions across the country were still reeling from her death, an unexpected tragedy.

Honorary pallbearers had included publisher William Randolph Hearst Jr. and *What's My Line?* moderator John Charles Daly. Among the celebrities attending were actress Joan Crawford, Ed Sullivan, jazz pianist Bobby Short, film producer Joseph E. Levine, and actress Betty White. Flower arrangements were present from Bob Hope, Elizabeth Taylor, Richard Burton, and New York City mayor John Lindsay whose sympathy card included the words, "Dorothy will be missed, not only by those who knew her, but also by the millions whose lives she reached daily." The day before the funeral, *United Press International* reported, "10,000 people walked past Dorothy Kilgallen's covered 'African mahogany' coffin for viewing at the Abbey Funeral Directors at 888 Lexington Avenue."

Of Kilgallen, celebrated newspaper columnist Bob Considine wrote:

There were two Dorothy Kilgallen's, three really, if you count the Dorothy Kilgallen of *What's My Line?* In the latter role, she was one of the best known women in America, chic, witty, trenchant and an absolute master of ferreting out the occupations of the mystery guests. Then there was

Dorothy Kilgallen, the "Voice of Broadway," saucy, provocative, and superbly informed about what was happening in the worlds of the theatre, café society, Hollywood, TV, Washington, London, Paris and Timbuktu.

The image of Dorothy as a journalist who drove up to assignments in a Rolls, which she did now and then, cannot evaporate in any reporter's mind the memory of her hard- digging, scrappy, dogged determination as a reporter... She had become more famous than most of the people she was covering.

Further research both before and after *Collateral Damage* was published and this book completed reveals the following, all pointing to an amazing career overshadowing any of the modern era including Oprah, Diana Sawyer, or Barbara Walters. A compendium of her achievements includes:

- At age twenty-three, a competitor with two men in the 1936 "Race around the World" restricted to commercial travel, where she became the first woman to fly across the Pacific while setting speed records. Famed aviator Amelia Earhart sent her good wishes and First lady Eleanor Roosevelt praised this accomplishment.

- In *Girl Around the World*, a book she wrote about the adventure, one of the most famous quotes is "I like danger and excitement."

- During the Christmas holidays in 1937 (Kilgallen was twenty-four), a surprise announcement appeared in Hearst newspapers across the country: "The first and only Woman Columnist Dorothy Kilgallen's *Voice of Broadway* Column Starts Monday. A Man's Job. Beginning Monday in the *New York Journal-American*, Dorothy Kilgallen will Report Daily on the Deeds and Misdeeds of Broadway. A Man's Job. But Dorothy has been doing a Man's Job and Doing It Better."

- During World War II, hosted radio program *Dorothy Kilgallen's Diary* to raise money through sale of war bonds.

- Appeared in movies, *Fly Away Baby, Pajama Party*, and *Sinner Take All*, on TV show *To Tell the Truth* and on radio program, *Boston Blackie*.

- Nominated for a Pulitzer Prize based on coverage of Queen Elizabeth's coronation in 1953.

- From 1950 to 1965, star panelist on the *CBS* program *What's My Line?* viewed by more than ten million people each week.

270

- *New York Journal-American* column Voice of Broadway syndicated to two hundred newspapers across America; her contemporaries were Walter Winchell, Bob Considine, and Louella Parsons.
- Powerful Broadway critic who made frequent appearances at such NYC "watering holes" as the Stork Club, El Morocco, P. J. Clarke's, and Sardi's.
- Articles appeared in *Good Housekeeping* magazine and photo on the cover of *Cosmopolitan*.
- From 1945 to 1963, cohosted with her husband, Richard Kollmar, an NYC radio program, *Breakfast with Dorothy and Dick*, listened to by a million people a day.
- Star status led to 1956 appearance on *Person to Person with Edward R. Murrow*, the *Sixty Minutes* of its day, as well as highly popular *Flintstones* show.
- Close friends: John F. Kennedy, Ernest Hemingway, Joan Crawford, Marilyn Monroe, Cary Grant, Ethel Merman, and Ella Fitzgerald.
- As a top-notch investigative reporter, covered the Lindbergh Baby kidnapping and Dr. Sam Sheppard and Jack Ruby trials.
- The most credible journalist to have investigated the JFK assassination in history.

And all this from a college dropout who had to withstand an era of gender discrimination abounding at every turn. *What's My Line?* episodes of interest may be watched at:

- Nudist Camp Owner: https://www.dailymotion.com/video/x3295so
- Father Jim Kilgallen on Program: https://www.youtube.com/watch?v=awvassUXswE
- Top Ten Moments on Show: https://www.youtube.com/watch?v=gPBFxn1EIHE
- Odd Questions asked by Dorothy: https://www.youtube.com/watch?v=0uFwTsHS2wg

* * *

This is the woman who died so tragically, the woman murdered by those who stole her motherhood, a motherhood that meant more to her than all the accolades showered on this famous journalist and media icon through the years. No doubt Kilgallen would have given up all of that to live a full life so she could enjoy her children, especially Kerry, whom she loved more than herself.

Recall that when JFK died, it was his fussing over Kerry during a White House visit that Kilgallen most cherished: "The picture that stays in my mind was the one of this tall young man bending over a small boy, carefully scrutinizing envelopes until he came to the name Kerry Ardan Kollmar—Grade 3B. This was the man who was assassinated in Dallas."

Regarding JFK's assassination, as noted in *Collateral Damage*, if Kilgallen had lived, arguably there would have been action-packed months and years ahead. Little doubt exists that after returning to New York City from New Orleans with her new evidence connecting Marcello, Lee Harvey Oswald, and Jack Ruby, Kilgallen would have completed her JFK and Oswald assassinations investigation. The resulting evidence would have been exposed in a series of *Journal-American* articles, or more likely, organized into manuscript form so that Bennett Cerf could have rushed her book into publication at Random House in early 1966. Either way, Kilgallen's conclusion that the JFK and Oswald assassinations were simply part of a very successful mob operation, it appears certain, would have shone through.

Soon after, the shocking evidence Kilgallen revealed would have triggered a full-scale grand jury investigation of the twin assassinations, including subpoenaing of relevant witnesses. With Dorothy as the star witness, the grand jury would, in all likelihood, have issued an indictment charging Carlos Marcello and his Dallas underlings with complicity in the murders of JFK and Oswald.

Based on the same evidence Kilgallen exposed, J. Edgar Hoover would, it seems certain, have been indicted. The charge would be obstruction of justice by deliberately preventing any investigation of the twin assassinations. He would resign pending the outcome of the court proceedings.

Through Kilgallen's disclosures, disbarment proceedings could be filed against Melvin Belli for having compromised Jack Ruby's constitutional rights to adequate representation. Ruby's new attorney would work on a plea agreement with the Dallas prosecutors that could have saved his life.

Instead of being forgotten through the years, Kilgallen's findings would be included in any and all discussions and debates about the JFK assassination. As a result of her relentless search for what really occurred in Dallas in November 1963, Dorothy's theories would have become part of the historical record. For her tireless dedication to truth and justice, Dorothy Kilgallen would have earned the Pulitzer Prize for Journalism. In the audience, husband Richard and children Dickie, Jill, and Kerry would have loudly applauded their wife and mother, a true beacon of inspiration whose work acumen serves as a role model to men and women alike.

Dorothy Kilgallen, Melvin Belli, and Joe Tonahill at the Ruby trial

* * *

Regarding President John F. Kennedy and his future, had he not been the victim of an assassination in 1963, the potential for what might have happened is muddied a bit by the possibility that during the 1964 election his various affairs, including the one with Marilyn, might have tainted his reputation enough to tilt the election to an opponent. Even if JFK had won, he would have faced continuing pressure to exit Vietnam, an uphill battle regarding the seething civil rights issue, the continuing Cold War battle with Khrushchev and the Russians, and his dreams about the space program pushing the envelope. Nevertheless, the potential was unlimited regarding what the president may have accomplished.

All this is speculation, but what is not concerns the human side of JFK, who, through his tragic death, never would enjoy seeing Caroline or John-John grow up. He wouldn't be able to help them with their homework, show them how to drive a car, take them on travels around the globe, and watch each enter grade school and high school and then college. He would never attend either one's wedding when they married, enjoy grandchildren, and so much more.

As noted in *Collateral Damage*, there seemed little credible information regarding the inside story of time spent by JFK with his children until 2011 when Caroline Kennedy was interviewed by *Parade*'s Dotson

JFK and Caroline

Rader. The information was based on interviews that noted historian Arthur M. Schlesinger recorded with Jackie Kennedy within months of JFK's death that Caroline permitted to be used in a new book entitled *Jacqueline Kennedy: Historic Conversations on Life with John F. Kennedy*.

Jackie's insight into the type of household Caroline and John-John grew up in was most revealing. She recalled:

> ... [John] used always come out in the [White House] garden during their recess in the morning and clap his hands, and all the kids from their school would come running...then [Caroline and John-John] would come in during the evening, just as he was finishing up for the day, and just play around his office.
>
> ... One of the last days, Charlie the dog came in and bit John on the nose and [we]had to get Dr. Burkley. You know the children were never bratty but he liked to have them underfoot, and then he'd take them swimming or else, if it didn't quite work that way when he'd come upstairs before dinner, no matter who we had for dinner, they'd come in. You know they'd have their time with them in their pajamas.
>
> He just loved to have them around... he really taught Caroline how to swim. He made her dive off the high diving board. [In] Hyannis Port or Newport or Palm Beach, he'd get on the floor, then he would really roll around with them.

JFK and John-John

None of that playing with the children could ever happen again when he was tragically killed as collateral damage in November 1963. The world had lost a US president, but the children had lost their father, and he had lost them forever.

* * *

Before her untimely death, the little girl, Norma Jeane Mortenson, who became the heartthrob Marilyn Monroe had, except for the Robert Kennedy disaster leading to her death, seemingly turned her life around, with movie offers galore and a better sense of mental health and the fame and fortune awaiting her. Little doubt exists that she could have become even more of a celebrity, the most beautiful woman on the face of the earth who would continue to warm the hearts of those who watched her on the big screen. This said, due to her tragic death, no remarriage for Marilyn to Joe DiMaggio was possible, nor was any future enjoyment of the home that she had always dreamed of living in for years to come. Perhaps worse, Marilyn would never be the mother she wanted to be, one who could have certainly given birth to a beautiful child who she would have loved and loved some more. She couldn't even play with her dog Maf or ever again enjoy the drives she took along the Malibu coast.

Marilyn backstage at the 1951 Academy Awards television program

As before, new evidence about Marilyn's life and times came to me from strange directions, unlikely for sure. Gary Kaskel, a noted Santa Monica screenwriter and playwright sent a link to two videos I never knew existed but ones that project a young Marilyn appearing on television for the very first time. The year was 1952 and the young starlet had appeared in the film *Monkey Business*, starring Cary Grant. For this role and others that year, Marilyn won the *Look* magazine Newcomer of the Year Award and appeared on television with Don Murray, who appeared with Marilyn in the film *Bus Stop* and was nominated for an Academy Award.

What the videos indicate is a somewhat shy Marilyn who seems overwhelmed with the attention she is receiving at age twenty-six. For certain, her best attribute, the smile that lit up the screen, is front and center, but less than ten years later that smile would disappear forever when she was murdered. The videos may be viewed at https://www.youtube.com/watch?v=pGW6ei82E0E and https://www.youtube.com/watch?v=zS9Ss EAK7PU.

This is the Marilyn who died, the Marilyn who would never again be able to speak with her half-sister Berniece or her niece Mona; the Marilyn who could never again interact with those in her profession that she loved, the Strasbergs, Dean Martin, and many more; the Marilyn who could never "mother" Joe DiMaggio during his times of turmoil; and the Marilyn whose fun-loving spirit on the big screen entertained millions who loved her like a daughter or sister. This was Marilyn the human being, the sometimes insecure Marilyn, arguably the most beautiful woman inside and out who ever lived, the real Marilyn Monroe.

While many tributes to Marilyn have come through the ages, including the eulogy performed at her funeral as included in *Collateral Damage*, perhaps it is the singer Elton John who best captured her life and times and her death in his masterpiece, "Candle in the Wind." Close inspection of just a few lines of his wonderful display as wordsmith in the ilk of Dorothy Kilgallen provides a window into the very soul of Marilyn.

Three incredible human beings, each possessing flaws of course, but for certain neither Marilyn Monroe, President John F. Kennedy, nor Dorothy Kilgallen, should have died. Three unique and never-to-be-forgotten souls—

each a victim denied justice whose life and times and deaths will bind them forever—Marilyn at age thirty-six, JFK at age forty-six, and Dorothy Kilgallen at age fifty-two.

CHAPTER 23

Having now laid out like a prosecutor would at trial the most credible evidence regarding why Robert Kennedy had the strongest motive[19] to have silenced Marilyn Monroe through the rather unorthodox method of investigating JFK's death first (1963), then Dorothy's (1965), and then Marilyn's even though she died first (1962), the following facts and conclusions seem quite plausible:

- John F. Kennedy was not killed by one man, Lee Harvey Oswald, but instead JFK's death was orchestrated by New Orleans Mafia don Carlos Marcello in 1963 so attorney general Robert Kennedy would become powerless and not destroy Marcello's multi-million-dollar empire.

- President Lyndon Johnson and FBI director J. Edgar Hoover covered up the truth about the assassination of JFK through manipulation of the Warren Commission to render a bogus "Oswald Alone" report.

- Dorothy Kilgallen did not die of an overdose of barbiturates in 1965 but instead was murdered when she came too close to the truth about Marcello having orchestrated JFK's death and arguably the cover-up of the truth by the Warren Commission.

---

19 One may recall that Brenda DeJourdan told this author that when Marilyn died, her father, Kilgallen's butler, quoted Dorothy as saying, "It's the Kennedys."

- Marilyn Monroe did not commit suicide but was silenced by "operatives" of then-attorney general Robert F. Kennedy in 1962 when she threatened to alert the media to the film legend's love affairs with JFK and RFK and matters of national security leaked to her during that affair.

- Connecting the life and times and the tragic deaths of Marilyn, JFK, and Dorothy for the first time based on motive points to Bobby Kennedy's abuse of power in the early 1960s having penetrated the lives of these three twentieth-century icons like a poisonous snake, causing directly or indirectly each to die at an early age.

With these facts in mind, the logical conclusion to be reached is that:

If Robert F. Kennedy had been prosecuted for complicity in Marilyn Monroe's murder in 1962 based on compelling evidence at the time, he would have been rendered powerless and there would have been no JFK assassination in 1963 and thus no Warren Commission investigation since those who killed the president to make Bobby powerless would have had no motive to do so. Further, Dorothy Kilgallen would not have been murdered in 1965 since there would have been no JFK assassination to investigate since her getting too close to the truth was why she was silenced, changing the course of history.

Cover-ups thus abound when it comes to the truth about the JFK assassination and the deaths of Marilyn Monroe and Dorothy Kilgallen. It is also not a stretch to believe that Joseph Kennedy utilized his friendship with Hoover to influence the Warren Commission investigation process to prevent any exposure of Joe's "fix" of the 1960 presidential election and RFK's complicity in the death of Marilyn.

In effect, as it has been proven in this book, certain government corruption, whether by administrative bodies such as the Warren Commission or via cover-ups by those touching on the judicial system including medical examiners, law enforcement, and district attorneys, have infected the very fiber of American justice, the bulwark of democracy. Only by righting these wrongs may distortions of history regarding Marilyn, JFK, and Dorothy be addressed sooner than later.

* * *

Without question, while the truth about what happened to JFK and Dorothy Kilgallen when they died has been the target of many cover-ups, Marilyn Monroe has been portrayed through the years in a continuing distorted manner, one infected with misinformation and downright lies regarding not only her death but her life and times. Yet another disturbing compilation of untruths about the cause of Marilyn's death occurred in April 2022, when a Netflix documentary covered up not only the homicide but Robert Kennedy's complicity. Even worse, aspects of the documentary violated the movie star's rights to privacy.

Based on Anthony Summers' 1985 book *Goddess: The Secret Lives of Marilyn Monroe*, the Netflix documentary *The Mystery of Marilyn Monroe: The Unheard Tapes* portrayed the legendary film star in a manner that was unjustifiably malicious, vindictive, defamatory, and downright degrading. While insisting that she committed suicide, Summers had as his agenda that pre-determined conclusion and then worked to fit an assorted set of facts to it while excluding significant evidence to the contrary. The result: an ill-advised documentary resulting in distortions of history about Marilyn's life and times and her death excluding the fact that she was murdered in August 1962 and that RFK had the strongest motive to have orchestrated her death so as to silence her.

Adding confusion to the documentary was Summers' comment toward the end. He told viewers: "I did not find out *anything* that convinced me that Marilyn had been deliberately killed."

Why the confusion? Because Summers and director Emma Cooper actually provided some compelling evidence to the contrary from audio-taped interviews that the Kennedys, specifically Bobby, were concerned with Marilyn's potential to cause a scandal enveloping JFK and RFK. The sound bites chosen from various sources indicated they were "playing with fire," that "we can't deal with Marilyn anymore," and that "she was raising a stink" during the months leading up to her death.

This said, to lead viewers away from such matters, Summers unnecessarily did everything possible to demean Marilyn including depicting her, based on interviews with unsavory sources, as a slut, a whore, crazy, a drug addict, one who used "sugar daddies" to get ahead, that she was "animal-like," "a Communist" and one who enjoyed orgies with both Kennedy brothers. In his 1985 book, Summers even included a grainy post-autopsy photo of Marilyn, disgraceful conduct for sure.

To then seal the "verdict" they were seeking, that Marilyn was suicidal, Summers and Cooper violated Marilyn's rights to privacy by utilizing the substance of conversations she had with her psychiatrist Dr. Ralph Greenson. In the documentary, Summers admitted that Greenson's wife Hildi "allowed [me] access to many of Dr. Greenson's papers, his letters, which were gold dust." Common sense dictates that Summers and Cooper must have known (most likely), or should have known, based on numerous years of research for the various editions of his book and the documentary that included a thousand interviews and discovery of numerous government documents, that Hildi would not have had the right to do so unless Marilyn gave her permission. That is virtually impossible yet Summers used the "gold dust" to damage Marilyn's persona, her reputation, in tandem with his suicide conclusion.

To confirm that only the patient can provide permission for any disclosure of conversations or notes regarding conversations Marilyn had with Dr. Greenson while she was in therapy, I interviewed noted psychiatrist Dr. Jacob Towery. He is a private practitioner who has written for the *New York Times* and the *Washington Post* as well as being adjunct clinical faculty at Stanford University School of Medicine and Department of Psychiatry and Behavioral Sciences. Dr. Towery, after reviewing Summers' conduct, told me,

> Within the field of psychiatry, it is agreed that the standard of care is to maintain the confidentiality of our patients at all times. This extends even after a patient has died. Patients often place a great deal of trust in their psychiatrist, revealing things they may not reveal to anyone else, and it is our duty to protect that confidentiality including notes we take about a patient. If Marilyn Monroe's psychiatry notes fell into the hands of her psychiatrist's wife, it would not have been appropriate for her to release these notes and violate Ms. Monroe's privacy.

Since the psychiatrist/patient privilege continues after the death of the patient, whatever Marilyn said to Greenson is confidential and any notes about those conversations privileged as well. Multiple emails sent in early May 2022 to both Summers through his book agent Olivia Edwards at Curtis Brown UK and Cooper through her website, asking whether either had permission from Monroe to expose her confidential discussions with Greenson or permit his thoughts about them to be included in a book or documentary, went unanswered leading to the belief no such permission exists. The result: Marilyn's right to privacy via the psychiatrist/patient privilege was apparently violated.

Nevertheless, in a highly unprofessional and unethical manner, Summers actually revealed many of Greenson's conclusions regarding Marilyn's mindset based on their privileged conversations. No explanation, no context was provided by Summers as to when and exactly what Marilyn told Greenson leading to the conclusions. This is quite unfair to her, for him to cherry-pick certain opinions the psychiatrist had about Marilyn in the documentary (none are included in Summers' book). Marilyn thus has no way to defend herself against the potentially misleading portrayal of her mental state, and documentary viewers have no idea what observations Greenson may have had about Marilyn's upbeat behavior perhaps in the days just before she died.

This said, what strong evidence did Summers and Cooper leave out of the documentary? Many examples exist but three major ones are of paramount importance.

Regarding Dorothy Kilgallen, recall that she penned one of her *New York Journal-American* articles about Marilyn *just two days* before her death.

It read:

Marilyn Monroe's health must be improving. She's been attending select Hollywood parties and has become the talk of the town again. In California, they're circulating a photograph of her that certainly isn't as bare as the famous calendar, but is very interesting. And she's cooking in the sex-appeal department, too; she's proven vastly alluring to a handsome gentleman who is a bigger name than Joe DiMaggio was in his heyday. So, don't write Marilyn off as finished.

To deal with Kilgallen's sunny words about Marilyn's mindset in the first two sentences (followed by a sure reference to RFK based on his being "a bigger name than Joe DiMaggio"), Summers took the approach, misleading for sure, in the 1985 edition of *Goddess* by leaving out the words, "Marilyn Monroe's health must be improving. She's been attending select Hollywood parties and has become the talk of the town again." In the updated paperback edition (2022), the same exclusion of Kilgallen's first two sentences occurs at page 441, and in the documentary, no mention whatsoever is made of any part of the column. This is deception for sure since Summers had to leave part of the quote out since it doesn't fit the mold of a woman being suicidal, one whose "health must be improving." In fact, Kilgallen, who was aware that Marilyn had Broadway offers, a dream of hers, later wrote of suspicions she had about Marilyn's death, stating, "The real story hasn't been told, not by a long shot."

Summers used a similar method of deception when dealing with a statement he knew about from Marilyn's housekeeper, Eunice Murray, whom Summers extensively interviewed and who is seen in the documentary. The statement is included in her 1975 book, *Marilyn: The Last Months* on page 122. It reads, "At least one thing is obvious. On Friday [August 4, day before she died] Marilyn had no somber plans to

Marilyn Monroe in all her glory

end her life. There was too much to look forward to." Again this statement about Marilyn's mindset is left out of the documentary as are the facts that she loved her dog "Maf" and would have never left him behind, and that she shopped with Murray hours before she died for furniture for the house that meant so much to her, another reason for never having killed herself.

Continuing a pattern of deception to even a higher disturbing level, Summers was aware that once the documentary aired, he would release an updated version of *Goddess* and thus decided he had to make certain anyone reading it would not question his conclusion in the documentary that Marilyn committed suicide. At some point, however, he must have realized a problem could exist since in the original *Goddess* published in 1985, he included a statement from LA Assistant District Attorney John Miner, assigned to Marilyn's case and an actual observer of the autopsy.

Miner was quoted as stating that he believed, based on a thorough investigation, that "it was 'highly improbable' Marilyn deliberately killed herself… since among other things, she had plans and expectations for her immediate future," once again calling attention to Marilyn not being suicidal.

How did Summers handle this problem with both the updated paperback book and the documentary? He simply removed nearly eight paragraphs from the first edition of *Goddess* that would have been included on page 387 of the updated edition. The intended result: Miner and his "highly improbable" statement as well as other important information about the assistant DA simply disappeared from view both there and in the documentary where Miner is never mentioned.

Investigator believed Monroe was murdered

This all said, arguably the most glaring evidence of Summers being deceptive deals with a "top secret" CIA document he must have been aware of or should have been, since he boasted of spending three years researching Marilyn's case and that he had to "dig, dig, dig" and "focus, focus, focus" on his investigation (1,000 interviews, 650 audio-taped accounts). Even one quick glimpse of the August 3, 1962 CIA memo noted in *Collateral Damage* makes one realize why Summers must have concluded that he had a real problem with his suicide conclusion since the memo's shocking revelations contradict it while providing evidence of the "romance and sex affair" with Marilyn.

Additional evidence of Summers' deception includes, among other subjects, the lack of interest or analysis in the documentary of conflicting forensic evidence pointing to a homicide, excluding any credible evidence of the cause of death, Dr. Thomas Noguchi's bogus autopsy leading to the unproven verdict of "probable suicide," and strong evidence detailing how RFK orchestrated Marilyn's death. Also, a statement by Dr. Ralph Greenson regarding Marilyn's death as portrayed in the YouTube video (https://www.youtube.com/watch?v=erdu8rtL5Vc) is left out of the documentary. Greenson, answering a reporter's questions on the run, said (emphasis added):

> I can't explain myself or defend myself without revealing things I don't want to reveal. You can't draw a line and say I'll tell you this but I won't tell you that. It's a terrible position to be in to have to say I can't talk about it because I can't tell the whole story. When asked to provide more facts, Greenson replied, **"Listen, talk to Bobby Kennedy."**

In Summers' book, he included Greenson's comments but purposely left out "Listen, talk to Bobby Kennedy." Why, again because the psychiatrist's pointing to RFK's complicity in Marilyn's death doesn't fit the suicide conclusion.

By excluding critical evidence and leaving out statements in the documentary that Summers himself made in his 2022 updated paperback book (page 437) such as "None of the people Marilyn spoke to thought she sounded depressed that last week before she died," he has broken the bond of trust with documentary viewers triggering a cover-up. Despite the deception, Summers had the audacity to state toward the end of the documentary:

> There have been several conspiracy stories. There are people, on very thin evidence, largely made-up evidence, who suggest that, people who want to hide the precise circumstances of her death because Marilyn was murdered. Although I made a lot of progress, in the work, and found out things to do with her dying and the circumstances of her dying, which had not been found out before, I did not find anything that convinced me that she had

been deliberately killed. She died committing suicide or taking a huge accidental overdose of drugs.

But I did find evidence, the circumstances of her death that had been deliberately covered up. If you say to me why were these circumstances covered up, I would say that the evidence suggests it was covered up because of her connection with the Kennedy brothers.

Curious as to why Summers stated that "I did not find anything that convinced me that she [Marilyn] had been deliberately killed," I emailed his book agent on May 5, 2022, requesting an interview. When there was no response, I followed up with emails on the ninth and sixteenth with several additional questions about Summers' research including knowledge of the CIA document, before Ms. Edwards replied, "Anthony is travelling at present and will address [your questions] on his return." Despite this promise, Summers did not respond and neither did Cooper to similar questions I emailed to her via her website.

This said, Summers' comment that Marilyn may have taken an "accidental overdose of drugs" is never proven in the documentary, and in the different editions of his book, he was more emphatic regarding complicity by the Kennedys, writing, "The circumstances of Marilyn's death, which *very much involved the Kennedys*, was deliberately covered up" (page 481, 2022 paperback edition, emphasis added). By leaving out that her death "very much involved the Kennedys" and that it "was deliberately covered up," Summers continues in the documentary the theme of protecting that family from responsibility for Marilyn's death and any cover-up.

In total, Summers' statement appears to be contradicting himself. It is as if he has presented his case, one, for all practical purposes, proving Marilyn committed suicide, but then re-examines the substance of the documentary, perhaps even what he has excluded pointing to the contrary, and decides he has to make a final catch-all statement to not only convince himself he is right, but also make certain viewers believe he is correct with his conclusion. Summers therefore denounces "conspiracy theories…based on very thin evidence…made up by those who want to hide the precise circumstances that Marilyn was murdered" without naming those who might have the motive to do so.

Tragically, the damage done by Summers and Cooper may very well impede any opportunity for a thorough, unbiased investigation of her demise that could very well result in the justice Marilyn deserves since they succeeded in portraying her as a sad, mentally ill woman with no reason to live. To the contrary, Marilyn had much to live for during the final days of her life, and were it not for the actions of Robert F. Kennedy, as proven in my books, this exceptional woman would have never died at the young age of thirty-six.

Shame on Summers and Cooper for disrespecting Marilyn, for perpetuating untruths about her, and for continuing to tarnish her reputation by connecting her name with the word "suicide" when nothing of the sort happened on that sad day in August 1962. As her "voice," as her paladin, I will continue to fight for the justice she deserves as the victim of a homicide.

* * *

Having exposed evidence of the cover-ups occurring in the deaths of Marilyn, JFK and Dorothy Kilgallen, much of it through the lens of the famous journalist, in effect resolving three true-crime murder mysteries that were not mysteries at all, my hope is the result will be fresh probes of each death for history's sake.

The truth must ring out as it should, and to that end, sixty years after Marilyn died, the cold cases involving the three twentieth-century icons must be reopened through congressional and independent grand jury investigation so as to expose cover-ups and rectify distortions of history. With this in mind, I strongly encourage readers of my book and their families and friends to take action demanding that a congressional committee reinvestigate JFK's death in light of Senator John Sherman Cooper's worthy criticism as exposed in this book for the first time. And I encourage those who condemn the failure of former NYC DA Cyrus Vance Jr. and former NYPD police commissioner Dermot Shea to reopen and fully investigate Kilgallen's death, despite promising to do so, to call or write those now in those positions of power. They are, as of mid-2022, Alvin Bragg and Keechant Sewell, respectively. Of assistance may also be New York attorney general Letitia James.

In addition, due to the faulty investigation of Marilyn's death, in effect, no investigation at all, action by readers is warranted to convince LA County DA George Gascón to convene an independent grand jury at once. His worship of the Kennedy image, the Camelot side, especially for RFK, has caused him to refuse to reopen Marilyn's case as demanded by this author despite the overwhelming evidence that she was murdered (2021 letter to Gascón at www.markshawbooks.com).

When you, as a reader of this book, do take action, you will join me in fighting for justice, a worthy cause for sure. The truth must shine down, and together, we can make it happen even if we fail, once, twice, or a hundred times over.

* * *

Certainly the cover-ups about the JFK assassination, from the day he died until now, boggle the mind, each a result of the distortions of history carried forth by the disgraceful, corrupt Warren Commission. Responsibility for their own set of distortions of history must rest with the plethora of authors (Vincent Bugliosi, Gerald Posner, Dan Abrams, James Patterson, and others) and so-called "experts" like filmmaker Oliver Stone who have perpetuated myths about what happened in Dallas in 1964 for six decades and counting as noted in *Collateral Damage*. Along with the Sixth Floor Museum at Dealey Plaza and the JFK Library (a whitewash of his life and times), the enablers should be ashamed for their conduct, for their continuing to wave the flag for the ludicrous untruth: that Lee Harvey Oswald acted alone to kill JFK.

This all said, the worst offenders today, those who distort history every single day, are the powers-that-be at the Sixth Floor Museum at Dealey Plaza in Dallas who continue to deceive students, teachers, researchers, and the general public. How so? By promoting the museum as a priority visit for those interested in learning about all sides of the story regarding the JFK and Oswald assassinations.

Attracting more than four hundred thousand visitors each year, the museum calls its home, the Texas School Book Depository building, "the landmark that changed the world" when it is nothing of the sort, since it was JFK's death that "changed the world." Touting itself as "celebrating the legacy of President John F. Kennedy," the museum claims its exhibits provide "accurate" and "impartial" information, including "the most recent developments" in evidence concerning the tragic events that happened on November 22, 1963.

One section of the outdated "exhibit" hall at the Sixth Floor Museum

Each and every one of the proclamations made by those who operate the museum and the board of directors at the Dallas County Historical Foundation, packed with old-line Dallas big-shot cronies who have no integrity, is untrue while the museum hides behind the mask of stating that it is "keeping the legacy of JFK alive." Through false advertising and deceptive practices on a daily basis, students, teachers, researchers, and the general public are hoodwinked into believing they will learn the truth about the JFK and Lee Harvey Oswald assassinations when, in reality, the museum is nothing short of being a shrine to Oswald, an extension of the ludicrous Warren Commission report and the ludicrous "Oswald Alone" theory which, to date, more than 85 percent of the American people believe is pure bunk.

Basically a cash cow that is a true stain on the city of Dallas, the museum restricts program speakers to only those who advocate the "Oswald Alone" theory and prohibits any research materials adverse to the theory, while providing outdated exhibits, an audio tour that includes information at least five years old, educational programs on its website that are completely misleading, and a bookstore that only stocks "Oswald Alone" books. When soliciting donations to the museum, the false advertising continues based on lies told about the worthiness of the museum's collection, which I exposed in *Denial of Justice* during a November 2019 Allen Public Library (near Dallas) presentation. As of late 2022, there are more than 3.8 million YouTube views. https://www.youtube.com/watch?v=VYDaqto22NY.

Currently, CEO Nicola Langford, Curator Stephen Fagin, Curator of Collections Lindsey Richardson, and the board of the Dallas Historical Foundation, which cares less about accurate history, must continue to promote the "Oswald Alone" theory so the museum stays relevant. Worse, Langford, Fagin, Richardson, and the board members are distorting history even to the extent of permitting an outlandish presentation about the Ruby police files by Dallas judge Brandon Birmingham and attorney Toby Shook, ignoring all aspects of the trial transcript evidence. If one watches the YouTube video (https://tinyurl.com/ya9gm75j, The Assassin's Assassin: A Case Study of the Jack Ruby Trial) and has any sense regarding the truth about what happened in Dallas, it is quite evident mistakes of historical importance run rampant especially matters regarding the Ruby trial and pre-trial publicity.

One indication of the museum's greedy practices was instead of permitting veterans of wars who risked their lives defending the US to enter the museum free on Veteran's Day in 2021, the museum provided the veterans a discounted price of nineteen dollars. Shame on them.

To make the public aware of the distortions of history, one may post Yelp reviews as I have done condemning the poisoning of those who visit, especially young people. As I have done, send a letter to Mike Morath, the Texas commissioner of education, protesting the museum's fraudulent practices.

EPILOGUE

O ver the course of the last six years or so, thousands of email or Facebook questions have been forwarded to me, with the main one being: Why do you believe so many never-before-exposed facts of historical interest touching on the JFK assassination, Dorothy Kilgallen's life and times, and even Marilyn Monroe have fallen into your lap?

It is a proper question—one I have asked myself many times since much smarter people, certainly much smarter researchers than me, could have dealt with the new evidence including follow-up and so forth. But, as whatever spirit guiding my life along apparently intended, the responsibility for taking what has come my way and doing my best to let the world know about it has been a destiny of sorts and certainly serendipitous in nature.

In effect, to date, I've been able to, at the least, justify contributing four significant monuments to history: Kilgallen's eighteen-month investigation of the JFK assassination including interviewing Jack Ruby at his trial, exposure of the Jack Ruby trial testimony, exposure of the Ruby Warren Commission testimony, and now the corrupt inner workings of that commission. Each has been possible due to my becoming "prepared," qualified, if you will, to do so through the early life experiences chronicled in the first six chapters of this book.

How have I handled that responsibility? Well, hopefully in good fashion for the most part, although I certainly admit some mistakes, matters of importance I've either overlooked or have not handled the best way possible, resulting in proper criticism in a civil manner and also criticism from those with a nasty tone to them. For the most part, I have respected the so-called "experts" who disagree even if it comes from a jealous point of view, taken the advice, and corrected any errors as my literary journey continued.

But this reply to the question—why me?—I can only answer by again pointing out that my possessing a legal acumen, criminal trial experience where I was required to piece together evidence for trial preparation including cross examination of witnesses and opening and closing arguments, and, without doubt, Dorothy Kilgallen being my inspiration, a "guide" of sorts, along the way, provided and continues to provide a huge advantage for sure. Due to that advantage, I believe I have earned respect as an investigative reporter, author of distinction, and serious historian while realizing that there are those who do not want to know the truth about any of the matters of importance included in my six books touching on the JFK assassination and the deaths of Marilyn Monroe and Dorothy Kilgallen.

Regarding Dorothy, recall that no less than F. Lee Bailey said of her, "She was a very bright and very good reporter of criminal cases. The best there was." William Randolph Hearst Jr. agreed, stating:

> Dorothy Kilgallen was as good a reporter as ever came down the line. She had three trademarks: a keen mind, a tailored exterior, and a steel rod as a backbone. Dorothy was life and death. She reached into the precipices of people's emotions, in both her writings and her personal confrontations with her own existence. She was enthusiastic, open, full of life.

In addition, most people who have watched *What's My Line?* agree, Kilgallen acted like a prosecutor by throwing out razor-sharp questions leading to her far exceeding any other panelist when it came to guessing a guest's unusual occupation.

In fact, I stand by a statement made during hundreds of interviews and presentations—if Dorothy and her research is not part of the equation when dealing with both JFK and Oswald's deaths, then that research is flawed from the start. No better proof exists than pointing at the Warren Commission investigation, if you want to call it that, and the report since its faulty nature, one packed with untruths start to finish as Senator John Sherman Cooper exposed to Morris Wolff, was completed without calling Dorothy to testify.

Hopefully, in the future, competent researchers will take my research, included in this book and the other five I've written touching on the assassination, Dorothy, and Marilyn, and use it to expose the truth to the world, especially to young people. That research, as noted briefly in the Introduction, is archived at Purdue University, my alma mater as announced in an October 2020 press release (https://tinyurl.com/3ecpce7w). The site where the collection is available is at https://archives.lib.purdue.edu/repositories/2/resources/1620.

In addition, an oral history of my life and times (most of it true!) compiled by Purdue's Dean of Libraries and School of Information Studies Beth McNeil, may be viewed at https://collections.lib.purdue.edu/oral-history/interviews/1031.

The journey to the Purdue honor has indeed been a strange one. This said, hopefully an inspiring one for all of those, who, like me, are not blessed with great intellect but instead a work-harder-than-anyone-else attitude and the courage of their convictions as well as a free spirit never afraid to try new things who has always treated rejection and failure as motivation for never giving up no matter the obstacles presented along the way. As Amelia Earhart, "the first lady of flight," once said, "There's more to life than being a passenger," and I've been blessed to be in the cockpit for nearly eight decades.

ACKNOWLEDGMENTS

First, and foremost, my loving thanks to my wife, Wen-ying Lu, for her support through the years since we married in 2006. She has put up with a very strange husband, whose wild adventures she has willingly shared, while providing a mainstream of wisdom that has been quite responsible for any of my accomplishments through the years.

Of course, Lu and I being together would have never happened if Black Sox had not cemented the relationship with his love toward her. My canine pal and best friend will always occupy a special place in my heart and soul and

Lu and I in Carmel, California, celebrating our wedding anniversary

one day when I get to visit doggie heaven, I will pet and play with him from morning until the end of the day.

To my sister Anne, thanks for all of your support. I miss chatting with you on a regular basis. And to all of my friends and supporters, I thank you for that friendship and support, especially Morris Wolff, Donna O'Laughlin, Kathleen Lieberman, and Dr. Charles Mathis, who not only provided insight into how Dorothy Kilgallen was murdered but also led me to discovering the LBJ/Hoover conversations on YouTube.

To those who have inspired my writings, I thank you as well. They include Greg Desilet, an editor of the first degree, Mike Hundert, Doreen

Serb, Greg Mullanax, and certainly highly competent researchers Kathryn Fauble and David Henschel. And to those who have supported me with media appearances, George Hammond, George Noory, and Tom Danheiser, among many others.

To Anthony Ziccardi, Megan Wheeler, Maddie Sturgeon, Devon Brown, Clayton Ferrell, Cody Corcoran, Mary Cantor, and the crew at Post Hill Press, many thanks for letting me tell my stories. Four books and counting and I am most blessed to have you all in my corner.

To Dorothy Kilgallen, thank you for inspiring me to tell your story. You are an amazing woman and I will do my best to seek the truth about what happened to you until my dying breath. What an inspiration you are for everyone—a person, a journalist of great integrity.

Above all, I thank the Holy Spirit for a life filled with adventure from start to finish. Why I have deserved your blessings I do not know, but I am so thankful for every single moment I have spent on this earth.

—Mark Shaw

REFERENCE NOTES

The content of *Fighting for Justice* is the result of accessing as many credible print sources as possible and interviewing those who have firsthand information about the life and times of the subjects mentioned in the book. Even though many of the events described happened nearly sixty years ago, people who actually knew the subjects are still alive. Special care was taken to locate these individuals but in many cases doing so proved futile.

Regarding print sources, only legitimate books, newspapers, magazines, and credible internet sites were considered, especially those published close to when important events happened. When possible, quotes used were confirmed through a second source.

Concerning the information focusing on the JFK and Lee Harvey Oswald assassinations, interviews conducted for the author's previous books, *Melvin Belli: King of the Courtroom, The Poison Patriarch, The Reporter Who Knew Too Much, Denial of Justice,* and *Collateral Damage,* were utilized when necessary. More than seventy individuals with firsthand accounts were woven into the text for this book. Each was an eyewitness to history; each had a different perspective of what occurred before, during, and after the Dallas killings fifty years ago.

Whenever possible, secondary sources regarding the assassinations were only included when other information corroborated whatever facts were discovered. Certainly all information collected from FBI and CIA files was accurate based on the author having secured the files through the Freedom of Information Act.

Without question, readers are welcome to dispute the author's sources and any and all theories proposed in this book. I welcome both positive and negative feedback and will revise further editions based on suggestions and corrections.

The following sections contain material for each book chapter as well as the Epilogue. Instances where individuals spoke to the author, and the source itself was noted in the text, are not listed here.

Chapter One

Belli quotes from *Melvin Belli, King of the Courtroom* by Mark Shaw, 2007. Shaw personal information from author accounts.

Chapter Two–Six

Shaw personal information from author accounts.

Chapter Seven

Melvin Belli: King of the Courtroom text based on author research. *The Poison Patriarch* (TPP) text based on author research. Kennedy 1960 election "fix" from TPP.

Chapter Eight

Dorothy Kilgallen life and times chronicle based on author research for *The Reporter Who Knew Too Much*. Kuhn comments from *New York Evening Journal*, 1938. Kilgallen Hauptmann trial coverage from *New York Evening Journal*, 1935. "Race Around the World" details from *The Reporter Who Knew Too Much* (TRWKTM) by Shaw, 2016.

Chapter Nine

Lenny Bruce trial details from court transcript. Queen coronation columns from *Evening Journal*. Dr. Sam Sheppard case information from TRWKTM, various newspaper sources and trial transcripts from National Archives. Bailey quote from TRWKTM.

Chapter Ten

Ruby trial chronicle from TRWKTM and *Denial of Justice* (DOJ) by Shaw. Tonahill letter to FBI from National Archives. Kilgallen columns from TRWKTM and National Archives. Ruby psychiatric examination from National Archives, Ruby polygraph information from National Archives, Tonahill interview from TRWKTM, Ruby comments from National Archives.

Chapter Eleven

Means letter from *Collateral Damage* (CD) by Shaw. Kilgallen columns from CD. US Department of Justice memos, etc. from National Archives. Marcello FBI file from National Archives. John Shear statements re Sirhan at https://patch.com/california/arcadia/santa-anita-hero-recalls-working-with-rfk-assassin Accounts re Kilgallen life and times from TRWKTM and DOJ. Sinclaire and Simpson accounts from TRWKTM. Stone account from TRWKTM. These interviews at www.thedorothykilgallenstory.org

Chapter Twelve

FBI files from National Archives. Levine, Gebbia, and Sinclaire accounts from TRWKTM and DOJ. Campisi and Civello accounts from DOJ.

Chapter Thirteen

Statements by Sinclaire, Simpson, etc. from TRWKTM. Kilgallen autopsy report from National Archives. Pataky poems from his website.

Chapter Fourteen

Photograph of Marilyn, Montand and Kilgallen from National Archives. Kilgallen columns from *Journal-American*, Marilyn Monroe Coroner's Report from National Archives. Noguchi statements from CD. Monroe Certificate of Death from National Archives. "Happy Birthday" photo from National Archives.

Chapter Fifteen

CIA document from National Archives. July 1964 FBI document from National Archives.

Chapter Sixteen

Hamel interview from various sources—confirmed through author contact with her business office. Hersh quotes from *The Dark Side of Camelot* published by Back Bay Books, 1998. Kilgallen UFO columns, etc. from *Los Angeles Times* and TRWKTM. 20th Century Fox RFK/Lawford landing from CD. Franklin quotes from his book, *The Beverly Hills Murder File*, published by Epic Books, 1999.

Chapter Seventeen

Nancy Gager Clinch quotes from *The Kennedy Neurosis* published by Grosset & Dunlap, NY. 1973. Photos of Marilyn/Presley, Monroe/Fitzgerald, and Steinbeck letter from National Archives. Morton Downey Jr.'s account of Joe Kennedy's antisemitic statements from Ronald Kessler's book, *Sins of the Father*, published by Grand Central Publishing, New York City, 2012.

Chapter Eighteen

Sinatra Toupee Photo National Archives. Sinatra Gangster photo National Archives. Shore Reprise Records info from TPP by Shaw. Sinatra comments about Kilgallen from TRWKTM, DOJ, and CD. Sinatra enabler with fix of 1960 presidential election from TPP. Grecco account re Marilyn from The Hollywood Reporter.

Chapter Nineteen

Tina Sinatra comments to author Cari Beauchamp from *Joseph P. Kennedy Presents: His Hollywood Years*, Knopf, NYC, 2009. Sinatra quotes about Kilgallen from CD. Sinatra mother quote about Frank from CD. Cohen comments from TPP and CD. Sands Hotel memo from CD. Quotes by Paul Anka from his book *My Way*, St. Martins Griffin, NYC 2014, Kilgallen column from *New York Journal-American*.

Chapter Twenty

Hoover list of Kilgallen "offenses"—TPP, DOJ, CD. Warren Commission information and LBJ/Hoover tapes from government documents release as noted. Kilgallen column from *Journal-American*.

Chapter Twenty-One

Cooper excerpts from LBJ/Hoover tapes. Hoover/LBJ tapes from government document release. as noted. Hoover re Kilgallen obsession from various Shaw books. Letter from LBJ to Warren from National Archives. Breckinridge Long quote from *The Patriarch: The Remarkable Life and Turbulent Times of Joseph P. Kennedy*, Penguin, 2012.

Chapter Twenty-Two

Kilgallen funeral from TRWKTM. Kilgallen achievements from various Shaw books. Considine article from *New York Journal-American*.

Chapter Twenty-Three

Summation of Conclusions from various Shaw books.

Epilogue

Hearst Jr. comments from *The Hearsts: Father and Son*, UNKNO Publishers, 1991.